PAUL / CA

Programmable Logic Controllers

Colin D. Simpson

REGENTS/PRENTICE HALL
Englewood Cliffs, NJ 07632

Simpson, Colin D. (Colin David)
 Programmable logic controllers / Colin D. Simpson.
  p.   cm.
 Includes index.
 ISBN 0-13-735861-X
 1. Programmable controllers.   I. Title.
 TJ223.P76S57 1994
 629.8'95—dc20
                                                    93-8439
                                                    CIP

Editorial/production supervision
 and interior design: *Julie Boddorf/Cathy Frank*
Cover design: *Mike Fender*
Prepress Buyer: *Ilene Sanford*
Manufacturing Buyer: *Ed O'Dougherty*
Acquisitions Editor: *Holly Hodder*
Editorial Assistant: *Melissa Steffens*

© 1994 by REGENTS/PRENTICE HALL
A Division of Simon & Schuster
Englewood Cliffs, NJ 07632

Printed in the United States of America

10 9 8 7 6 5 4 3 2 1

ISBN 0-13-735861-X

PRENTICE-HALL INTERNATIONAL (UK) LIMITED, *London*
PRENTICE-HALL OF AUSTRALIA PTY. LIMITED, *Sydney*
PRENTICE-HALL CANADA INC., *Toronto*
PRENTICE-HALL HISPANOAMERICANA, S.A., *Mexico*
PRENTICE-HALL OF INDIA PRIVATE LIMITED, *New Delhi*
PRENTICE-HALL OF JAPAN, INC., *Tokyo*
SIMON & SCHUSTER ASIA PTE. LTD., *Singapore*
EDITORA PRENTICE-HALL DO BRASIL, LTDA., *Rio de Janeiro*

Contents

Preface

The primary objective of this book is to provide a comprehensive treatment of programmable controllers at a level suitable for 2- and 3-year programs in electrical and electronic engineering technology. The content is suitable for colleges, technical institutes, and vocational/technical schools. Electrical apprentices and journeymen will also find this book to be invaluable due to the extensive coverage of installation and maintenance of PLCs. For students in advanced programs, an indepth discussion of algorithms and Proportional-Integral-Derivative (PID) control is provided.

This book is written for students who have no prior knowledge of programmable controllers. It is an entry-level text that is both comprehensive and easy to read. Students in related programs, such as mechanical engineering, will find this book to be particularly useful since it was written assuming a minimum background in electricity and electronics. The sequence of chapters represents a logical progression through the fundamentals and advanced concepts of PLC programming and application. The first four chapters discuss the basic components of a typical PLC system. This is followed by a comprehensive discussion of troubleshooting and safety precautions. The fundamentals of relay logic and ladder logic are covered in chapters six and seven. Timers, counters, and sequencers are discussed in subsequent chapters. This is followed by a thorough discussion of process control and math functions. Number systems, digital logic, and alternative programming languages are also covered in this book. Boolean algebra and its application to programmable controllers is presented with an emphasis on practical examples.

Acknowledgments

This book could never have emerged in its present form without the help of many people. I would like to express my appreciation to the editorial staff of Regents/Prentice Hall, particularly Julie Boddorf, Cathy Frank, Melissa Steffens, and Judy Casillo. A special thanks goes to Holly Hodder, for her enthusiasm, support, and editorial expertise.

I am grateful to the hundreds of technicians, apprentices, and engineers that I have had the pleasure of teaching the subject of programmable controllers. It is these students whose valuable input has contributed greatly to the development of the original manuscript.

My thanks are also extended to Mr. Bud Skinner of Applied Physics Specialties. I would also like to express my appreciation to Mr. Chuck Hansman of Timroc Industrial Sales for his suggestions regarding the chapter on process control. Special thanks are also owed to the members of IBEW locals 424, 353, and 1788 for their contributions to the chapter on installation and maintenance of PLCs.

I would like to thank my colleagues at George Brown College, particularly Ed Larocque, Kurt Van de Kraats, Al Peat, Ross Roberts, and Malcolm Forge. I would also like to express my gratitude to the following reviewers for their insightful suggestions: Nazar M. Karzay, Indiana Vocational Technical College, Evansville, IN; Sohail Anwar, Penn State, Altoona, PA; Robert Leung, Guilford Technical Community College, Jamestown, NC; Lee Rosenthal, Fairleigh Dickinson University, Teaneck, NJ.

This book is dedicated to Chantal.

Overview of Programmable Controllers

Upon completion of this chapter, you will be able to

▶ Understand the purpose of a control panel.

▶ Define a programmable controller.

▶ List six factors affecting the original design of programmable controllers.

▶ Name three advantages of PLCs compared to relay logic systems.

▶ List the three main components in a PLC system.

▶ Understand the term "ladder logic."

1-1 INTRODUCTION

A programmable controller, or Programmable Logic Controller (PLC), is a device which is capable of being programmed to perform a controlling function. Before the advent of the programmable controller, the problem of industrial control was usually solved by the use of electromechanical relays or by hardwired solid-state logic blocks. These systems were very flexible in design and easy for maintenance personnel to understand. However, they involved a vast amount of inter-connection from relay to relay, and logic block to logic block. For the wiring cost to be minimized, relays and logic blocks had to be kept close together. This led to the development of the *control panel* concept for larger and more complex logic control systems.

Another important factor in the development of the control panel was the ability to check field devices at a common point. A control system with 1000 sensors, limit switches, pushbuttons, and output devices could easily cover a very

1-2 HISTORY

The PLC was first conceived by a group of engineers from the Hydramatic division of General Motors in 1968. The following design criteria were outlined by GM for the first generation of PLCs:

1. The machine must be easily programmed. It must have its sequence of operations changed readily, preferably in the plant.

2. It must be easily maintained and repaired using a modular format of plug-in assemblies.

3. The unit must be capable of operating more reliably in the plant than a relay control panel.

4. It must be physically smaller than a relay control panel to minimize expensive floor space.

5. The unit must be capable of outputting data to a central data collection system.

6. The unit must be competitive in cost with relay and solid-state panels that were presently in use.

Programmable controllers were originally designed to provide flexibility in control based on programming and executing logic instructions. Major advantages were realized by adopting the ladder diagram programming language, simplifying maintenance, and reducing the cost of spare parts inventories. Also, PLC allowed for shorter installation time and faster commissioning through programming rather than wiring.

Table 1-1 highlights key developments in the evolution of PLCs.

In 1968, the prime focus of programmable controllers was simply to replace relays. In relay ladder diagrams, a contact is either closed or open. Therefore, it was convenient to have instructions that enabled the controller to examine a particular contact to determine its closed or open condition. Likewise, two instruc-

large area in a manufacturing plant. Thus, it would take a considerable amount of time for a technician to check each device at its location. By having each device wired back to a common point, each device could be checked for operation fairly quickly.

TABLE 1-1

1968	• Concept of the programmable controller
1969	• Hardware-based central processing unit
1972	• Logic instruction, 1k memory, 128 input and output
1974	• Source code edit
	• Multiprocessing PLC
	• Logic, timer/counter, data move, arithmetic
	• 12k memory, 1024 input and output
1976	• Remote input/output system
1977	• Microprocessor-based PLC with logic coprocessor
1978	• Universal input/output structure
1979	• Bit-slice processor architecture
1980	• High-performance remote input/output with intelligent input/output modules and block transfer
1981	• Medium-speed data highway (token passing)
1982	• Microcoded, multiprocessing 4th generation PLC
1983	• Basic language coprocessor
	• Bulk storage
1986	• Flexible multilanguage programmable controllers

tions were provided to energize, or *set*, the appropriate output. Programs were entered into the memory using a manual loader.

In the mid-1970's, program entry made a major step forward by utilizing a graphic Cathode-Ray Tube (CRT) program panel. This panel provided a high-level, graphical, function-oriented programming tool that allowed the user to edit, modify, document, and maintain ladder diagram programs. Hard copy records and program loading were accomplished by a teletype connected to the CRT terminal. Digital cassette systems were later introduced to facilitate reprogramming and reloading of programmable controller systems.

In 1978, the National Electrical Manufacturers Association (NEMA) released a standard for programmable controllers—NEMA Standard ICS3-1978, part ICS3-304. NEMA defined a programmable controller as follows:

A digital operated electronic apparatus that uses a programmable memory for the internal storage of instructions for implementing specific functions, such as logic, sequencing, timing, counting, and arithmetic, to control machines or processes through digital or analog input or output modules, various types of machines or processes.

There are presently over 50 different manufacturers of programmable controllers. Because there are so many different PLCs in use, it is impossible to cover all the different types of equipment on the market. Fortunately, it really isn't necessary to understand every available PLC. All machines share a number of similarities. Although a manual would be required to determine the method of entering an individual contact or timer on a particular PLC, the function of this contact or timer is virtually identical for all PLCs.

1-3 ADVANTAGES OF USING PROGRAMMABLE CONTROLLERS

The rapidly growing market for PLCs, combined with the wide variety of PLCs available, indicate that all other previous systems used for industrial control will eventually become obsolete. Conventional relay and pneumatic systems are severely restricted in flexibility. For example, if the sequence of an assembly machine would require alteration, such as stages being added or eliminated, a great deal of time would have to be spent reconnecting the electrical and pneumatic systems.

Although first and second generation PLCs were very expensive, the cost of these machines has drastically reduced due to increased competition and technological advancements. In many cases, a small PLC is now *less* expensive than a comparable hardwired relay logic system.

The following points outline some of the other numerous advantages derived from using PLCs:

1. PLCs are easy to program and install. Most PLCs are provided with quick release type screw connections for fast wiring of input and output devices. PLC editing features allow program changes, corrections, and loading procedures to be accomplished in a matter of seconds in most cases.

2. The speed with which internal timers operate is much faster than conventional time delay relay systems. For example, a typical time delay relay can produce a short delay as fast as 150 milliseconds (ms), with a reset period of 300 ms. A PLC can produce a short delay of 15 ms, with a reset period of approximately 15 ms. In terms of speed difference between the two systems, a PLC is roughly 13 times faster. An assembly machine using a PLC would therefore have a higher productivity rate.

1-4 PROGRAMMABLE CONTROLLER COMPONENTS

Regardless of size, complexity, or cost, all PLCs contain a basic set of components, or parts. Some of these parts are hardware items, and others represent the functional characteristics of the PLC software, or programs. All programmable controllers have input and output interfaces, memory, a method of programming, a Central Processing Unit (CPU), and a power supply. These functions are shown in the functional block diagram of Figure 1-1.

The input interface provides a connection to the machine or process being controlled. The principal function of this interface is to receive and convert field signals into a form that can be used by the CPU. This conversion involves changing contact closures, current signals, analog voltages, etc. into simple voltage levels that can be understood by the CPU. The input interface is modular and can be expanded by adding more modules to allow more inputs when the control task increases. The number of possible inputs are usually limited by the CPU and the size of memory.

The output interface performs the opposite function of the input interface. It takes signals from the CPU and translates them into forms that are appropriate to produce control actions by external devices such as solenoids, motor starters, etc. The output interface is also modular in nature, so that additional output functions can be incorporated when required.

3. Access to PLCs is restricted by hardware features such as keylocks, and by software features, such as *passwords*. Timers and their timing values can also be protected through special commands.

4. Problem-solving with PLCs is a major advantage over any other type of control system. Many PLCs are provided with diagnostic indicators which monitor power supply, central processing unit faults, low battery power for memory backup, input and output conditions, forced output conditions, etc.

5. PLCs can be designed with communications capabilities that allow them to converse with local and remote computer systems or to provide human interfaces. These interfaces range from simple light or annunciator systems with alphanumeric displays, to elaborate video screens that allow the current state of a process to be viewed.

6. PLCs are extremely reliable control devices and can be obtained in forms that can survive and function in harsh conditions. They can meet almost any set of installation code requirements.

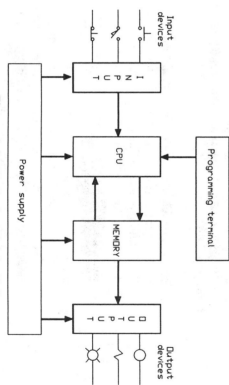

Figure 1-1 Block diagram of a PLC.

The CPU and memory provide the main intelligence of a PLC. Fundamental operating information is stored in memory as a pattern of electrical charges (bits) that is organized into basic working groups called *words*. Each word stored in memory is a piece of data, an instruction, or part of an instruction. Data come from the input section and, based on the stored program, the CPU performs logical decisions and drives outputs. The CPU continually refers to the program stored in memory for instructions concerning its next action and for reference data. It also uses memory as a scratch pad to store outside data for future use or for intermediate action when some sort of decision-making operation is involved.

The power supply provides all the voltage levels needed to operate the PLC. The power supply converts 120V or 240V AC into the DC voltage required by the CPU, memory, and Input/Output (I/O) modules.

A program that is written by a user and stored in a PLC's memory is a representation of the actions required to produce the correct output control signals for a given process condition. Such a program includes sections that allow process data to be brought into the controller memory, sections that represent decision-making, and sections that deal with converting a decision into physical output action.

Programming languages have many forms. Like all languages, the language of a PLC has grammar, syntax, and vocabulary that allow the user to write a program stating what the CPU is required to do. Each PLC manufacturer uses a slightly different language to do this. Most PLC languages are based on *ladder logic*, which is an advanced form of relay logic. In addition to specifying contact closure types and coils, ladder logic programs allow entry of math functions, analog control, complex counter and timer operations, etc. Alternative languages use Boolean representation of these control schemes as the base of the computer representation. Flowchart programming language is also used with some PLCs. A flowchart is a pictorial language that shows the interconnections of variables within a process.

A programming device, or programming terminal, allows a user to enter instructions into memory in the form of a program. The programming device produces the pattern of electrical signals that correspond to the symbols, letters, or numbers entered by the user. Programming devices vary widely in complexity, ease of use, and cost. They can be small, hand-held units, or they may contain large CRT screens allowing better overviews of programs and often providing some form of automatic program documentation. Many PLCs can now be programmed using a Personal Computer (PC). By purchasing special PLC software, a PC can function as a programming terminal, allowing program entry and editing directly from the PC's keyboard.

REVIEW QUESTIONS

1-1. PLCs were originally designed as replacements for
(a) microcomputers.
(b) analog controllers.
(c) relay logic.
(d) numerical control equipment.

1-2. List four advantages of using programmable controllers.

1-3. The control plan stored in a PLC is called
(a) a Boolean ladder.
(b) a CPU.
(c) words.
(d) a program.

1-4. The input interface
    (a) allows a user to input a program.
    (b) connects the CPU to signals from a process.
    (c) allows the CPU to input messages to a CRT screen.
    (d) provides inputs to motor controllers and similar field devices.

1-5. The output interface
    (a) connects the CPU to signals from a process.
    (b) provides data for the CPU to analyze.
    (c) allows the program in memory to be output to the CPU.
    (d) connects the CPU to the process and produces control signals.

1-6. Name three types of programming languages.

1-7. Define the difference between an input interface and an output interface.

1-8. The central processing unit
    (a) understands only ladder logic.
    (b) looks at the output interface, makes a decision provided by the program, and sets the input interface.
    (c) looks at the input interface, makes a decision provided by the program, and sets the output interface.
    (d) serves only to store a program in memory.

1-9. Review the chapter and determine the names of the two main types of information stored in the memory of a PLC.

1-10. The programming device, or programming terminal,
    (a) is the device used by the PLC to bring process signals into the output interface.
    (b) is always a CRT screen device.
    (c) allows a user to enter a program into the PLC.
    (d) is a term that applies to the method used to enter flowchart programs.

2

Central Processing Unit

Upon completion of this chapter, you will be able to

▶ Define the term "CPU."
▶ Explain the purpose of the executive program.
▶ Understand the application of buses in a CPU.
▶ List two types of CPU diagnostics.
▶ Differentiate between fatal and non-fatal errors.
▶ Explain the advantage of multiprocessing.
▶ Describe the two general classes of memory devices.
▶ Name four types of memory.
▶ Define memory protect.
▶ Understand memory utilization and how it applies to PLC systems.
▶ Describe the scan function.

2-1 INTRODUCTION

This chapter provides a more detailed discussion of the Central Processing Unit (CPU) and its associated memory. Figure 2-1 illustrates the relationship between the CPU and the other parts of a typical PLC. The CPU and memory act together. The term "CPU" is often used interchangeably with **processor**, or microprocessor. However, the actual CPU includes all the necessary elements that form the intelligence of a system, while the processor, or microprocessor, is a component of the CPU.

2-2 MICROPROCESSORS

The CPU is the "brain" of a PLC. This part of the machine contains the memory circuits, decision-making circuits, and power supply for the CPU. In Figure 2-1, the power supply is contained inside the CPU block enclosure, although it may actually be in a separate unit mounted next to the enclosure that contains the processor and memory.

The microprocessor in a PLC system is controlled by a program called the *executive*, or *operating system*. The executive is a collection of supervisory programs that are permanently stored in memory. The executive program changes the generalized computing power of a microprocessor into a specialized PLC. By executing the operating system, the microprocessor can perform all of its control, processing, communication, and other related functions.

A typical microprocessor-based CPU will be capable of the following four basic types of operation:

1. Input and output operations. These functions allow the PLC to communicate with the outside world.

2. Arithmetic and logic. Operations such as add, subtract, and AND and OR functions are performed by the CPU.

3. Reading or changing contents of memory locations. The bit patterns accessed by the microprocessor may be data or instructions.

4. Jump operations. These functions allow portions of the user program to be bypassed when requested.

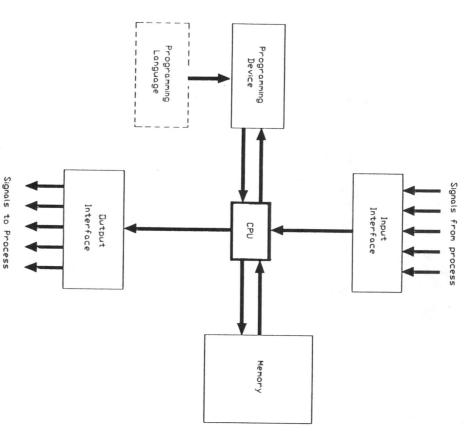

Figure 2-1 The relationship between the CPU and other parts of a PLC.

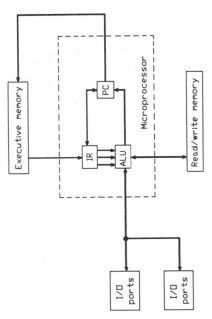

Figure 2-2 Basic components of a microprocessor.

Figure 2-2 shows the basic components of a microprocessor (MPU). The executive memory circuits hold the operating system. The **Arithmetic Logic Unit (ALU)** performs all arithmetic and logic operations. Also inside the microprocessor is the *program counter (PC)*. The PC keeps track of which step of the program's instructions the microprocessor is executing. When branches or jumps occur in the program, the PC is set forward or backward so that it keeps track of program execution at all times.

The *Internal Register (IR)* of the MPU stores data as commanded by the ALU. The IR receives information from the executive memory and stores these data until the ALU requests them.

The *Read/Write (R/W) memory* stores a program written by a user. Also stored in this memory are the general parameters for total system operation. Separate memory units in the read/write memory are typically referred to as **registers.**

The I/O ports shown in Figure 2-2 are used by the MPU to communicate with other circuits in the PLC system. Data are transferred by the I/O ports using **buses.** Figure 2-3 illustrates the connections of the buses used in a microprocessor system. The two main buses associated with the microprocessor are the *address bus* and *data bus*. A typical address bus contains 16 unidirectional lines. Unidirectional means data can only flow in one direction, like traffic on a one-way street. An address bus allows the microprocessor to select an address, which is then decoded, and the appropriate memory location or I/O device is chosen. An address bus's sole purpose is to activate devices and memory locations at the proper times for further use by the data bus.

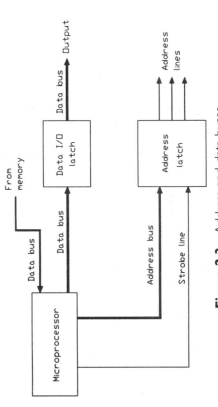

Figure 2-3 Address and data buses.

A data bus is bidirectional and is typically eight lines. Bidirectional means that data and information are allowed to flow in either direction. Data lines are used to transfer bits out of or into the microprocessor. A data bus can be used to read and write information such as the state of a coil or contact, or the value stored in a timer or counter.

Additional circuitry devices utilized by the microprocessor are required for the storage of data until the proper cycle time of the processor is reached. These peripheral devices are called **latches**. Figure 2-3 shows the two types of latches used by a microprocessor, the *address latch* and *data I/O latch*. The address latch receives an address location from the microprocessor and temporarily stores these data until the microprocessor commands the information to be sent. The command signal is transmitted through a line called a *strobe signal*. The I/O data latch is used by the microprocessor to temporarily store data being sent to the output system.

The power of a microprocessor can be defined in terms of the number and variety of instructions to which it can respond. There is an overall limit based on the sizes of the locations, or registers, of the microprocessor in which the instructions are stored. For example, an 8-bit register can hold only about 250 combinations, compared with the 65,000 combinations that can be held by a 16-bit register. This size difference between 8- and 16-bit microprocessors has an effect on the speed and precision with which mathematical operations are carried out.

2-3 CPU DIAGNOSTICS

The program entered into a PLC by a user is often referred to as a *control application program*. The executive program responds to the control application program and translates the application's program requirements into specific instructions appropriate for PLC action. Figure 2-4 illustrates the general functions of the executive program and its relationship to a control application program.

The executive program is responsible for *diagnostic procedures* performed by the CPU. The two most common types of CPU diagnostics are:

1. Self-checking on startup, or initialization.
2. User-initiated diagnostics.

Typical self-checking diagnostics include memory ok, processor ok, battery ok, and power supply ok. If the tests are successful, there is often an indicator light(s) on the CPU to make this fact apparent. User-initiated diagnostics normally test all memory and check other features, such as communications ports.

In some systems, the errors revealed by diagnostic checks are classified as *fatal* or *non-fatal* and are stored in a specially designated group of registers. Fatal errors, such as memory failure, or low-power supply activate a fault relay. The fault relay is controlled by the microprocessor and is activated when one or more

Figure 2-4 Function of executive program.

Central Processing Unit

EXECUTIVE
- I/O interface
- Handling
- Diagnostics
- Execution of applications program

Control Application Program

specific fault conditions occur. PLC systems which contain fault storage registers can be accessed by a programming terminal, and the specific failure area may be diagnosed.

The test of communications ports is performed as part of system procedures for communicating with the input/output subsystems. These techniques verify the validity of the data received and transmitted.

2-4 MULTIPROCESSING

The CPU of a PLC system may contain more than one microprocessor. The advantage of using multiprocessing is that control and communication tasks can be divided up, and the overall operating speed is improved. Under these circumstances, each microprocessor has a specific set of operations to look after. Some PLC manufacturers use a control microprocessor and a logic microprocessor. The control microprocessor carries out the more complex computations and data manipulations. The logic microprocessor executes the timing, logic, and counting operations, as well as looks after the applications program. Figure 2-5 shows a block diagram for a dual microprocessor CPU.

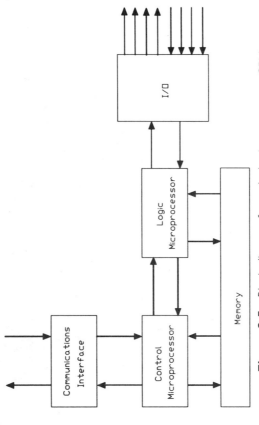

Figure 2-5 Block diagram for a dual microprocessor CPU.

In Figure 2-5, the logic microprocessor is shown to interact with the control microprocessor, memory, and I/O. It examines the control program and combines input data with internal data to produce a control output. When the logic microprocessor encounters a functional operation that exceeds its designated tasks, it transfers the problem to the control microprocessor. The control microprocessor signals the logic microprocessor when it has completed the task, allowing the result to be accessed and incorporated into the system output.

2-5 MEMORY

Data are stored in memory locations by a process called **writing**. Data are retrieved from memory by what is referred to as **reading**. The total number of binary digits, or bits, that can be stored in the RAM memory of a PLC is called the *memory capacity*. Memory capacity is often expressed in terms of 8-bit groups, or *bytes*. For example, if a PLC is said to have a memory capacity of 4K, this would mean that the machine is capable of storing four kilobytes of information, or 32 thousand bits.

The total memory system in a PLC is divided into the executive program and control application program. Because storage and retrieval requirements are not the same for both types of memory, they are not always stored in the same manner. For example, the application memory must be in a temporary storage medium because it must be changed whenever required. On the other hand, the executive program requires a memory that permanently stores its contents and cannot be deliberately or accidentally altered.

There are two general classes of memory devices: **volatile** and **nonvolatile.** Memory devices are classified according to how stable the stored data are when electrical power is removed. Volatile memory will lose data with loss of power; programs stored in these devices are usually protected by the use of backup battery power that operates when system power is removed. Volatile memory is easily altered and is ideally suited for application memory. Nonvolatile memory will retain its programmed contents, regardless of whether operating power is applied or not. The contents of nonvolatile memory are essentially permanent, requiring special operations to clear and reprogram the memory circuits.

Memory devices can be manufactured from either semiconductors or magnetic cores. Both types can be used for either volatile or non-volatile memory storage, although magnetic core is used mainly as non-volatile memory. Magnetic core memories have been in use since the 1950's, and it was an extremely popular storage medium in the first generation of PLCs. Semiconductor memory is generally faster, in terms of data retrieval time, and is gradually replacing magnetic core memories in all types of digital equipment.

Semiconductor memories are divided into two categories: **bipolar and MOS.** Bipolar memories are constructed using miniature bipolar transistors, while MOS memories use Metal Oxide Semiconductor Field Effect Transistors, or MOSFET's. Bipolar semiconductor memories contain more complex circuitry than MOS memory, thus limiting the amount of memory that can be placed on a silicon chip. Bipolar semiconductor memory is also referred to as Transistor-Transistor Logic, or TTL. MOS memory is slower than TTL but requires less power to operate, which makes MOS memory much more advantageous in situations such as volatile storage, where a battery is used to retain memory contents when power is removed.

2-6 MEMORY TYPES

Read Only Memory (ROM) is designed to permanently store fixed programs and data. The contents can be examined or read, but not written or altered. The bit patterns that represent a program are fixed in the device at the time of its manufacture. ROM memory Integrated Circuits (ICs) can be either TTL or MOS. PLC systems frequently use ROM chips known as Mask-programmed ROM, or *MROM.* A photographic negative, called a *mask,* is used to supervise the electrical interconnections stored in the ROM silicon chip. Generally, PLCs rarely use ROM for their application memories. Although in some situations, small, dedicated PLCs with limited programs and fixed data will use ROM memories for their application programs.

Random Access Memory (RAM) is also referred to as *Read/Write (R/W) memory,* and is designed so that information can be written into or read from any unique location. Random access memory is primarily constructed using TTL or MOS memory chips. There are two types of RAM: *static* and *dynamic.* Static RAM uses digital storage devices called *flip-flops.* Dynamic RAM uses a different technique that basically involves storing charges on a tiny capacitor element. The advantage of dynamic RAM is that it is physically smaller than static RAM. However, dynamic RAM requires a voltage signal to the logic states of dynamic memory at frequent intervals due to the leakage of charge from capacitor elements. Special silicon IC chips called *refresh controllers* are used to constantly recharge capacitive storage in a dynamic memory chip. RAM memory is the most popular approach for applications program storage.

Programmable Read Only Memory (PROM) is a special type of ROM that can be programmed. This type of memory is generally used to provide a permanent storage backup to RAM memory. Special programming equipment is required to enter a program, and once entered, it cannot be changed.

Erasable Programmable Read Only Memory (EPROM) is a specially designed PROM that can be reprogrammed, after being entirely erased, with the use of an Ultra-Violet (UV) light source. EPROM has a small window over the memory array. Exposure to a UV light will erase the contents of memory. For a typical mercury discharge light source, the erasure process requires about 20 minutes of exposure. EPROM is well-suited to applications programs in which nonvolatility is required, but which do not require changes to be made via a programming terminal.

Electrically Erasable Programmable Read Only Memory (EEPROM) is an IC memory which can be programmed using a typical PLC programming terminal. However, EEPROM must be totally erased before any new information can be entered. The erase/write process takes approximately 10 milliseconds, which can be a significant drawback when data are written as part of the execution of an application program.

Magnetic core memory uses a small toroidal (round) piece of ferromagnetic material called a *ferrite core*. Figure 2-6 shows a ferrite core with a conductor and a *sense line*. In reality, the core is approximately 20 mils in diameter. Ferrite cores have a high value of retentivity, which allows them to remain magnetized for very long periods of time. The core also has a very low reluctance, which means it is easily magnetized. Each core represents a single binary digit. The binary digit is considered to be either a 1 or a 0, depending on the direction of the flux in the core. When current passes through the core, magnetic flux is produced around the core in a direction determined by the *right hand rule*. When the current in the conductor is reduced to zero, flux is retained by the core. The two states of magnetism act in a similar manner to a flip-flop.

In a ferromagnetic core, when the flux direction is clockwise around the conductor, it is considered to have a binary 1 value. When the flux direction is counter-clockwise, the state of the memory core is said to be 0.

For a PLC to determine the state of its magnetic core, a sense line must be used. If the core has a small value of flux, it is implied that the core must be in a binary 0 condition, and the voltage induced in the sense line will be low. If the core is in a 1 state, the induced voltage in the sense line will be high.

The primary disadvantage of using magnetic core memory is that it uses what is known as *destructive readout*. Because all cores end up being reset to zero at some point, the information previously stored is erased, meaning that each time the status of the core is read, the data are cleared. The only way to retain the information after reading is to somehow write the data back into the magnetic core.

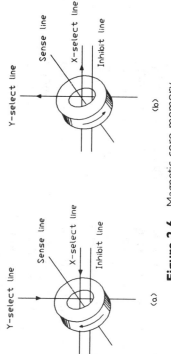

Figure 2-6   Magnetic core memory.

Another type of magnetic storage is Magnetic Bubble Memory, or MBM. An MBM uses a tiny cylindrical magnetic domain, which is embedded in a thin magnetic film. The domain bubbles move laterally in the film by applying a magnetic field parallel to the film. By continuously changing the magnetic field, the bubbles circulate in a loop inside the magnetic film. MBMs are capable of storing large amounts of data and are nonvolatile. If power is removed, the bubbles remain frozen in position. When power is restored, the bubbles resume circulating in a loop. Loops in an MBM are in the shape of continuous, elongated paths of major and minor loops. The minor loops are the memory cell arrays where the data are stored, and the major loop is a path used to retrieve data from the minor loops.

2-7 MEMORY PROTECT

Most CPUs are equipped with memory protect switches. These switches are key-operated, and when removed, will *lock out* the program stored in RAM memory. The program will still run when the memory protect is activated, however, it is impossible to alter the program once the memory protect is on. This protective system was designed to prevent unauthorized personnel from altering a program stored in the machine's memory. On some PLCs, the keylock switch is exclusively used for memory protect. Other machines, such as the Allen-Bradley PLC, also use the keylock switch on the CPU to operate the Run/Program operation, which will be discussed later.

CPUs also determine the number of I/O devices which can be accessed by a PLC. Most PLCs have CPUs which are capable of accessing 256 I/O points, although much larger and much smaller systems are available and in use by industry.

As the amount of I/O requirements increase, the amount of memory in the CPU must also increase. Most PLCs have expandable memory. That is, additional memory modules can be purchased to increase the size of memory in the CPU. Very small PLCs, which have less than 64 I/O points, usually do not have expandable memory, but systems with greater than 64 I/O are generally expandable in increments of 1K, 2K, 4K, etc. (The abbreviation K represents 1024 memory locations.)

2-8 MEMORY UTILIZATION

A memory location is an address in the CPU's memory where a binary word can be stored. A word, or register, consists of usually 8 or 16 binary digits, or bits. A single contact may use one location in the machine's memory. In systems where only eight bits are used in a memory location, the memory capability is 1/2 that of a CPU with 16 bits in a location.

The term memory utilization refers to the number of memory locations required to store each type of instruction. For example, an analog input requires more memory than a discrete input because it contains more variables. However, a rule of thumb for memory locations is one location per coil, or contact. 1K of memory would allow a program containing 1000 coils and contacts to be stored in RAM.

Two terms that often arise when programming PLCs are: *input tables* and *output tables*. These terms simply refer to a location where the status of an input or output device is stored. If a PLC has 32 inputs connected at the I/O rack, an input table containing 32 bits would be required. Each bit is either a 1 or 0 depending on whether the input is open or closed. A closed contact, such as a Stop switch, would have a binary 1 stored in its respective location in the input table. A solenoid which is de-energized would have a 0 in its output table. Input and output tables are constantly being revised by the CPU. Each time a memory location is examined, the table changes if the contact or coil has changed state.

Most PLCs also contain coils and contacts which are not accessible at the I/O rack. These software coils are used for interlocking purposes, in the same way control relays are used in relay logic circuits. These internal coils and contacts are referred to as internal storage bits, and have a portion of the CPU's memory set aside for their functions.

CPUs also have memory locations set aside for storing data from timers, counters, and analog modules. These addresses are called *storage registers*, and contain values stored in binary form.

2-9 MEMORY ORGANIZATION

Each PLC manufacturer uses a slightly different method of organizing the information which is stored in the memory of the machine. Although all PLCs have similarities in their memory structure, such as RAM and ROM chips, the locations where bits of information are stored and the method the CPU uses to read these data can vary quite substantially.

Memory organization takes into account the way a PLC divides the available memory into different sections. Because ROM memory contains information that is not alterable, this portion of memory is a fixed quantity. However, application memory is usually quite flexible in terms of how many bytes of information are allocated for any particular function. For example, if you are programming a PLC system which requires a large number of counters and timers, it is possible on some PLCs to alter the size of the memory allocated for these instructions.

The entire processor memory of a typical PLC is divided into three major parts: data table, user program, and message storage area. These sections store information about the status of an input or output device, and are also used to store program instructions and messages. Figure 2-7 shows the standard memory layout for an Allen-Bradley PLC. Each of the three sections is capable of handling various amounts of information. The memory itself is divided according to how many binary digits, or bits, it is capable of handling.

The left side of Figure 2-7 shows the total words allocated for each portion of memory. The factory-configured data in the data table has 128 words, or

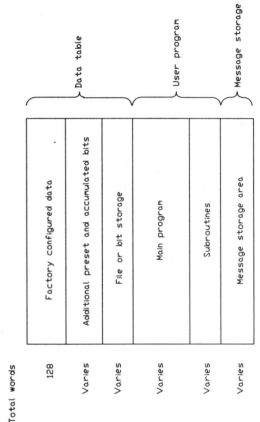

Figure 2-7 Allen-Bradley memory layout.

128 × 16 bits, set aside for programs and subroutines that were installed by the manufacturer. This portion of the memory would be considered part of the ROM memory because factory-configured data cannot be erased. The two other headings in the data table are used for storing information accumulated by timers, counters, sequencers, and other file functions. Because the total number of timers and counters available can be slightly adjusted, the total words allocated for these two sections is considered to vary.

The main program, subroutines, and file or bit storage are in the portion of memory set aside for the user. This portion of the memory is also referred to as the application memory. The application memory stores programmed instructions. The data table also shares the file or bit storage. It is inside the data table that information about devices such as coils and contacts is stored. The data table consists of the input table, output table, internal storage bits, and storage registers. The data table stores the status of a bit. For example, if a coil is energized, the bit in the data table for the coil's address will be 1, if the coil is de-energized, the bit will be 0. The data table also stores information about timers and counters, such as the accumulated value of a timer.

The input table stores information about input devices connected to the PLC. If there are 24 inputs connected to a machine, 24 bits are required for the input table. Each bit indicates the status of the device connected to the PLC. The output table also has a size which corresponds to the number of output devices connected to the machine. Internal storage bits are also referred to as "software coils". These coils and contacts can be used in the program, but are not accessible at the I/O rack. Internal coils are used for interlocking purposes in the control program. For example, if a control relay operates a motor, the control relay may not be required at the I/O rack because it is not physically connected to any device. Therefore, an internal coil could be used as a control relay, and the motor itself could be an output coil that actually has a physical location at the I/O rack. Because timers and counters themselves are not accessible at the internal addresses, the addresses of these types of functions are considered to be internal addresses.

Storage registers include input, output, and holding registers. Input registers store data obtained from analog and word input devices such as thermocouples, thumbwheel switches, shaft encoders, etc. Output registers contain binary information which can be sent to output modules such as analog output cards, or word output cards. This type of information is used when controlling devices such as variable speed drives for motor control, or decimal indicating devices such as tachometers, temperature displays, or any type of numerical indicator. Holding registers hold information regarding the accumulated value of timers, counters, etc.

A user program is the memory which is set aside for ladder logic programs written by the user. This portion of the machine's memory is used to store all PLC instructions that have been programmed by the user into memory. The addresses of all inputs and outputs are stored in the user program. When the PLC is operating, the processor is constantly reading the user program and controlling the bits that are stored in the data table. The size of the user program is determined by the size of the PLC itself. That is, the amount of user program is determined by the number of inputs and outputs that the PLC is capable of addressing.

A portion of the PLC's memory is also allocated for subroutines. This portion of the memory is allocated for the storage of relatively small programs that are periodically accessed by the main user program. The subroutine area itself is not scanned by the CPU unless instructed to do so by a subroutine instruction. When the processor receives a subroutine command, it jumps to this portion of the memory, scans the subroutine program, and essentially acts as an end-of-program statement for the main program itself.

The last major part of the memory system on the Allen-Bradley PLC is the message storage area. This area is allocated for storing user-programmed messages to be displayed on the CRT screen or printed out in hardcopy form. A standard T3 dedicated programming terminal will allow storage of up to 70 messages. These messages can be used in a similar manner to REM statements in computer programming. Message storage will be displayed after the end statement of a ladder logic program. Each binary word allocated in this portion of memory will store two alphanumeric characters.

Virtually all portions of Allen-Bradley memory are variable, which allows for considerable customizing of this type of PLC. For example, if you are doing a lot of programming which involves timers and counters, the data table can be expanded to accommodate up to 488 counters and timers using the PLC-2 system. The data table will allow expansion up to a maximum of 7,808 words using a PLC-2/17, or it can be left in the factory-configured size of 128 words, depending on the application.

2-10 SCAN FUNCTION

For a CPU to execute a program stored in memory, it must be able to *see* what is occurring in the various memory locations. The procedure of reading the status of all inputs and outputs, examining application program instructions, and executing the control program is referred to as the *scan function* of a PLC.

The CPU is constantly interacting with system memory to interpret and execute the application program that controls the machine, or process. The amount of time required for the CPU to read the program stored in RAM memory, execute the control program, and update all outputs on the I/O rack is called **scan time.**

Scan time is a very important factor in a PLC. For example, if an input signal changes states twice during one scan, the PLC will never be able to "see" the signal. This situation occurs if the change in input signal is faster than the scan time. If it takes 7 ms for the CPU to scan a program, and an input contact is opening and closing every 3 ms, the CPU does not know that the contact is changing state. Most PLCs have a scan time which can be adjusted for different operations such as troubleshooting, or program debugging.

Each instruction entered into a program requires a certain amount of time for the instruction to be executed. The amount of time required depends on the instruction. For example, it takes less time for a processor to read the status of an output coil than it does to read the accumulated value of a timer. The overall length of the program itself will also have an effect on scan time. Table 2-1 shows the average length of time required for the CPU to process some typical instructions.

The length of time required to scan an entire program once varies between 1 ms and 255 ms, depending on the manufacturer and model number of the machine being used. The amount of RAM memory allocated by a manufacturer will have

TABLE 2-1

Instruction	Average Time if Instruction Is Energized	Average Time if Instruction Is De-energized
Normally open contact	7 μs	6 μs
Normally closed contact	5 μs	5 μs
Output coil	8 μs	8 μs
TDON timer	50 μs	35 μs
TDOFF timer	55 μs	40 μs
Up-counter	40 μs	30 μs
Down-counter	35 μs	30 μs
Math function	30–300 μs	15 μs
Sequencer	400 μs	50 μs
Data transfer	200 μs	50 μs

an effect on total scan time as well. Typically, 2 ms is added for each 1K of memory available. When a programming terminal is connected to the CPU, scan time also increases because it takes longer to transmit the status of I/O to the CRT screen.

2-11 POWER SUPPLY

A PLC's power supply provides all the voltage levels required for operation. The power supply converts 120 or 220 VAC into the DC voltage required by the CPU, memory, and I/O electronic circuitry. The PLC operates on +5 and −5 V DC. Therefore, the power supply must be capable of rectifying and stepping-down the AC input voltage to a usable level of DC voltage. Conversion is accomplished by using two Full Wave Bridge rectifiers (FWB) and a center-tap transformer, as shown in Figure 2-8. This circuit also illustrates voltage waveforms at various points in the power supply.

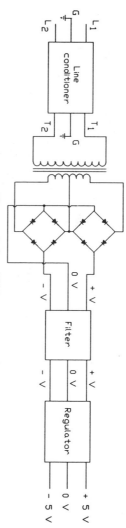

Figure 2-8 CPU power supply.

In Figure 2-8, L₁ and L₂ represent incoming AC power. The neutral conductor is indicated as N. The line conditioner prevents AC voltage spikes from affecting the power supply. Terminals T₁ and T₂ represent the primary connections for the voltage transformer. The two FWBs are used to rectify the stepped-down AC voltage. One bridge produces +5 VDC and the other produces −5 VDC. This dual voltage is required to operate many of the IC chips in the CPU.

The filter circuit is used to smooth out the pulsating DC voltage from the rectifiers. The internal circuitry of a filter is generally comprised of combinations of resistors, capacitors, and/or inductors. In some cases, filtering is accomplished electronically.

The regulator circuit is designed to ensure a constant voltage level at the output of the power supply, regardless of the loading conditions that occur. An ideal power supply should produce the same output voltage whether it is fully loaded or if no load is applied. The regulator electronically monitors the output voltage to maintain steady values of +5 VDC and −5 VDC at the output.

REVIEW QUESTIONS

2-1. The CPU in a PLC
    (a) is stored in RAM.
    (b) is usually a microprocessor.
    (c) contains the applications program.
    (d) can be erased using UV light.

2-2. Which task does a CPU in a PLC NOT perform?
    (a) Arithmetic functions
    (b) Basic data manipulation
    (c) Provide direct connection to process sensors for control
    (d) Change the executive and applications programs

2-3. What are the two main functions of the ALU?

2-4. What are the two main buses associated with a microprocessor?

2-5. A program entered into a PLC by a user is generally referred to as
 (a) the executive program.
 (b) the control application program.
 (c) ROM.
 (d) RAM.

2-6. A microprocessor is used in a PLC as
 (a) ROM.
 (b) a CRT.
 (c) a bus.
 (d) a CPU.

2-7. What are the two most common types of CPU diagnostics?

2-8. Errors revealed by diagnostic checks are
 (a) fatal or non-fatal.
 (b) invalid.
 (c) caused by user programs.
 (d) not serious in nature.

2-9. Memory size in a PLC is NOT measured in
 (a) baud.
 (b) words.
 (c) bits.
 (d) bytes.

2-10. Volatile memory
 (a) is always ROM.
 (b) is never used in PLCs.
 (c) loses data if power is removed.
 (d) is always core memory.

2-11. Core memory
 (a) is faster than semiconductor memory.
 (b) is never used in PLCs.
 (c) is always used in PLCs.
 (d) has a high value of retentivity.

2-12. What are the two categories of semiconductor memories?

2-13. Programmable Read Only Memory (PROM)
 (a) is also referred to as read/write memory.
 (b) is a specially-designed PROM that can be reprogrammed with UV light.
 (c) is generally used to provide a permanent storage backup to RAM memory.
 (d) can be programmed easily via a PLC programming terminal.

2-14. Magnetic bubble memory
 (a) is volatile.
 (b) is nonvolatile.
 (c) can only store small amounts of data.
 (d) is programmed by UV light.

2-15. The most common form of memory used to store the applications program in a PLC is
 (a) EEPROM.
 (b) EPROM.
 (c) ROM.
 (d) RAM.

2-16. Memory protect
 (a) locks out the program stored in RAM.
 (b) prevents RAM memory from being lost when power is removed.

(c) locks out the program stored in **ROM.**

(d) prevents UV light from erasing programs.

2-17. Typically, a word stored in PLC memory consists of

(a) 8 bytes.

(b) up to 26 letters.

(c) 8 or 16 bits.

(d) 8 or 16 registers.

2-18) Define the term "memory utilization".

2-19. 1K of memory is actually

(a) 1000 bits.

(b) 1000 words.

(c) 1024 bits.

(d) 1024 words.

2-20. What is a data table?

2-21. True/False: The executive software in most PLCs is backed up by a battery.

2-22. A PLC with a maximum of 256 outputs would require an output table of

(a) 256 bytes.

(b) 256 bits.

(c) 128 bits.

(d) 128 bytes.

2-23. A PLC system has an 8-bit microprocessor with a 16-bit memory structure. How many bits will the memory have if it has a memory capacity of 8K?

(a) 131,072 bits

(b) 8,192 bits

(c) 8,000 bits

(d) 128,000 bits

2-24. An area NOT commonly allocated in the memory map of a PLC is

(a) the applications program.

(b) the data table.

(c) the CPU

(d) the executive program.

2-25. What is "scan time"?

2-26. If a PLC has a total scan time of 5 ms and is required to monitor a signal that _____, the CPU will never notice that the signal has changed state.

(a) changes state once in 10 ms.

(b) changes state very slowly.

(c) changes state once in 20 ms.

(d) changes state twice in 4 ms.

3

I/O System

Upon completion of this chapter, you will be able to

▶ Explain the purpose of the I/O system.
▶ Understand I/O addressing.
▶ Define discrete inputs.
▶ List four tasks performed by an input module.
▶ Describe the basic operation of a discrete output.
▶ Explain the purpose of data I/O interfaces.
▶ Define analog I/O.
▶ Describe the resolution of an analog I/O module.
▶ List three applications for advanced I/O.
▶ Explain the purpose of remote I/O.

3-I INTRODUCTION

The I/O system provides an interface between the hardwired components in the field, and the CPU. The input interface allows status information regarding processes to be communicated to the CPU and allows the CPU to communicate operating signals through the output interface to the process devices under its control.

The CPU has timing and control lines that connect to the input and output interfaces. During the operating cycle, these lines provide the signals that control the transmission of information between the CPU/memory system and the I/O interfaces. During each cycle, the inputs are signalled and their registers are updated. While this interchange is taking place, the revised output register contents

3-2 I/O ADDRESSING

are transferred to the output interface circuits under the control of these timing lines.

Early versions of today's PLCs were limited to interface circuits that could translate voltage level signals from ON/OFF type devices in the field to the logic voltage signals required by the electronics in a PLC. This limitation allowed the PLC only partial control of many processes. As applications multiplied, so did I/O interfaces. Today's PLCs have a large variety of I/O interfaces available. These interfaces interact with almost every conceivable process element. The demand for faster control has also led to intelligent I/O interfaces. Intelligent I/O speeds up CPU scan time by assuming some data manipulation and timing duties.

The I/O system basically consists of two components: the I/O rack and the I/O module. For most PLCs, the location of where a module is inserted defines the address of each connected device. A module usually consists of either eight inputs or eight outputs, and a rack will, in most cases, hold eight modules. Therefore, the standard number of I/O points in one rack is 64. This number can certainly be larger or smaller, but 64 I/O is still considered to be relatively standard. High-density modules consist of 16 inputs or outputs, and some PLC manufacturers have I/O modules containing 32 input or output points.

Programmable controller I/O is divided into two general classes: those with fixed or nonflexible addressing schemes and those with flexible, adaptable addressing schemes. Addressing is the way that the control program in the CPU relates to a particular real-world sensor or actuator. The design of a PLC determines whether or not the system is capable of being addressed flexibly, or is rigid in its addressing method.

Flexible addressing schemes allow PLC systems to be designed and installed in several sections, or stages. This installation scheme allows system designers to create control logic software without being constrained to follow a sequential I/O assignment, resulting in a randomly addressed and installed I/O system. The disadvantage of flexible I/O addressing is that in large PLC systems, such a design may make it difficult to diagnose and correct problems when they occur. This is particularly true when proper PLC documentation I/O is not provided.

Addressing is either in decimal or octal form. The decimal method follows a sequential assignment of I/O points, such as inputs 1 through 8 for the first module, 9 through 16 for the second module, 17 through 24 for the third, etc. The octal numbering system is based on 8 digits, 0 through 7. An 8-point I/O module using the octal number system would have addresses 0 through 7 for the first module, 10 through 17 for the second, and 20 through 27 for the third module.

In flexible addressing schemes, I/O is addressed by either physically setting a series of Dual Inline Package (DIP) switches associated with a particular slot in the I/O rack or, in some newer PLC systems, using EEPROM memory to hold I/O address data. Addressing is generally established during initial system configuration, and is considered to be permanent. Figure 3-1 illustrates a typical configuration of DIP switches for I/O rack selection.

In nonflexible systems, individual slot and point addresses are normally determined by the sequence in which the I/O racks are connected together. In the case of some small PLCs, the system contains one rack and therefore has I/O addressing fixed by the manufacturer.

Actual address labelling varies greatly from manufacturer to manufacturer. Generally, four or five digits are used in a typical I/O address. For example, an Allen-Bradley input address would be 11000. The first digit in this address identifies

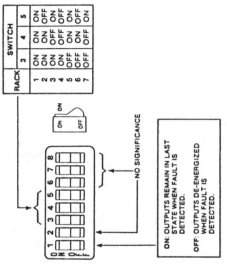

RACK	SWITCH		
	3	4	5
1	ON	ON	ON
2	ON	ON	OFF
3	ON	OFF	ON
4	ON	OFF	OFF
5	OFF	ON	ON
6	OFF	ON	OFF
7	OFF	OFF	ON

NO SIGNIFICANCE

ON: OUTPUTS REMAIN IN LAST STATE WHEN FAULT IS DETECTED.

OFF: OUTPUTS DE-ENERGIZED WHEN FAULT IS DETECTED.

Figure 3-1 Configuration of DIP switches. (Courtesy of Allen-Bradley.)

whether the device is an input or output; if it is a 1, it is an input device, if it is 0, it is an output device. The second digit is the rack number. The third digit identifies the module number. Because Allen-Bradley PLCs use the octal numbering system, the number 0 means that this is the first module in the rack. The last two digits identify the connection point in the module itself. These numbers are typically 00 to 07.

3-3   DISCRETE INPUTS

The most common type of I/O interface is the *discrete* type. A discrete component is something that can be in only one of two possible states—either ON or OFF. A Start switch would be an example of a discrete input, and a motor starter coil would be a type of discrete output. The classification of discrete I/O covers bit-oriented inputs and outputs. In this type of input or output, each bit represents a complete information element in itself, providing the status of some external contact or advising of the presence or absence of power in a process circuit. Several types of discrete inputs and outputs are shown in Table 3-1.

Discrete I/O interfaces receive their module voltage and current for proper operation from the back plane of the rack enclosure into which they are inserted. Power from the supply is used to power the electronics, both active and passive, that reside on the I/O module circuit board. The relatively higher currents required by the loads of an output module are supplied by user-supplied power. Table 3-2 shows the standard ratings for discrete I/O interfaces.

TABLE 3-1 Discrete Inputs and Outputs

Field Input Devices	Field Output Devices
Pushbuttons	Control relays
Selector switches	Alarms
Limit switches	Valves
Relay contacts	Motor starters
Motor starter contacts	Solenoids
Relay contacts	Fans
Photoelectric eyes	Lights
Proximity switches	
Thumbwheel switches	
Circuit breakers	

TABLE 3-2 Standard Discrete I/O
Interface Ratings

Input Interfaces	Output Interfaces
24 V AC/DC	24 V AC/DC
48 V AC/DC	48 V AC/DC
120 V AC/DC	120 V AC/DC
220 V AC/DC	220 V AC/DC
TTL level	TTL level

A typical input module performs the following four tasks:

1. Senses the presence or absence of an input signal at each of its input terminals.
2. Converts an input signal to a level usable by the interface's electronic circuit.
3. Electronically isolates the input and output stages of the module.
4. Produces an output to be sensed by the CPU with its electronic circuit.

A block diagram of a typical AC/DC input interface circuit is shown in Figure 3-2. Notice the bridge rectifier circuit to detect AC. This component is present regardless of whether the module is AC or DC. The bridge is usually followed by signal conditioning, which protects against signal bouncing and electrical noise on the input power line. This filter causes a signal delay of typically 9-25 ms. The threshold decision circuit detects whether the incoming signal has reached the proper voltage level for the specified input rating. The threshold decision is usually based on both voltage level and time above the critical level. If the input signal exceeds and remains above the threshold voltage for a time period of at least the

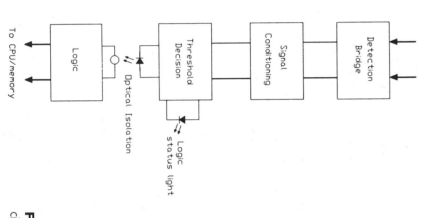

Figure 3-2 Block diagram for AC/DC input circuit.

filter delay (9–25 ms), the signal will be recognized as valid input. After this block has determined that input is valid, it is usually passed through an isolation stage so that external circuit problems are unlikely to reach inside the interface.

The optical isolation in the circuit of Figure 3-2 is generally accomplished by a Light-Emitting Diode (LED) phototransistor, or some other type of opto-coupler device. This optical isolation ensures that there is no electrical connection between the field device (power) and PLC (logic). The separation between these two circuits will help prevent large voltage spikes from damaging the logic side of the interface, and is an important feature that contributes to the reliability of the system in the event of wiring accidents.

The last step of interfacing involves conditioning the signal to correspond with correct logic 1 or 0 voltage levels. There is usually provision to indicate the current status of the input, using an LED that lights in the logic 1 input condition.

An AC input device, such as a switch, will have the power applied to the switch, and when the switch is closed, the signal will arrive at the input module. The AC voltage is then rectified and stepped down to a value that the CPU can process. Figure 3-3 shows the internal circuitry of an input module. The capacitor, C, is used to filter the ripple voltage produced by the rectifier circuit. The isolation between the input voltage and the voltage to the CPU is accomplished by an opto-coupler. The opto-coupler contains an LED encapsulated in plastic with a phototransistor. The LED is placed inside the plastic so its light shines directly onto the phototransistor. When a rectified DC signal passes through the LED, the transistor switches ON and passes current to the logic circuitry of the PLC. An indicating LED is also used to show whether there is power flow to the input point.

Most input circuits will have an LED (power) indicator to show that the proper input voltage level is present at the module. In addition to a power indicator, many input modules also have an LED to indicate the presence of a logic 1 at the logic section. If the input voltage is present, and the logic circuit is functioning properly, this LED is illuminated. Figure 3-4 illustrates a typical input module. The electronic circuitry is housed inside a plastic case.

Most of the discrete I/O modules currently on the market have common user-driven features. In most cases, the faceplate to which the field wiring is attached can be removed from the I/O module circuit board to make servicing the PLC system easier, because disturbing the field wiring on an installed system may cause various problems. Most faceplates and I/O modules are keyed to prevent putting the wrong faceplate on the wrong module. In other words, an output module cannot be placed in the slot where an input module was originally located. Figure 3-5 shows two different methods of keying modules. In Figure 3-5(a), the I/O rack backplane connector is keyed to prevent any module, other than the type for which the connector is keyed, from being installed in that particular slot. In Figure 3-5(b), a connector keying pin is used to prevent any other module from being installed in that connector.

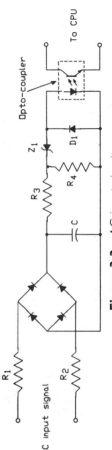

Figure 3-3 AC input circuit.

Wiring connections on a faceplate are typically of the box lug terminal type, and allow wire up to No. 12 AWG to be easily attached. A typical I/O faceplate also includes a space designated for labelling the physical I/O points for real-world identification. This label space is usually adjacent to the status indicators for troubleshooting ease.

Figure 3-6 shows a typical wiring diagram for an input module of a PLC. This wiring technique is valid for almost any type of PLC. In Figure 3-6(a), the AC input power is identified as L1 and L2. All input devices are shown connected

Figure 3-4   Typical input module.

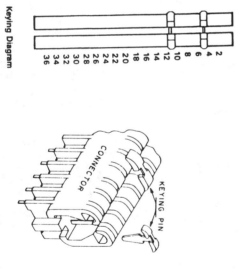

Keying Diagram

2
4
6
8
10
12
14
16
18
20
22
24
26
28
30
32
34
36

CONNECTOR

KEYING PIN

Figure 3-5   Keyed connectors and slots.

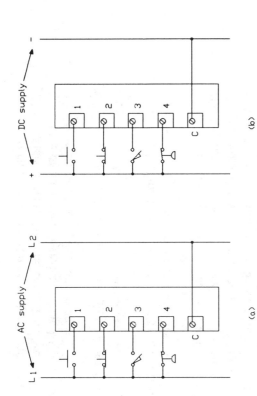

(a)   (b)

Figure 3-6 Typical connection diagram for (a) AC; and (b) DC input modules.

in parallel to L1, while L2 is brought directly to the module itself. If this were a 120 V input card, L2 would represent the neutral connection.

In Figure 3-6(b), the supply voltage is DC and the input devices are shown connected in parallel with the + DC and the common point, C, of the module is connected to the −DC of the supply.

A TTI, or Transistor-Transistor Logic, level is a 5 V DC I/O point which allows interfacing with TTL-compatible devices, such as solid-state controls and sensing instruments. TTL input modules generally receive their power from within the rack enclosure, although some interfaces may require an external +5 VDC power supply. TTL output interfaces to all of the PLC to drive output devices that are TTL-compatible, such as 7-segment LED displays, Integrated Circuits (ICs), and assorted +5 VDC devices. TTL output modules usually require an external +5 VDC power supply (rack- or panel-mounted) with specific current requirements.

The TTL input module has a configuration similar to AC/DC inputs; however, the time delay caused by filtering is usually much shorter with a TTL input. Figure 3-7 shows a typical TTL input connection diagram. The input cable to the TTL

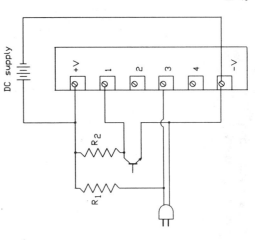

Figure 3-7 Typical TTL connection diagram.

module is shielded and certain precautions must be taken when installing this type of cable (see Chapter 5). The cable shield reduces the effects of electrical noise.

One of the newer developments in I/O technology is the mixed I/O module. This module has two distinct advantages:

1. It has the ability to be distributed in an I/O system all the way down to the sensors and actuators. Consequently, the installation costs of the control system are reduced.

2. The I/O module has the capability to detect failures, both in the module, as well as in the sensors and actuators connected to it.

In addition to the above features, a mixed I/O module allows each point on the module to be selectable as either an input or output point. For example, an 8-point module can be configured as seven in and one out, or as four in and four out, or three in and five out. Some PLC manufacturers already have mixed I/O modules available as dedicated four-in, four-out modules, but without the added benefits of cost-effective distribution and enhanced diagnostics.

3-4 DISCRETE OUTPUTS

A discrete output module operates in the opposite manner from an input module. A DC signal from the CPU is converted through each module section to a usable output voltage. A block diagram of an output module is shown in Figure 3-8. The logic signal generated by the PLC is passed through an electrical isolation stage, followed by a switching circuit. This circuit handles the externally-supplied power and is usually provided with protection against surge currents, as well as normal overload fusing. A signal from the CPU is received by the logic circuitry, one for each scan. If the CPU signal code corresponds to the assigned number of the module, the module section is energized. The identification numbers of a module are determined by the setting of the module's microswitches. A typical discrete output module may have 4, 8, or 16 output points.

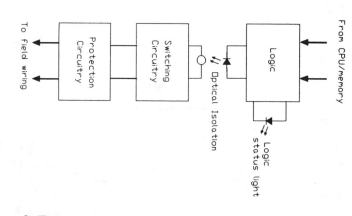

Figure 3-8 Block diagram of an AC or DC output interface.

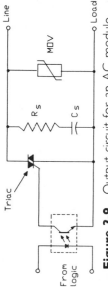

Figure 3-9 Output circuit for an AC module.

Output modules usually have indicator lights to indicate point status. These lights may be of a neon type if used on the field side of the connections. Fuses are generally required here, and are provided on a per circuit basis, thus allowing for each circuit to be protected and operated separately. Some modules also provide visual indicators for fuse status. Newer modules provide circuit protection on a programmable, nondestructive basis, thus eliminating the need for fuses. Voltage isolation and transient protection are also provided.

Figure 3-9 shows the internal circuitry of an AC output module. Once again, isolation between the small CPU voltage and the larger output voltage is accomplished by an opto-coupler. The opto-coupler is connected to the gate of the triac and switches the triac ON when a signal is received. The triac is the equivalent of two SCRs in inverse parallel connection with a common gate that controls the switching state. Once the breakover voltage point on the gate is reached, the triac conducts in either direction. The gate pulse which turns the triac on is controlled by a logic level signal from the CPU. The logic signal is isolated to prevent a failure in the output module from damaging the CPU.

When a triac is switched, a large inductive voltage spike may develop, which can damage electronic circuitry. In Figure 3-9, the potential for damage is reduced by the use of an RC snubber and Metal Oxide Varistor (MOV). The RC snubber consists of a resistor, R_s, and a capacitor, C_s, connected in series across the triac. The MOV is also connected across the triac to help suppress any voltage spikes which may occur.

Figure 3-10 shows a typical wiring diagram for an AC output module. When an output signal is received at each output, it enables that circuit's triac, and an output current is applied at the module's output terminal. Because the output current of a typical AC output module is about 20 mA, a standard Control Relay (CR), which has a small inrush and seal-in current, is connected to the output module. The contacts of the CR are then used to control the larger load.

A DC output interface is used to switch DC loads. Instead of a triac or SCR, a DC output generally uses a power transistor to switch the DC voltage. Power transistors are also sensitive to excessively applied voltages and surge currents, which could result in overdissipation and short-circuit conditions. To prevent

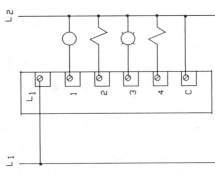

Figure 3-10 AC output module connection diagram.

these conditions from occurring, a power transistor is usually protected by a *free wheeling diode*. By placing a diode across the output field device (i.e., motor starter coil), the counter emf (electromotive force) developed by the inductive load is dissipated by the diode and the transistor is protected. Figure 3-11 shows a typical DC output circuit and a wiring method for a DC output module.

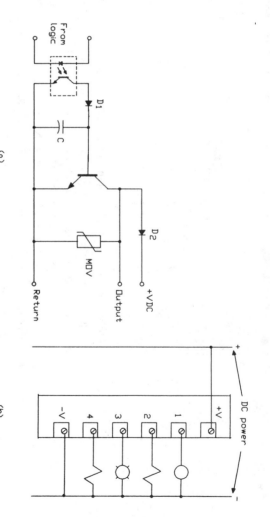

Figure 3-11 (a) Typical DC output circuit; (b) Device connection.

3-5 DATA I/O INTERFACES

Numerical data I/O interfaces can be divided into two general classes: those that provide interface to multibit digital devices and those that provide interface to analog devices. In this section, we will examine the modules that provide interface to multibit digital devices.

Multibit digital devices are discrete (ON/OFF) in nature and allow a group of bits to be input or output as a unit. One type of multibit input module is the register, or BCD (Binary Coded Decimal). This type of module allows groups of bits to be input as a unit to accommodate devices that require bits to be handled in parallel form. Examples of such devices include thumbwheel switches with BCD outputs, absolute shaft encoders with Gray code, and a variety of panel meter instruments. A typical input module may contain four input channels, each capable of handling 16 bits.

A typical data interface module is used to input data into specific register or word locations in memory to be used by the control program. Register input modules usually accept voltages in the range of 5 VDC (TTL) to 24 VDC. Data manipulation instructions such as GET and MOVW are used to access data from the register input module.

Inputs are filtered and isolated, and output power is supplied for the interface circuitry that lies outside the opto-coupler. Field data are received under the supervision of the timing signals generated by the module itself, and these data are temporarily stored in an input buffer register. This register is updated independently from the CPU scan cycle by interface timing signals. However, a synchronizing signal between the CPU and module is used to prevent the buffer from being overwritten while it is being read by the CPU. Figure 3-12 shows a block diagram of the functional relationships of a typical data input module.

Figure 3-13 shows a data input interface (register input module) connected to thumbwheel switches. In this illustration, it is assumed that the CPU is programmed to convert the BCD value into an equivalent binary value, and to load

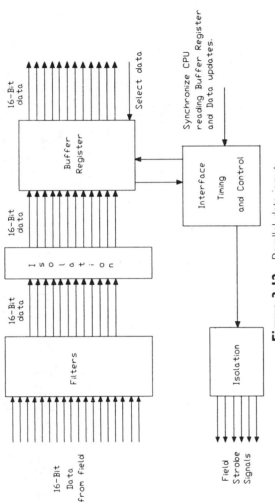

Figure 3-12 Parallel data input.

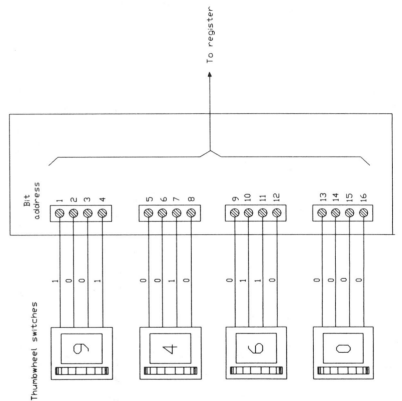

Figure 3-13 BCD input interface module.

the binary number into the register. Typical parameters are timer and counter presets, and setpoint values. Each input operates in a very similar manner to that of the TTL or DC input modules mentioned previously.

By using **multiplexing,** more than one input line can be connected to each terminal of a data I/O module. Multiplexing essentially allows one transmission line to carry several digital signals. This sharing of transmission lines is accomplished by each line being used in short intervals at prescribed times by each signal source. Therefore, a switching effect is observed as the multiplex circuitry alternately switches from one signal source to another. Figure 3-14 illustrates a

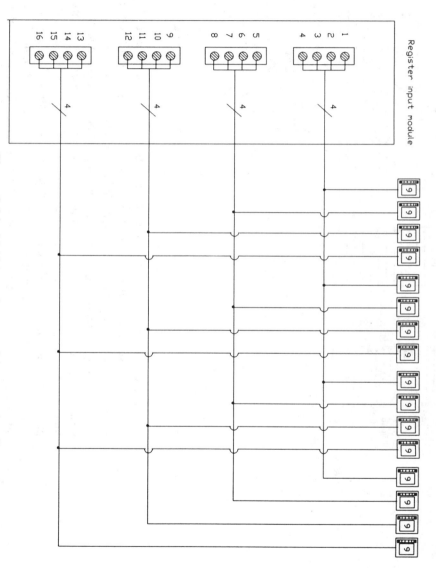

Figure 3-14 Multiplexer input module connection diagram.

block diagram connection for a module which is capable of multiplexing four 4-digit thumbwheel switches. In this circuit, each thumbwheel switch provides four lines of data to each four groups of input bits in the multiplexer module.

For multiplexing to be properly executed in data I/O modules, it is necessary to apply strobe signals to indicate the timing. This technique requires that various device outputs use tri-state, open collector outputs, or diode isolation, and that the device have a strobe or enable capability. Figure 3-15 shows the timing and data transfer sequences for a typical multiplexed interface.

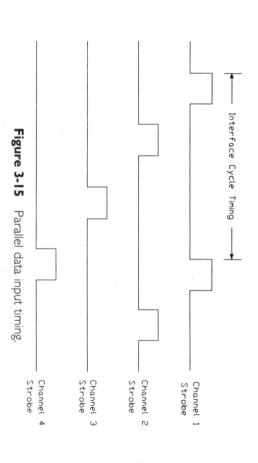

Figure 3-15 Parallel data input timing.

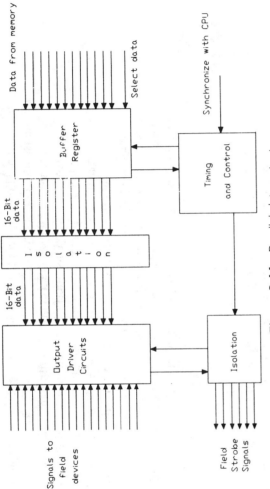

Figure 3-16 Parallel data output.

Data output interfaces provide outputs that are word-oriented, typically providing 16-bit parallel outputs. These outputs are used to drive devices such as 7-segment displays and process elements capable of being driven by multibit parallel instructions. Once again, it is not unusual for multiplexing to be used to drive multiple systems, although to achieve this task, it is necessary for the field devices to be activated to receive the data signals by some timing pulse. Figure 3-16 shows a block diagram of the basic functional relationships of a parallel output data interface. The outputs are opto-coupled and protected, and an external power supply is required to the circuitry beyond the opto-coupler. The timing and control

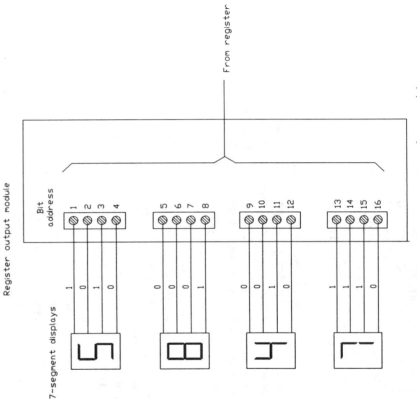

Figure 3-17 Data output interface module.

3-6 ANALOG I/O

circuitry allows the contents of the data registers or output buffers to be fed to the isolation circuitry.

Figure 3-17 shows a register (BCD) output interface connected to a 7-segment LED display board. This interface is used to output data from a specific register or word location in memory. Register output modules generally provide voltages that range from 5 VDC to 30 VDC and have 16 or 32 output lines, corresponding to one or two I/O registers, respectively. When information is sent from the CPU through a data transfer or I/O register instruction, the data are latched in the module and made available at the output circuit. In Figure 3-17, it is assumed that the CPU is programmed to convert the BCD value into an equivalent binary value, and then to load that binary value into the register.

Analog I/O devices are components whose input or output varies in both time and magnitude. A sine wave is an analog signal. A thermocouple would be considered to be an analog input because it produces voltages which vary with temperature. An AC drive would require an analog output signal from a PLC because the drive causes a motor to operate at an rpm which is determined by the voltage applied to the drive's control circuit. Analog input and output modules are utilized whenever the sensors and actuators chosen are of the continuously variable type, in contrast to the discrete I/O ON-OFF type. Analog input modules generally have eight available channels, while a typical output module has either two or four channels. Some of the newer analog modules have both analog inputs and analog outputs on the same module, typically with four input channels and two output channels.

Analog interfaces are available in unipolar (positive) and bipolar (positive and negative) ratings. Standard ratings found in analog modules are shown in Table 3-3.

An analog input module performs what is known as an Analog-to-Digital (A/D) conversion. That is, the card takes an input voltage and converts it to a discrete signal that the CPU can process. By using A/D converters, voltages and currents can be detected and converted into digital word equivalents for examination as part of a control program. An analog output module converts a digital signal to an analog value (D/A). The analog output module receives numerical data for the CPU, which are then converted into a proportional voltage or current to control an analog field device. The digital data pass through a Digital-to-Analog Converter (DAC). Optical isolation between digital and analog signals is generally accomplished by an opto-coupler.

The *resolution* of an analog I/O module is an important consideration for controlling precision when using a PLC. A converter that uses an 8-bit word will have a full-scale resolution of one part in 256. Therefore, a 10 V signal can be divided into increments of about 0.04 V. A more precise method of control involves using a 10-bit word that gives one part in 1,024, or using a 12-bit word that gives one part in 4,096. The higher the resolution, the more accurately an analog value can be represented digitally. Figure 3-18 shows how an input signal is divided into smaller increments for increased accuracy.

TABLE 3-3

Analog Inputs	Analog Outputs
4 – 20 mA	4 – 20 mA
0 to +5 VDC	0 to +5 VDC
0 to +10 VDC	0 to +10 VDC
0 to + or –10 VDC	0 to + or –10 VDC

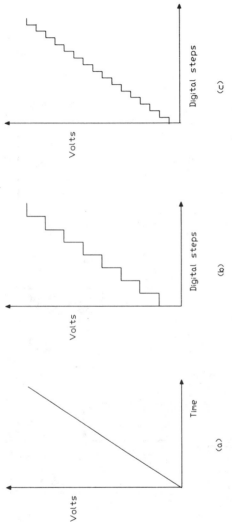

Figure 3-18 Analog-to-digital signal conversion.

Although accuracy and resolution are related, accuracy of a module is actually how well and intact a signal passes into and out of a PLC system, and is a function of the entire board's design. It is normally a function of temperature, and is expressed as a percentage of full-scale at a given temperature. For example, <±0.025% of full-scale at 25°C would be an indication of a module's accuracy.

The following four factors should also be considered when evaluating analog I/O:

1. *Power requirements:* Does the module draw a large amount of power from the power supply, or does it require special external power supplies?

2. *Temperature coefficient and total output drift:* These factors refer to the module's ability to maintain accuracy over a certain temperature range, and are usually expressed in the form of fractions of full-scale per degree of change.

3. *Input impedance and capacitance:* These values must be known to match the external device to the module. Typical ratings are in megaohms (MΩ) and pico Farads (pF).

4. *Common mode rejection ratio:* Refers to a module's ability to prevent noise from interfering with data integrity, on a single channel and from channel to channel on the module.

A typical analog input module usually has four multiplexed inputs with separation provided by the interface input. A block diagram of a four-channel analog input module is shown in Figure 3-19. The initial input stage provides protection, filtering, limiting, and multiplexing. The limiting feature prevents signals of incorrect magnitude and/or polarity from reaching the A/D converter. The analog signal is transmitted to the A/D converter, where it is changed to a digital signal and passed through the isolation stage into the data buffer. Timing and control circuits are used to set channel selection and transfer the digital signals into and out of the data buffer. Once again, the timing and control of the data buffer is independent of the CPU scan cycle.

Reference and calibration control allow the user to calibrate a module using reference voltages generated by the interface. Some of the newer analog modules available are digitally designed and provide automatic linearization and engineering unit scaling at the module level. This means that when data are received by the CPU, they have been converted to values relative to the physical parameter being considered, i.e., position, flow, etc.

A typical analog input module has a very high input impedance, which allows

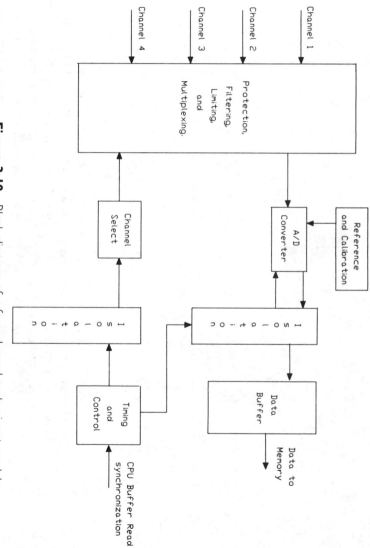

Figure 3-19 Block diagram of a four-channel analog input module.

for the interface of high source-resistant outputs from input devices. Figure 3-20 shows a typical analog input connection diagram. The shielded cable shown in the diagram helps reduce line impedance imbalances to provide good common mode rejection of noise levels. The power supply for the module shown in Figure 3-20 provides both positive and negative DC voltages, which means that the interface is capable of bipolar operation.

An analog output module receives numerical data from the CPU. These data are then translated into a proportional voltage or current to control an analog field device. Data from a specific register or word location in memory are passed through the CPU's data bus to a D/A converter. Analog output from the converter is then used to control an analog field device. Isolation between the output circuit and logic circuit is usually provided by an opto-coupler. Generally, an analog

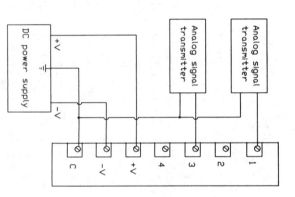

Figure 3-20 Typical analog input connection diagram.

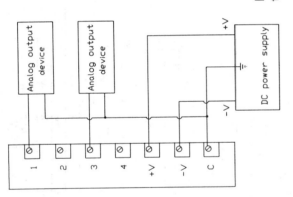

Figure 3-21 Typical analog output connection diagram.

output interface requires an external power supply that meets certain current and voltage requirements. Figure 3-21 illustrates a typical device connection for an analog output module.

The output voltages and currents for an analog card are always DC values. However, this doesn't mean that a device such as an AC drive cannot be controlled. AC drives still have DC control circuit voltages, which is where the output voltage from the analog card can be applied. As the 0 to 10 VDC output of the module is applied to the AC drive, the output of the drive causes the AC motor to vary in speed.

Discrete and analog output modules are very sensitive to power surges, or spikes, occurring on the line. For this reason, surge suppressors are often installed. These suppressors can be either RC snubbers and/or MOVs, which hold the output voltage at the desired level.

3-7 ADVANCED I/O

Ninety percent of all I/O requirements were discussed in the previous sections dealing with discrete, numerical, and analog interfaces. However, there are some signals that cannot be processed by a PLC efficiently using these three types of modules. In these special cases, I/O modules are required to respond to the following application demands:

Applications that require fast input response. In some cases, certain devices generate signals that are much faster than CPU scan time and cannot be detected through standard I/O modules.

Applications that require sending and receiving alphanumeric data between peripheral equipment and the PLC.

Motion control problems.

Complex control problems such as three-mode (PID) process control.

Fast response module. A fast response input module is used to detect input pulses of very short durations. This microprocessor-based module is designed to accommodate input pulses that occur too rapidly for the CPU scan to accurately detect. The high-speed interface counts and accumulates the pulses, and provides the results to the CPU during the normal I/O scan window. The input voltage and frequency range can be up to 24 VDC at 50,000 Hz, and the logic data signal can be activated by the leading or trailing edge of the triggering input.

LSB
LEAST SIGNIFICANT BIT

			MSB				
			MOST SIGNIFICANT BIT				

BINARY →	000	001	010	011	100	101	110	111
HEX →	0	1	2	3	4	5	6	7
0000 0	NUL	DLE	SP	0	@	P	`	p
0001 1	SOH	DC1	!	1	A	Q	a	q
0010 2	STX	DC2	"	2	B	R	b	r
0011 3	ETX	DC3	#	3	C	S	c	s
0100 4	EOT	DC4	$	4	D	T	d	t
0101 5	ENQ	NAK	%	5	E	U	e	u
0110 6	ACK	SYN	&	6	F	V	f	v
0111 7	BEL	ETB	'	7	G	W	g	w
1000 8	BS	CAN	(	8	H	X	h	x
1001 9	HT	EM	)	9	I	Y	i	y
1010 A	LF	SUB	*	:	J	Z	j	z
1011 B	VT	ESC	+	;	K	[	k	{
1100 C	FF	FS	,	<	L	\	l	|
1101 D	CR	GS	-	=	M	]	m	}
1110 E	SO	RS	.	>	N	^	n	~
1111 F	SI	US	/	?	O	_	o	DEL

Figure 3-22 Standard ASCII Control Code and Character Set.

ASCII module. The ASCII I/O interface is used for sending and receiving alphanumeric data between peripheral equipment and the PLC. Typical peripheral devices include video monitors, printers, etc. ASCII is an acronym for the American Standard Code for Information Interchange, and is a 7-bit code for representing letters, numbers, and symbols appearing in written material. Figure 3-22 shows the 128 standard ASCII control codes and character set with both binary and hexadecimal numbering systems. An ASCII module will usually have either limited communication circuitry or advanced communication circuitry, including a RAM buffer and dedicated microprocessor. A module with limited communication circuitry allows a user to generate, store, and output messages in standard ASCII code for report generation, logging, alarm indication, etc. An ASCII module with advanced communication circuitry is mainly used in network communications which require high-speed data transmissions. Both modules use RS-232C, RS-422, or 20 mA current loop standard communications links.

Motion control modules. PLCs are ideally suited for both linear and rotary motion control applications, and can meet requirements for precision of up to 0.001 in. of error relative to commanded position. The basic requirements of a motion

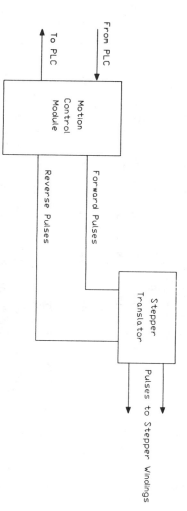

Figure 3-23 Open-loop motion control.

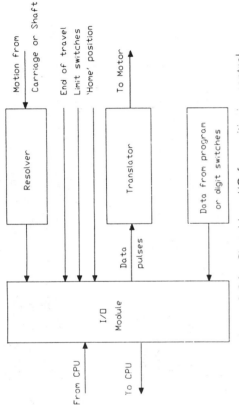

Figure 3-24 Closed-loop I/O for positioning control.

control module is to provide an intelligent, closed-loop motion control ability to effectively interface the PLC sequencing operation with precisely-executed positioning commands to a servo-drive positioning system. Open-loop control with stepper motors is also accomplished using motion control modules, as shown in Figure 3-23. In a typical application, the PLC transmits a block of data containing distance, rate, and direction information to the module. The module then generates the signals to be sent to the stepper motor. The speed of the stepper motor is set by the number of pulses transmitted by the module. This type of system is considered to be of open-loop control because the PLC has no way of determining the accuracy of the commands sent to the motor.

In more refined systems, such as three- to five-axes positioning, it is common to provide sensors to transmit information regarding the status of an operation and to allow for error corrections, as shown in Figure 3-24. A motion control I/O module takes selected commands from the CPU and executes those commands, reporting back to the CPU when requested. A typical position loop may

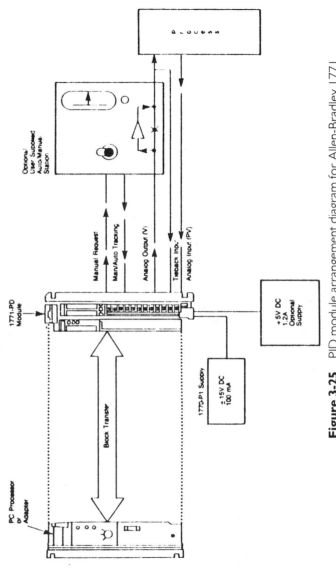

Figure 3-25 PID module arrangement diagram for Allen-Bradley 1771. (Courtesy of Allen-Bradley.)

be solved and updated as often as every 2.2 ms. The module takes in a current position reference directly from a position sensor such as a resolver or optical encoder. This current position information is compared to the commanded position at that time and a resulting voltage is sent to the connected servo-drive system. In placement operations, it is possible to store multiparameter motion profiles as a library that can be called by sending an identifying code to the module.

PID module. The Proportional-Integral-Derivative (PID) module is used in process control applications in which PID algorithms are used in what is commonly referred to as three-mode closed-loop feedback control. An algorithm is a complex program based on mathematical calculations. The principles of process control are discussed in Chapter 14. A PID module allows process control to take place outside the CPU. This arrangement prevents the CPU from being burdened with complex calculations. The microprocessor in the PID module processes data and compares the data to setpoints provided by the CPU and determines the appropriate output signal. Most PID modules have at least four channels or loops of control per module. Status and diagnostic indicators are provided to allow easy maintenance of the system once it is installed. Configuring a PID module includes configuring the types of analog signals, types of digital signals, and other signal conditions. Figure 3-25 shows a typical PID module connection arrangement.

Local I/O is applied to PLC systems in which the I/O and CPU are mounted together in one control cabinet. *Remote I/O*, or *serial I/O*, has the ability to be used where applications call for the distribution of I/O racks over large distances.

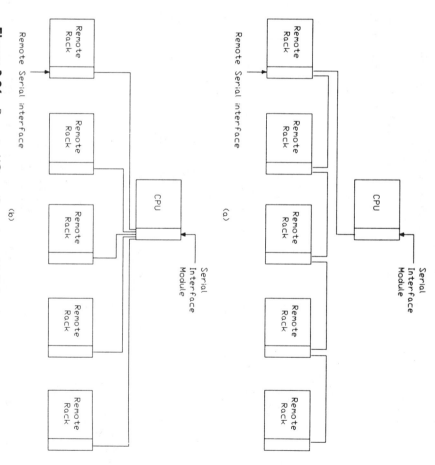

Remote Serial interface

(a)

Remote Serial interface

(b)

Figure 3-26 Remote I/O configurations: (a) Daisy chain; (b) Star.

In situations where a large number of I/O devices are required to be controlled by one CPU, it is good practice to use remote I/O locations. That is, install I/O racks at various locations throughout a plant, rather than run all the I/O cables back to one location. In a factory with large square-footage, the cost of routing I/O cables to one location can be extremely high. Also, as the length of cable increases, the chances of noise interference and troubleshooting problems also increase.

If fiber optic cable is used between the CPU and I/O rack, it is possible to operate I/O points from distances greater than 20 miles with virtually no voltage drop. Coaxial cable will allow remote I/O to be installed at distances greater than two miles. Two methods of connecting remote I/O are shown in Figure 3-26. Both methods require each individual I/O rack to drive the logic circuitry of the modules, as well as contain a remote I/O adapter module to allow communication with the CPU. The remote racks can be connected using either a *daisy chain* or *star* configuration.

REVIEW QUESTIONS

3-1. An I/O system basically consists of two components:
    (a) input modules and output modules.
    (b) ON and OFF devices.
    (c) an I/O rack and I/O modules.
    (d) discrete and analog devices.

3-2. The I/O system provides an interface between
    (a) input modules and output modules.
    (b) the I/O rack and I/O modules.
    (c) the CPU and I/O rack.
    (d) the CPU and field equipment.

3-3. What is the most commonly-used type of I/O interface?
    (a) Discrete inputs
    (b) Analog I/O
    (c) Discrete I/O
    (d) A PID

3-4. Which of the following statements does *not* apply to input interface modules in a PLC?
    (a) Input modules are used to control the power to field devices.
    (b) Each output module point is energized by an output in the program.
    (c) The condition of each module is specified each time a program scan occurs.
    (d) The state of each module is specified by an entry in an output register in memory.

3-5. High-density modules
    (a) are not practical in PLC applications.
    (b) consist of 64 inputs or outputs.
    (c) consist of 8 inputs or outputs.
    (d) consist of 16 inputs or outputs.

3-6. What are the two general classifications for PLC I/O?

3-7. A discrete I/O interface will only respond to which of the following field device conditions?
    (a) Open/Close
    (b) ON/OFF
    (c) Switch opening
    (d) All of the above

3-8. List six examples of discrete input devices.

3-9. List four examples of discrete output devices.

3-10. What are the four tasks that a typical input module performs?

3-11. The bridge rectifier section in a discrete input module converts the input signal to

    (a) a low AC level.

    (b) a DC level.

    (c) a low frequency level.

    (d) a high AC level.

3-12. Which of the following is *not* a primary source of delay in a discrete input module in a PLC?

    (a) A slow detection bridge

    (b) Opto-couplers that are slow to respond

    (c) Triacs operating on zero crossing

    (d) The threshold operation taking time

3-13. Typical input signal delays range from

    (a) 20 - 45 ms.

    (b) 9 - 25 s.

    (c) 20 - 45 μs.

    (d) 9 - 25 ms.

3-14. An input signal is considered to be valid if

    (a) it exceeds the threshold voltage and remains ON for at least the filter delay.

    (b) it stays ON for one scan.

    (c) it exceeds the threshold voltage.

    (d) it reaches 90% of the threshold for 10 ms.

3-15. A TTL level signal has a typical voltage of

    (a) 10 VAC.

    (b) 10 VDC.

    (c) 5 VAC.

    (d) 5 VDC.

3-16. What is a freewheeling diode?

3-17. What are the two general classifications of data I/O interfaces?

3-18. Multiplexing

    (a) allows one transmission line to carry several signals.

    (b) eliminates the need for discrete inputs.

    (c) reduces the switching effect caused by triacs.

    (d) eliminates unwanted signal noise.

3-19. A data output interface will typically provide

    (a) 8-bit parallel outputs.

    (b) 16-bit parallel outputs.

    (c) 32-bit parallel outputs.

    (d) 16-byte parallel outputs.

3-20. An analog signal

    (a) can only be in one of two possible states.

    (b) is repetitious over a given period of time.

    (c) varies with time but not magnitude.

    (d) varies with time and magnitude.

3-21. Define unipolar and bipolar analog interfaces.

3-22. What are the four factors that should be considered when evaluating analog I/O?

3-23. An 8-bit DAC will have a resolution of

    (a) one part in 1024.

(b) one part in 256.

(c) one part in 4096.

(d) one part in 512.

3-24. The precision with which analog I/O modules in a PLC handle voltages

(a) depends on the word size of the CPU.

(b) depends on the number of bits in the A/D or D/A range.

(c) depends on the speed of the interface.

(d) requires that the field device be strobed.

3-25. List four types of advanced I/O modules.

3-26. Which of the following is not a standard communication link for an ASCII module?

(a) 10

(b) RS 232C

(c) RS 422

(d) 4 - 20 mA

3-27. What level of precision can be achieved using a PLC in motion control applications?

(a) 0.01 in.

(b) 0.001 in.

(c) 0.1 cm

(d) 0.001 cm

3-28. PID control is also referred to as

(a) two-mode closed-loop control.

(b) Proportional-Integral-Differential control.

(c) Proportional-Inverse-Derivative control.

(d) Proportional-Integral-Derivative control.

3-29. What is an algorithm?

3-30. What is the advantage of remote I/O compared to local I/O?

3-31. What are the two methods of connecting remote I/O racks?

Programming Terminals and Peripheral Devices

4

4-1 INTRODUCTION

Upon completion of this chapter, you will be able to

▲ Define "programming terminal."

▲ Understand the application of dedicated programming terminals.

▲ List the two types of dedicated terminals.

▲ Describe the purpose of mini-programmers.

▲ Define computer-based programming terminals.

▲ Differentiate between programming software and documentation software.

▲ Describe the function of a host computer-based PLC system.

A programming terminal provides the user with a method of entering and monitoring a program in the CPU's memory. Programming terminals vary widely in complexity, ease of use, and cost.

There are two basic methods of entering a program into a PLC. It can be done with either a dedicated programming terminal, or with a computer using PLC software. In both cases, the programming terminal is connected to the CPU via the connector on the processor. This connector is typically a 25-pin RS-232 serial communications port, which is compatible with most IBM computers.

A dedicated controller is still the most common method of entering a program into a CPU. Although the computer is popular with engineers for PLC programming, on the shop floor, a dedicated controller is capable of withstanding more rigorous use. For example, a portable laptop computer is in itself very rugged and durable, but the hard-disk required to store programs is sensitive to shock and corrosion. If a hard-disk is dropped, it can easily be destroyed, whereas a dedicated controller is capable of withstanding tremendous abuse.

Although most PLCs will perform the same basic functions, the most noticeable difference between products is the keyboard. For example, Texas Instruments uses a set of function keys marked F1 to F8 to access a wide variety of operations, including access to timers, counters, sequencers, math functions, etc. AEG Modicon and Allen-Bradley utilize shift key functions to increase the number of functions on the keyboard, as well as providing keys such as search and supervisory, which are multi-function keys.

4-2 DEDICATED PROGRAMMING TERMINALS

A dedicated programming terminal is a device which is used exclusively for program entry and PLC monitoring. It is dedicated to operate with only one brand of PLC and is generally limited to the range of functions it can control. A typical dedicated terminal consists of a Cathode Ray Tube (CRT), keyboard, and the electronic circuitry required for developing, modifying, and loading a program into CPU memory. A CRT provides the user with a visual representation of program and ranges in screen sizes from 5 in. to 12 in. (diagonally). Figure 4-1 shows a photograph of a dedicated programming terminal.

There are two basic types of dedicated programming terminals: dumb and intelligent. Dumb terminals have been extensively used over the past twenty years and are relatively inexpensive programming devices. This type of terminal relies entirely on the CPU for software documentation, and it must be connected to a processor to make any changes to the control program.

An intelligent dedicated programming terminal is a microprocessor-based device that has its own memory and software. This type of device allows programs to be developed and altered without the programming terminal being connected to a CPU. Some intelligent terminals also have the feature of network interfacing which allows the terminal to be connected to a manufacturer's Local Area Network (LAN). This configuration allows the programming terminal to access any PLC in the network, and perform editing and monitoring functions. In most cases, an intelligent dedicated programming terminal will also have a floppy-disk port on the front of the terminal. This port allows programs to be loaded and retrieved

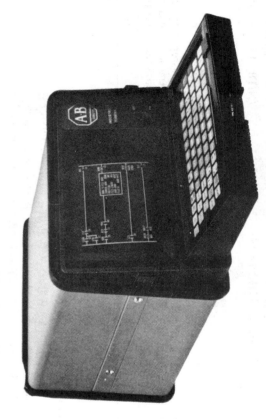

Figure 4-1 Dedicated programming terminal.

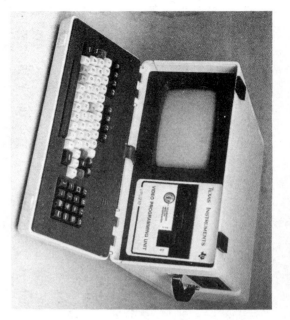

Figure 4-2 Intelligent dedicated programming terminal.

from the PLC by the terminal itself. Consequently, programs can be stored and written anywhere, and then loaded into the CPU via the floppy-disk port. Figure 4-2 shows an intelligent programming terminal.

The keyboards of all dedicated terminals share a certain amount of common functions, such as coils, contacts, timers, counters, force, print, cursor movement, insert, delete, get, put, etc. The keyboard shown in Figure 4-3 is for the Allen-Bradley T-3 dedicated programmer. This keyboard allows access to a wide variety of coil functions directly from the keyboard itself, including the MCR function, latching relays, timer and counter coils, get and put instructions, as well as math functions. Because Allen-Bradley PLCs have special requirements for entering rungs or ladders, the dedicated keyboard also has branch end and branch start instructions.

The T-3 also contains program instructions for writing subroutines to allow the CPU to "jump" to different points in a program and branch back and forth.

The SEARCH instruction on the T-3 programmer is used for a wide variety of tasks. Table 4-I illustrates some SEARCH function capabilities. The column identified as *Mode* indicates what mode of operation the CPU should be in, either Program, Run/Program, or Run. If the word "any" appears below the **Mode** column, it indicates that the CPU may be in any of the three possible states.

The Allen-Bradley T-3 programming terminal also contains a series of HELP directories which are designed to assist you in programming with an A/B PLC. Many of the keys shown on the keypad of the T-3 have more than one function. By using the HELP directory, it is possible to obtain a display of all the different features accessible by a single key. Table 4-2 is a listing of some of the functions

TABLE 4-I

Function	Mode	Keystrokes	Description
Locate first run of program	Any	[SEARCH][1]	Moves cursor to first line of program.
Locate last rung of program	Any	[SEARCH][1]	Moves cursor to end of program.
Locate specific address	Any	[SEARCH][8] [address]	Locates address in program.
Print	Any	[SEARCH] [43]	Prints single line of program.
Print	Any	[SEARCH] [44]	Prints entire program.
Display first 20 lines of data table configuration	Any	[SEARCH] [5] [0]	Displays first 20 lines of data table on CRT.
Change CPU status to RUN/PROGRAM mode	R/P	[SEARCH] [590]	Allows on-line programming change.

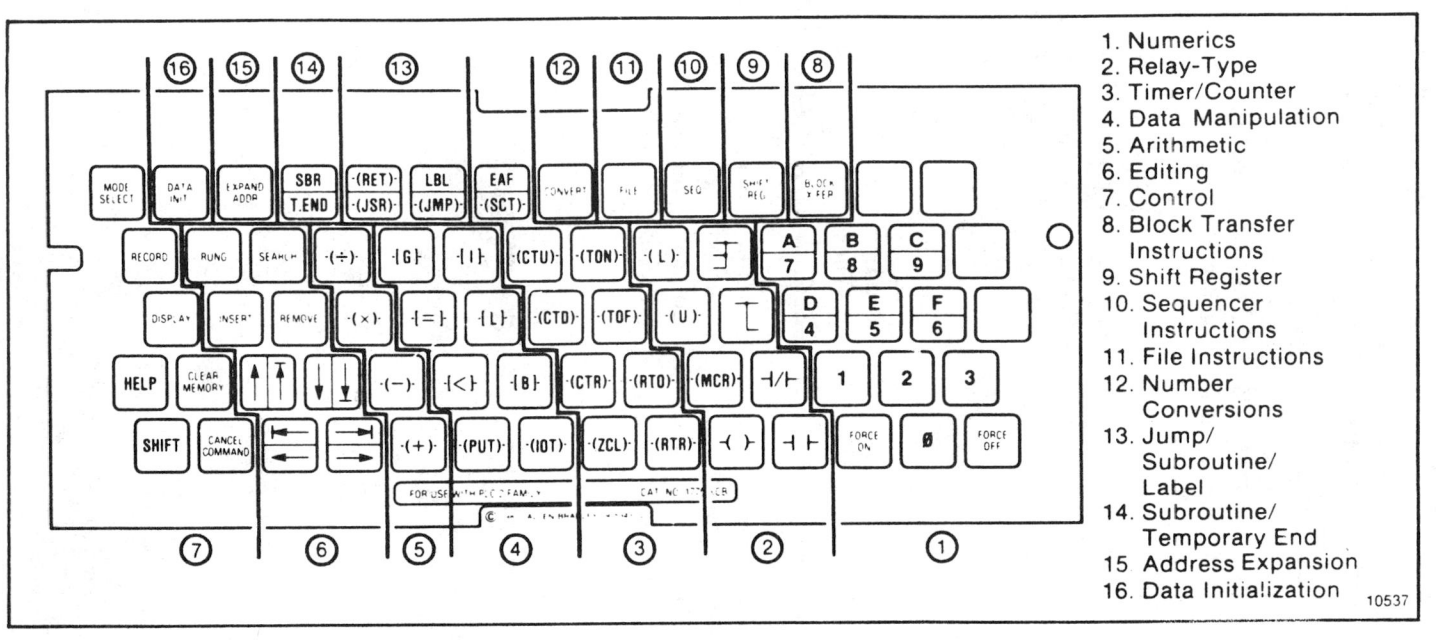

Figure 4-3 Keyboard for Allen-Bradley T-3 terminal.

1. Numerics
2. Relay-Type
3. Timer/Counter
4. Data Manipulation
5. Arithmetic
6. Editing
7. Control
8. Block Transfer Instructions
9. Shift Register
10. Sequencer Instructions
11. File Instructions
12. Number Conversions
13. Jump/Subroutine/Label
14. Subroutine/Temporary End
15. Address Expansion
16. Data Initialization

47

TABLE 4-2

Function	Mode	Keystrokes	Description
Help directory	Any	[HELP]	Provides description of keys used to obtain additional directories.
Control function directory	Any	[SEARCH] [HELP]	Lists control functions that use SEARCH keys.
Record function directory	Any	[RECORD] [HELP]	Lists all functions that use RECORD key.
Clear memory directory	Any	[CLEAR] [MEMORY] [HELP]	Provides listing of all functions using the CLEAR MEMORY key.

available by pressing the HELP key. The three main directories which can be accessed from the help instruction are

Control functions: Accessed by pressing [SEARCH] [HELP]
Record functions: Accessed by pressing [RECORD] [HELP]
Clear memory functions: Related functions of the Clear memory command, accessed by pressing [CLEAR MEMORY] [HELP]

4-3 MINI-PROGRAMMERS

A mini-programmer, or hand-held programmer, is an inexpensive and portable means of programming small PLCs. These devices are often the size of hand-held calculators and usually have LED or dot matrix LCD displays. The keyboard consists of numeric keys, programming instruction keys, and special function keys. Figure 4-4 shows a typical mini-programmer.

Mini-programmers can be either intelligent or dumb terminals depending on their make and model. A dumb terminal is very similar to a large CRT terminal in that it has basic features for entering and editing programs. An intelligent mini-

Keyboard

Display

Figure 4-4 Mini-programmer.

programmer is microprocessor-based and provides the user with features such as system diagnostic routines, message displays, etc.

4-4 COMPUTER-BASED PROGRAMING TERMINALS

In recent years, a definite trend has been developing toward the use of personal computer-based program development systems. Some manufacturers offer products that use an industry standard personal computer (i.e., IBM) as the base of their product offerings. Some offer the personal computer as part of the product, while many offer just the software to be used with the user's choice of personal computer hardware. Personal computers made by PLC manufacturers are generally much more rugged and durable than those found in typical office environments. For example, computer keyboards are often sealed to prevent spills and other dirt from entering and damaging the electronics of the system. There are also some types of filter systems that protect the disk drive of the computer, as well as extended temperature and humidity tolerances similar to those which the PLC would be exposed to in normal operating conditions.

Personal computers allow the development of simpler and more convenient PLC programming techniques. For example, a menu can be extended to the function keys, allowing *soft key* prompting on the screen. Self-learning programs can be offered. The personal computer is also available for ancillary, i.e., non-PLC-related activities such as word processing, file handling, etc. With personal computers, further refinement of graphical programming methods is possible, including a real-time color graphics operator interface. Also, the user requirement for programming with symbolic addressing and adequate text inclusion is readily available by virtue of the massive memory capacity of these units.

Programming software is the essential software required for the creation of contacts and coils using a personal computer. In addition to contacts and coils, programming software allows for the programming of any special mnemonic functions specified by the manufacturer in the instruction set. *Documentation software* is used in conjunction with the programming software to allow for the customizing of each coil and contact in a program. A full-function documentation software package will allow tor extensive comments to be added in the middle of ladder logic, to provide an explanation of a particular portion of the control program for the user's reference.

Data collection and *analysis software* is becoming increasingly popular in personal computers for industrial control. This software is based on a spreadsheet format. That is, it has the ability to collect data from single or multiple PLC CPUs. By using this type of software, data can be displayed in more traditional computer-related formats, i.e., graphs, charts, etc.

Another newer type of personal computer software for PLC applications is *real-time operator interface software*. This type of software allows supervisory control to be established using images on a CRT screen to advise an operator of process conditions and to provide a warning system in the event of process failure. Using real-time software, an operator can input information via a keyboard to control a process. Some of the newer software packages are combined with *touch screens* to allow an operator on the plant floor to make process revisions by simply touching a CRT screen at an appropriate point.

Computer-based programming terminals also have *simulation software* available that allows the computer to be used to simulate the operation of a process control program. The advantage of this type of software is that it allows an existing system to be effectively measured and analyzed, and it allows process designers to simulate various process conditions prior to the actual construction of a particular PLC system. In this way, system deficiencies and potential bottlenecks can be identified early in the system design process and costly miscalculations can be reduced.

4-5 HOST COMPUTER-BASED SYSTEMS

A **host computer** is defined as a multi-user system which is centrally located in a facility and is used for a variety of tasks. These tasks can range from the supervision of numerous PLC systems, to shop floor scheduling, maintenance and tool management, and broader tasks including production cost analysis, etc.

In very large PLC-based control environments, it is quite common for a host computer to be used with associated software and communications hardware for monitoring and editing programs from a centralized location. The resident software in a host computer is designed to allow PLC program development and documentation. When a program is written and entered into the computer, the program can then be directed to any CPU in the system by the plant communications network. Figure 4-5 shows a typical host computer-based programming system.

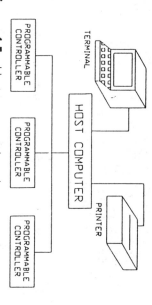

Figure 4-5 Host computer-based programming terminal.

4-6 PERIPHERAL DEVICES

A **peripheral device** is a device connected to the PLC that is not essential to the PLCs operation. By this definition, a programming terminal would be considered a peripheral device. Peripheral devices also include program loaders, which are components designed for loading and reloading programs into the PLC's RAM memory. Program loaders are often used as a memory backup system. In the event of the program stored in the PLC being erased or accidently altered, the program can simply be reloaded from the program loader. One very common type of program loader is the cassette recorder. The recorder is interfaced with the CPU by use of a standard RS-232 serial communications port.

When peripheral devices such as program loaders and printers operate by serial transmission, it means that the program data is transferred sequentially, instead of simultaneously. Since the binary digits, or bits, are transmitted in series, it is necessary to specify the speed which the data is to be sent or received. **Baud rate** is the term which defines the transmission speed of binary data, and is measured in bits per second. Some PLC's will automatically set the baud rate while others, such as T.I. and Allen-Bradley, require that it be specified. Standard baud rates are 110, 300, 600, 1200, 1800, 3600, 4800, 7200, and 9600.

Many PLC manufacturers also have programming terminals which contain built in disk drive systems. These disk drives allow programs to be stored on 5 1/4", or 3 1/2" disks. The program stored on disk can then be reloaded into the CPU at a later date. Disk storage systems will transmit and receive data faster than tape storage. Also, some disk storage systems will store up to 1.4 megabytes of information on a single disk, which is considerably more data storage than is available on a single cassette tape.

A modulator-demodulator (MODEM) device is a peripheral component that allows ladder logic programs in information in data tables to be transferred via a telephone link. By use of the modem, it is possible to transmit and receive program data almost anywhere in the world. The modem allows the CPU to interface with peripherals such as printers, computers, and program loaders from remote locations. The modem modulates digital signals to transmit over telephone lines, and demodulates incoming signals back into digital form. Modulation is a method of using digital information to control the amplitude of a high-frequency signal known as a *carrier*. The carrier signal is usually in the audio spectrum, which means it can be transmitted over a standard telephone circuit. When the signal is demodulated, it is converted from an audio signal back into a digital signal.

Electronic memory modules are peripheral devices which use EPROM or EEPROM integrated circuit chips to store and retrieve data. EPROM IC's are chips which use a special programmer to write, or burn, the coded program into the IC's memory. Since EPROM chips are non-volatile, or ROM, memory, once the program has been written into the EPROM it does not require a battery backup to retain its memory contents. The EPROM IC can only be erased by using an ultraviolet erasing device. EEPROM chips are very similar to EPROM in terms of program entry and storage. The main difference between the two is that EEPROM can be electronically erased, while EPROM needs a special ultraviolet erasing device. The fist generation of memory modules contained PROM IC chips. These ICs could only be programmed once, and were not erasable.

Peripheral devices also include display components such as seven-segment displays and alphanumeric displays. The seven-segment display uses I.FDs or liquid crystal displays, LCDs, to provide a numeric readout in groups of usually 4, 5, or 6 digits. These displays are used to indicate values such as timer and counter contents, analog values, word values, etc. The interface to a seven-segment display is provided by a seven-segment decoder driver. The input for a typical decoder driver is binary coded decimal, or BCD. When a BCD code is sent from a word location at the I/O rack, the decoder driver interprets this information, and converts it into an appropriate decimal value. It is possible to display alphabetic information using a seven-segment display, although message size is limited due to the number of seven-segment displays in a typical group. Nine-segment displays have more alphabetic capability and are also easier to read.

Alphanumeric displays can provide actual messages regarding the operating state of the machine or process being controlled. These messages are pre-programmed, and when a specific function occurs in a ladder logic program, they will display an appropriate message. Typical alphanumeric displays will show up to 24 characters and store over 100 messages.

Thumbwheel switches are peripheral devices which are used to enter data into the CPU's memory. These switches are rotating numeric inputs which, depending on their position, will enter or modify data such as the preset value of timers and counters. Each dial on a thumbwheel switch has ten positions, 0 thru 9, and typically there are 4 or 5 dials on a switch. The switching capability of a thumbwheel switch is limited to logic levels, with very small values of current. The output of a thumbwheel switch is generally either decimal, binary coded decimal (BCD), or hexadecimal.

One of the most common peripheral devices is the printer. This device allows you to obtain hardcopies of the program stored in the CPU's RAM memory. Since most peripheral ports are serial, it is necessary to use a printer which will accept serial transmission of data. Printers are typically either dot matrix or thermal. Dot matrix printers use standard paper, while thermal printers require a special type of paper which uses a heat-transfer process to produce ladder logic diagrams. Thermal printers operate on a similar principle to fax machines.

REVIEW QUESTIONS

4-1. A programming terminal is used to
(a) enter and monitor a program in the executive memory.
(b) enter and monitor a program in the application memory.
(c) enter and modify I/O modules.
(d) all of the above.

4-2. What are the two basic methods of entering a program into a PLC?

4-3. A typical CRT screen on a programming terminal ranges in size from
(a) 7 in. to 12 in. diagonally.
(b) 12 in. to 21 in. diagonally.
(c) 5 in. to 12 in. diagonally.
(d) 5 in. to 7 in. diagonally.

4-4. An intelligent dedicated programming terminal has
(a) a microprocessor.
(b) memory.
(c) software.
(d) all of the above.

4-5. What is a mini-programmer?

4-6. True/False: Mini-programmers can be either intelligent or dumb terminals.

4-7. What are two advantages of using computer-based programming terminals?

4-8. What are four types of software packages available with computer-based programming terminals?

4-9. What is a host computer?

5

Installation and Maintenance of Programmable Controllers

Upon completion of this chapter, you will be able to

▶ List three safety precautions when installing PLC systems.
▶ Define "system layout."
▶ Describe three safety measures that should be observed when installing PLCs in control panels.
▶ Understand proper grounding techniques for PLCs.
▶ Name three precautions to avoid electrical interference.
▶ Define "cross-talk interference."
▶ Explain I/O installation.
▶ Describe the need for I/O documentation.
▶ Understand leakage current and bleeder resistors.
▶ Explain the field checkout of PLC systems.
▶ Provide periodic maintenance for a PLC system.
▶ Troubleshoot PLCs.
▶ Describe redundant PLC architecture.

5-1 INTRODUCTION

The primary source of information regarding the installation and maintenance requirements of a PLC is its manufacturer. A manufacturer will usually provide installation notes for each module type and I/O rack as well as for the CPU/ memory. Once the relevant data are obtained from the manufacturer, they are then combined with engineering drawings and specifications for the installation in question.

To ensure that all PLC equipment operates satisfactorily and safely, all applicable local and national codes that apply to installing and operating the equipment must be followed. Because these codes can vary geographically and can change with time, it is the responsibility of the individual or company installing a PLC system to determine which standards and codes apply, and to comply with them. Failure to comply with applicable codes and standards can result in damage to equipment and/or serious injury to personnel.

All PLC equipment should be installed and operated in accordance with all applicable sections of the National Fire Protection Agency (NFPA), National Electrical Code (NEC), and the National Electrical Manufacturer's Association (NEMA). In Canada, installation must comply with the Canadian Electrical Code (CEC), and the Canadian Standards Association (CSA). Before beginning a PLC installation, the local Fire Marshall and Electrical Inspector should be contacted to determine which codes and standards apply to a particular installation.

Safety devices and techniques must be used in all industrial control systems to prevent injury to personnel and equipment. Control devices can fail under unsafe conditions. Therefore, unless proper safeguards are incorporated into the installation of equipment, some malfunctions of devices can result in sudden equipment startup. Such a startup could result in property damage and/or severe injury to the equipment operator. The following section describes the NEMA ICS 3-304 programmable control recommendations that generally apply to the installation of solid-state PLC devices.

ICS 3-304.81 Safety Recommendations:

Consideration should be given to the use of an emergency stop function which is independent of the programmable controller.

Where the operator is exposed to the machinery, such as in loading or unloading a machine tool, or where the machine cycles automatically, consideration should be given to the use of an electromechanical override or other redundant means, independent of the programmable controller, for starting and interrupting the cycle.

If provision is required for changing programs while the equipment is in operation, consideration should be given to the use of locks or other means of assuring that such changes can be made only by authorized personnel. These recommendations are intended as safeguards against the failure of critical components and the effects of such failures or the inadvertent errors that might be introduced if programs are changed while the equipment is in operation.

(Courtesy of the National Electrical Manufacturers Association.)

Pre-installation planning and site preparation must include consideration of potential hazards to personnel during PLC, system, or operator-induced failures. The equipment connected to a PLC should include independent interlocks and safety switches to minimize potential safety-related failures. The following safety precautions should be observed when installing a PLC system:

1. Do not exceed the manufacturer's ratings. To help reduce the possibility of injury to personnel, do not exceed the manufacturer's specified ratings for PLC equipment. Refer to the manufacturer's installation manual for more information regarding equipment limitations.

2. Provide emergency stop switches. A means for removing power from the

output should be provided in the event of an emergency condition occurring during a process operation. Output power must be removed by a non-semiconductor switch or a physically- wired relay contact.

3. Provide a JOG switch. The PLC should be bypassed with an external JOG or INCH switch during machine loading or setup operations.

During design, installation, start-up, operation, and maintenance of PLC controlled systems, the worst-case scenario, or **catastrophic failure** should be kept in mind as the first concern. Catastrophic failure includes not only the programmable controller, but also any equipment controlled by the PLC. The term **fail-safe** is a term used to describe a system that, when control is lost, will do the least amount of damage. In fact many fail-safe systems are designed so that the damage resulting from system failure is predictable. Why do we need fail-safe system? For the simple reason, people make mistakes and machines break down. It is extremely likely that at some point in time a system failure will occur. These failures can be caused by human error, or by mechanical breakdown of equipment. The following steps outline some fundamental safety considerations that should be taken into account when designing and installing a PLC controlled system:

1. **Provide backup.** Redundant design of not only the PLC components such as I/O and CPUs, but also equipment to be controlled by the PLC. For example if a pump motor has a 1 in 10 chance of breaking down or failing to start, a backup motor will reduce the chance of failure to 1 in 100.

2. **Utilize safety devices.** The use of fuses, circuit breakers, relief valves, etc. will help protect human life. These devices are absolutely critical in the design considerations of any PLC controlled system.

3. *Provide intrinsic fail-safety.* An intrinsically fail-safe system will help prevent injury and damage to equipment. For example, if a pump impeller breaks, the housing will contain the damage.

4. *Install alarms.* Alarms will help to alert personnel of impending trouble, and allow them to take remedial action beyond that normally provided by the PLC system. An alarm should always operate in a fail-safe mode so that if the alarm itself should fail, i.e. power interruption, the device will be energized by a battery backup.

5. *Use interlocks.* Mechanical interlocks on devices such as switches and valves will greatly reduce the possibility of human error. Interlocks must also be designed to be fail-safe so that if the interlock itself should fail, the system will shut down safely.

6. *Provide proper maintenance.* By applying preventive maintenance techniques to all equipment controlled by the PLC, the chances of system failure are substantially reduced. Proper maintenance also includes upgrading and replacing equipment when required, accurate record keeping and documentation.

7. *Allow for tolerance in equipment operation.* When designing and installing a PLC controlled system, it is important to keep in mind that some equipment is more reliable than others. Any rotating equipment subjected to many hours of continuous use will eventually break down. All possible system failures should be carefully analyzed before proceeding with a PLC installation.

5-3 SYSTEM LAYOUT

When a programmable controller system is to be installed, a primary consideration must be the system layout. In other words, how is the PLC hardware to be installed? The installation procedure must take into account where the system is being installed. The following questions should be addressed before the actual installation of a programmable controller system begins:

1. What is the current task to be performed? Define the objectives of the PLC installation.

2. Is there a possibility for expansion? Initial planning of an installation should take into account any plans for future expansion of the PLC system.

3. What are the load requirements for the system? Determine the discrete, data, and analog I/O requirements.

4. Where will the PLC be located? Is the PLC as close as possible to the machine or process that it will be controlling? Will remote I/O be required? Will a communication network be needed?

5. What are the environmental considerations? Is it a hazardous location? If so, the installation must conform to NEMA or CSA standards for this type of location. Is the temperature in the location extremely high? Are there large amounts of condensation in the area? Could the PLC be affected by large inductive loads such as transformers or welding machines?

If the I/O rack is installed inside an MCC (Motor Control Center) cabinet, the cabinet must be built to NEMA or CSA specifications. It is not necessary to install a PLC inside an enclosure, but it is generally recommended. Enclosures provide protection from atmospheric contaminants such as moisture, dust, and magnetic radiation. Because most PLCs are of an open or partially enclosed design, it is assumed that the proper cabinet is chosen for the particular application area. A NEMA 12 type enclosure is quite common for PLC installations. Most I/O racks can be mounted in either a panel-type mounting arrangement or a 19-inch rack mounting.

When a PLC is installed inside an enclosure, such as in an MCC cabinet, the temperature inside the enclosure should not exceed the maximum operating temperature of the PLC, which is typically 60 degrees Celsius. If the temperature inside the enclosure becomes too high, a fan or blower should be installed. In situations where condensations occur inside the enclosure, it is necessary to install thermostatically controlled heaters. To allow maximum convection cooling, all PLC components should be mounted in a vertical (upright) position.

If a PLC is installed inside an enclosure, the enclosure should be placed in a position that allows the doors to be opened fully to allow for access to wiring and the PLC components. If possible, accessories such as an AC power outlet and interior lighting should be installed inside the system enclosure. The back panel of the enclosure should be removable, and an emergency disconnect switch should be mounted inside the cabinet in an easily accessible location. Any electro-magnetic components such as magnetic starters, contactors, or relays should be mounted near the top of the enclosure with a space of at least six in. between the electro-magnetic components and the controller components. This gap will help reduce inductive interference caused by magnetic devices.

There are certain precautions which must be taken when installing PLCs in control panels. Some of these precautions and installation procedures are as follows:

1. Viewing windows installed in the doors of control panels help facilitate maintenance and troubleshooting chores for factory personnel. Figure 5-1 is a typical PLC control panel door layout. The windows are located to make the I/O modules clearly visible. Pushbutton switches and thumbwheel inputs enable the operator to enter input conditions and register data, either for testing purposes or for receiving data.

2. All PLCs in the control room must be grounded solidly according to the

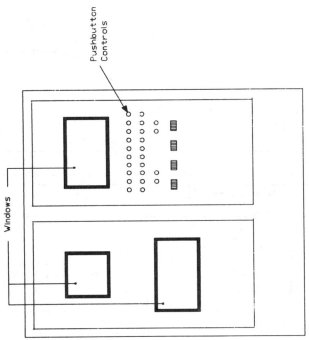

Figure 5-1 Typical door layout.

manufacturer's specifications. Some PLC designs have individual grounding connections from rack to faceplates and other system components, so care must be taken to follow good electrical practice in system grounding during electrical installation.

3. Wire terminals are installed inside the control panel, to which the user field equipment wiring and I/O module wiring terminals are joined. This extra step provides convenient tie-in for grouped field equipment. Figure 5-2 shows wiring terminal blocks used in a control panel. Note that the user's field wiring is connected to these terminals and not to the I/O rack directly.

4. Control panels containing PLCs may require heating, air conditioning, or ventilation to accommodate the PLC's operating temperature range. In some cases, the factory temperature, combined with heat from power supplies, memory, etc., will produce excessive cabinet temperatures. Temperatures can be driven up 10 or 20° C by this internally-generated heat. If plant temperatures are above the 40° to 45° C range, special cooling may be needed.

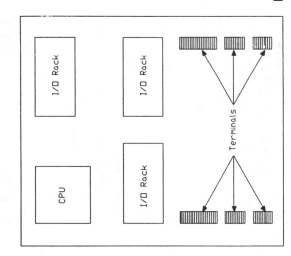

Figure 5-2 Terminal layout.

5-4 PROPER GROUNDING TECHNIQUES

Figure 5-3 shows a typical PLC system layout. Termination points for the hardwired field equipment would be made at the terminal strips. An emergency disconnect switch and isolation transformer are mounted inside the enclosure. A hardwired MCR is also included in this example system layout. The hardwired MCR is used to interrupt power to the I/O rack in the event of a system failure, but it will still allow power to be maintained at the CPU. A main power supply and auxiliary power supply are shown in Figure 5-3. Tandem power supplies are often used in situations where down-time is critical. If one power supply fails, the auxiliary can be either manually or automatically switched into the circuit to ensure continuous levels of voltage and current at the CPU.

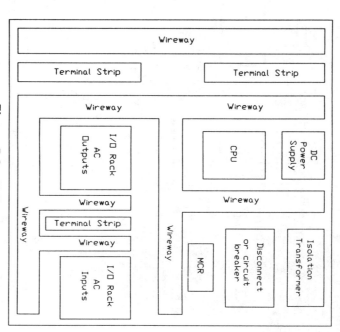

Figure 5-3 PLC system.

A good grounding system is essential for overall personnel safety and proper operation of a PLC installation. Some electrical systems have a metal conduit connected to the neutral phase at the circuit-breaker box. Depending on site conditions, it is possible for the metal conduit to conduct current from other sources in the system. To reduce the possibility of this occurring, isolate the earth ground and neutral from the conduit (except at the service entrance housing). Ensure that the power for the PLC and related equipment is wired in accordance with applicable electrical code and observe the following guidelines for power system grounding:

1. Any protective ground wires must have a resistance value of less than 0.1 Ω.
2. The resistance from the system ground to the earth ground must have a value of less than 0.1 Ω.

When installing a PLC system, use the ground connections to attach the supplied ground lug to the grounding conductor. The grounding conductor is connected to earth ground following applicable electrical codes. Generally, system

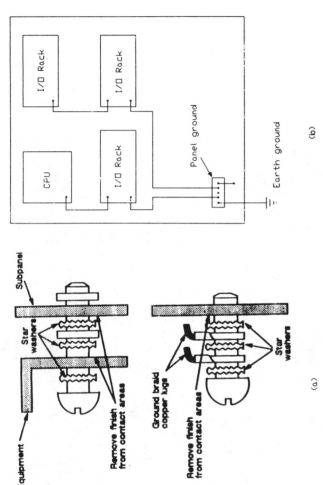

Figure 5-4 (a) Detail of ground lug connections; and (b) Equipment grounding connections.

grounding conductors are #8 AWG in size, and should always be as short as possible in length. When the PLC is mounted inside an enclosure, ensure that a good cabinet ground is achieved by removing existing paint and attach to the grounding connector using a bolt, washers, and nut, as necessary. Proper care should always be taken when terminating all grounding points in the system, lug to subpanel, device to lug, device to subpanel, etc. The area of termination should always be cleared of paints, coatings, and corrosion to ensure good continuity and low impedance.

Figure 5-4(a) shows two examples of ground connections where either PLC equipment or conductors are to be connected to a panel. Figure 5-4(b) illustrates a ground bus that is to be connected to earth ground by a customer as per applicable electrical codes. Panel sheet metal, as well as all CPU and I/O rack chassis, are grounded via the ground bus.

5-5 SOURCES OF ELECTRICAL INTERFERENCE

To ensure that PLC equipment has an adequately low susceptibility to electrical interference, suitable precautions must be taken starting at the specification stage of PLC installation. After the design of the PLC system is complete, it becomes more difficult to apply corrective measures. The following points should be adhered to in the design stage:

1. Limit the interference produced by "noisy" equipment by using suppression devices.

2. Install PLC cabling so as to minimize the coupling between the interference equipment and PLC communication cables.

3. Perform susceptibility tests on the equipment after the installation is complete.

The frequency of the power supplied by utility companies in North America is unlikely to vary by more than about 1%, and is therefore unlikely to cause problems unless used in critical timing functions. The voltage level supplied by utility companies may occasionally fall below the nominal voltage because of problems in the generating distribution network or overloading of the local supply.

In situations where the incoming power to a PLC is subject to fluctuations, it is good practice to install constant voltage transformers. If the rated voltage of a CPU drops below the minimum acceptable level, the processor will shut down and the PLC will fail to operate. Installing a constant voltage transformer will insure a constant power supply to the CPU.

The following processes may cause interruptions in the main power supply for brief instants or prolonged periods: large motors starting, load switching in the distribution network, and the operation of protective devices following lightning discharges to the network.

On any given day, power supplied to a factory may be subject to at least ten transient spikes with amplitudes in excess of 200 V. In plants which produce transient spikes, system power is even more prone to voltage surge. Even a domestic refrigerator can produce spikes of amplitude in excess of 400 V. Equipment containing contactors that switch the power to large electrical loads can produce pulse amplitudes exceeding 2 kV. Other examples of spike-producing interference are: SCR switching circuits, radio-frequency apparatus, local high-power radio communication equipment, AC/DC motors, and lighting.

Electrostatic Discharges (ESD) cause very severe interference and are quite common in environments with low humidity levels, particularly if synthetic floor coverings are used. In some circumstances, a person can be charged with up to a voltage of around 20 kV. As a rule of thumb, if a discharge to a grounded object can be felt, the person is charged with an amplitude in excess of about 5 kV.

Due to large charging voltages, the duration of ESD pulses is very short (approximately 30 ns), and their currents are quite high (50 A), which makes equipment very susceptible to both induced voltages and electromagnetic radiation from the discharge. Therefore, PLC equipment may be affected if a discharge occurs to any grounded object in close proximity.

Radiated electromagnetic interference is caused by devices such as local radar installations, radio, and TV transmitters. In many industrial situations, portable transceivers are frequently used, and these devices also cause electromagnetic interference.

If data cables and power cables are close to each other, i.e., in the same conduit, **cross-talk** interference may occur. Cross-talk interference is generally caused by placing high-voltage conductors and low-voltage conductors in the same raceway. To avoid this noise interference, it is good practice to group I/O modules with the same voltage ratings together in the I/O rack, and whenever possible, use only conductors with the same voltage rating in a conduit. For example, if an I/O rack contains 4-24 VDC modules and 4-220 VAC modules, group the four similar modules together and use two separate conduits for the different voltage ratings. This will keep cross-talk interference at a minimum.

If I/O wiring must cross an AC power line, it should only be done at right angles to minimize the possibility of electrical noise being picked up by the PLC conductors. I/O rack interconnect cables and I/O power cables may be routed in the same conduit because the danger of cross-talk between the two systems is remote. Wherever possible, a gap of at least two inches should be kept between the I/O modules and any raceway. When using terminal strips, a space of two inches should be maintained between both the terminal strip and wire duct, as well as the terminal strip and I/O modules.

As mentioned in Section 5-4, proper grounding of a PLC system is very important for personnel safety and to assure proper equipment operation. To assure continuous grounding, the ground conductor must not be soldered at any point. In the event of a high value of ground current, the temperature of the conductor could cause the solder to melt, resulting in the ground connection being interrupted. When using conductors containing ground wires, the ground wire

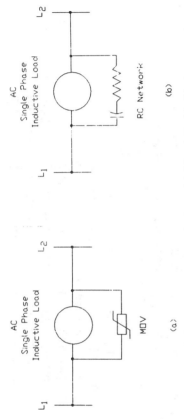

Figure 5-5 Surge suppression devices: (a) Metal Oxide Varistor; and (b) RC snubber.

should be separated from the other wires at the point where the conductor enters the enclosure.

It is also important to keep the ground wire as short as possible so the ground reference, or termination point, is as close as possible to the ground point of the building. All I/O racks, power supplies, motors, solenoids, etc. should be grounded to a central ground bus. The enclosure that the PLC is mounted in should also be grounded to the ground bus.

Equipment such as large AC motors and high-frequency welding machines are capable of introducing noise into power lines which can be disruptive to the operation of PLCs. This interference can also occur when low-voltage conductors are run in the same raceway as high-voltage conductors. Other devices which can cause noise problems are relays, solenoids, and motor starters, especially when operated by discrete components such as pushbuttons. Some protection from noise generators can be provided with isolation transformers.

To protect a PLC from power surges, or spikes, suppressors are installed in parallel with the device generating voltage surges. Typically, a surge suppressor, such as a Metal Oxide Varistor (MOV) or an RC snubber, is installed to limit the voltage spike caused by the electrical equipment. An MOV functions in the same manner as back-to-back zener diodes. One zener diode holds the positive AC signal to a constant value, while the second zener diode prevents the negative-going AC signal from exceeding a predetermined value. Figure 5-5(a) shows an MOV connected in parallel with an AC inductive load. An RC snubber circuit is shown in Figure 5-5(b).

5-6 I/O INSTALLATION

When installing an I/O system, preliminary wiring considerations must take into account factors such as wire size, labelling of wire and terminal points, and the grouping of conductors in the I/O rack. To determine the number of I/O modules required for a new system, it is necessary to lay out a diagram of the process that you intend to control. This diagram should include a *system abstract*, which is used to provide a clear statement regarding the objectives of the control problem as well as a concise description of the method to be used to solve the problem. The abstract also includes the system configuration. The system configuration is an illustration of the actual hardware components which will be controlled by the PLC.

At this stage in the initial design, it is possible to determine the type of I/O that will be needed. The types of I/O modules include discreet, analog, TTL, etc. When the number of modules has been determined, it is possible to draw a diagram of the I/O racks and where the racks will be located on the process control floor. The modules should be grouped in racks according to the actual location of the machine to be controlled. If possible, the modules should also be grouped inside the rack so that DC modules are kept separate from AC modules. This will help to prevent noise interference in the PLC system.

Once rack locations have been determined, a wiring diagram can be developed showing the actual field connections between hardwired components in the field and the I/O modules in the I/O rack. Figure 5-6 shows a typical wiring diagram using Allen-Bradley addressing. The wiring terminations in the module are identified by black dots. Figure 5-6(a) shows the wiring diagram for an input module. The eight input location numbers for the module are 0 through 7. The box marked C is the termination point on the module for the neutral wire. Figure 5-6(b) shows the eight termination points for an output module. Because power is applied directly to an output module, a termination point for the line voltage is shown as a box marked AC.

When wiring I/O devices and racks, it is good practice to have an orderly sequence when performing these tasks. The following steps illustrate such a sequence:

1. Use proper wiring techniques. This step is essential in any electrical installation. Proper wiring techniques include
   -Avoiding joining cables to increase length
   -Using a minimum 3-inch radius on cable bends
   -Separating signal types as much as possible
   -Using the shortest possible cable runs
   -Leaving emergency stops hardwired for each machine under PLC control.

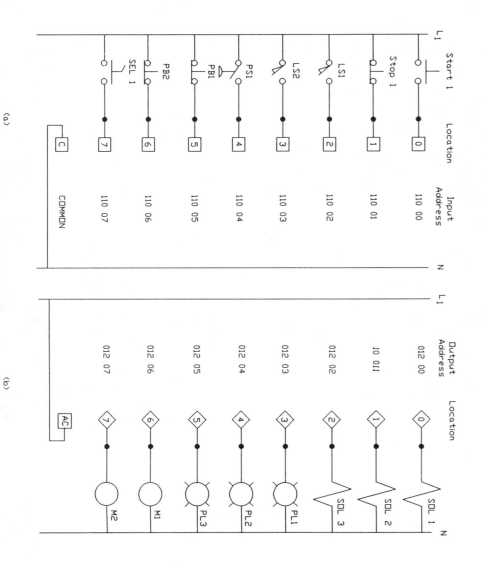

(a)

(b)

Figure 5-6 Wiring diagram.

Chapter 5 / Installation and Maintenance of Programmable Controllers

TABLE 5-1

Address	I/O Type	Device	Function
110 00	110v In.	PB	Start pushbutton
110 01	110v In.	PB	Stop pushbutton
110 02	110v In.	LS	Conveyor limit switch
110 03	110v In.	FS	Filling tank float switch
.	.	.	.
.	.	.	.
012 00	110v Out.	M	Motor magnetic
012 01	110v Out.	Sol	Hydraulic solenoid valve
012 02	110v Out.	PL	Motor pilot light

2. Verify that power is locked out from the PLC and all associated power supplies.

3. Verify that all I/O modules are of the proper type for the installation and are correctly situated in the rack.

4. Prepare and label the wire bundles for each module and all terminals.

5. Route the wire bundles through proper electrical raceways to the correct module locations.

6. Terminate each wire at its correct location at the module I/O points. Proper wiring techniques include stripping 3/8 in. of insulation off each wire, inserting each wire in the terminal, and tightening the terminal screw. Cable connections for data I/O should also be completed.

7. To minimize electrical interference, ground shielded cable at one end only.

8. After the termination of each wire, check wiring connections for durability by tugging on each wire.

Prior to installing I/O modules, it is essential that a list be prepared, detailing I/O placement and connections. It is also good practice to make a list of all inputs and outputs, identifying their addresses in the PLC program. This list is considered to be part of the *I/O documentation* and is very useful when troubleshooting, or debugging, PLC programs. A thorough documentation package should include a system abstract, I/O wiring diagram, I/O address assignment, internal address assignment, and register assignment. An example of an Allen-Bradley I/O address assignment chart is shown in Table 5-1. A typical address assignment chart will include the designated address in the PLC program, the type of input or output device at that address, and the function being performed by the device.

Internal I/O address assignments are the part of the I/O documentation that provides information on output coils which are not accessed at the I/O rack, but are still used in the actual ladder logic diagram. These internal coils are used for applications such as programming timers, counters, control relays, etc. Any function which requires a coil or set of contacts to operate an instruction that is not physically related to the I/O system can use internal coils. An example of an internal I/O address assignment chart for a Modicon 484 PLC is shown in Table 5-2.

TABLE 5-2

Internal Address	Description of Function
0258	Control relay for Start Pushbutton 1.
0259	Seals in Timer 4002.
0260	Output coil for Add instruction 4005.
0261	Output coil for Sequencer 4053.

TABLE 5-3

Register	Contents	Description
WY39	Analog output 1	Data for Variable Frequency Drive #1.
WX41	Analog input 1	Data obtained from Thermocouple 1.
TCC1	Timer 1	Accumulative value of Timer 1.
TCP2	Counter 2	Preset value of Counter 2.

A complete I/O documentation package should also include a register assignment chart. A register is a memory location used to store data that are to be used by the PLC. Counters, timers, and math functions use registers to hold information for the PLC system. Registers are also used for storing digital values obtained through analog input modules, and digital information which is to be transmitted via analog output modules. An example of a Texas Instruments register assignment chart is shown in Table 5-3.

When installing I/O modules that control analog functions, extra care should be taken to insulate the I/O conductors from noise generated by other equipment. I/O modules such as thermocouple inputs, TTL input/outputs, and analog input/outputs require shielded cable to prevent electrical noise from interfering with the operation of the module. A cable shield is generally made of aluminum foil and is wrapped around the conductors. When installing this type of cable, it is necessary to ground only one end of the shield. The shield at the I/O rack should be grounded, while the shield at the device, such as a thermocouple, should be left ungrounded. If the shield is grounded at both ends, it is possible for a ground loop to be introduced into the system. Ground loops generate Radio Frequency Interference (RFI), and can cause false triggering of I/O devices. Shielded cables are characterized by having at least 12 twists per foot.

When interfacing analog I/O, it may be necessary to install a voltage divider to match a field transmitter voltage range to that of an analog input module. A typical voltage divider circuit is shown in Figure 5-7. When using voltage dividers, resistances should be selected to provide as much current from the field device as possible to provide the maximum signal-to-noise ratio at the input. The value of resistance for a particular application can be determined by Ohm's law. For example, a field device has a voltage range of 0 - 30 V and can supply a current of 20 mA (max). If we assume that a device is to be connected to an analog input module with a range of 0 - 10 V, the resistors must be sized so that excess voltage is dropped across resistor R_1 and 10 V drops across resistor R_2 when the field voltage is 30 V. The size of resistors is calculated as follows based on a maximum field current of 20 mA:

$$R_1 = 20\ V/20\ mA = 1{,}000\ \Omega$$

$$R_2 = 10\ V/20\ mA = 500\ \Omega$$

Therefore, a total resistance of 1,500 Ω will draw 20 mA when the field voltage is 30 V.

The power-handling capabilities of the resistors in the voltage divider network is based on I^2R calculations, and is rounded up to the nearest wattage rating. For the previous example,

$$W_1 = I^2R = (0.02)^2(1{,}000) = 0.4\ W \text{ (nearest size is 1/2 W)}$$

$$W_2 = I^2R = (0.02)^2(500) = 0.2\ W \text{ (nearest size is 1/4 W, although 1/2 W would be recommended)}$$

When the input current is greater than the analog input module's rating, a current divider may be used. Figure 5-8 shows an example of a current divider

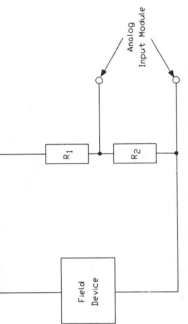

Figure 5-7 Voltage divider for analog input.

circuit. By placing a resistor in parallel with the input module, excess current is passed through resistor R_f. The current flowing through R_f will be the difference between the input from the field device and the current flowing into the module. For example, if the field device produces 50 mA at 20 V and the analog input module is rated at a maximum of 10 mA, 40 mA must flow through R_f. Once again, Ohm's law is used to calculate the resistance of R_f.

$$I_f = 40 \text{ mA, } V_f = 20 \text{ V}$$

$$R_f = V_f/I_f = 20/0.04 = 500 \ \Omega$$

When manufacturers refer to typical operating conditions, they are usually considering that 60% of the inputs are ON at any given time, and that 30% of the outputs are operating. Also, the ambient temperature is considered to be approximately 40°C during this typical operating condition. Typical operating conditions are design characteristics established by the manufacturer to guarantee that the PLC will function for prolonged periods of time under these conditions.

Even when they are in the OFF state, some devices have a very small value of current flowing. This current is called **leakage current** and is often present in semiconductor devices such as triacs and SCRs. Proximity switches are also notorious for allowing leakage current. This leakage current can cause the input of a module to flicker, or it can be sufficient to actually switch a module into a conducting state. Leakage current can be corrected by using *bleeder resistors*, as shown in Figure 5-9.

When triacs and SCRs are connected to an inductive load, there may be problems caused by *outrush*. When power is removed, the power stored in the

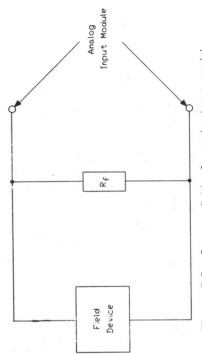

Figure 5-8 Current divider for analog input module.

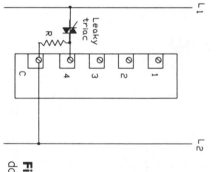

Figure 5-9 Bleeder resistor used to pull down leaky triac field device switch.

inductive load will try to force its way to ground and will often take a path across a device such as a triac in the OFF state. This problem is especially common when the current to the inductive load is cut off at the voltage peak, and can be subtle because it will not be detected until the power is switched back to ON. Outrush problems can be alleviated by installing a capacitor across the secondary side of the disconnect that supplies power to the inductive loads, as shown in Figure 5-10.

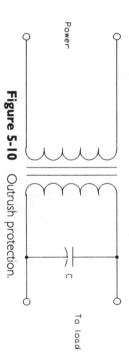

Figure 5-10 Outrush protection.

In most cases, solid-state outputs are provided with fusing on the module. This fusing protects the triac or transistor from moderate overloads. In situations where the module has no internal fusing, fusing should be installed externally during the initial installation. It is very important to adhere to the manufacturer's specifications when installing external fusing to a particular module. The fuse must have a proper rating which will insure that in the event of an overload condition, the fuse will open quickly to avoid damaging the output switching device.

Depending on the nature of a PLC installation, the CPU may or may not be separate from the I/O system. The CPU to I/O rack configuration is determined by the overall size of PLC operation. If remote I/O is being used, the CPU will have to be connected to the I/O rack via communication cables. These cables can be either *serial communication* or *parallel communication cables*. Parallel cables use 16 twisted pair of conductors, while serial conductors typically use two twisted pair of conductors. Serial cable installation is more economical, in terms of cost. Parallel communication cables are often installed in systems where high communication speed performance is essential.

5-7 FIELD CHECKOUT OF PROGRAMMABLE CONTROLLERS

After a PLC system has been installed, it is necessary to thoroughly inspect the installation to ensure that all connections were made correctly. Only after a system has been carefully inspected should power be applied to the system. Once power is applied, all inputs and outputs must be checked to verify their operation. This pre-start-up inspection procedure is commonly referred to as *field checkout*, or **commissioning**. The following steps should be taken whenever a pre-start-up of a system is required:

1. Inspect the CPU and I/O system visually. This step is necessary to verify that I/O modules are in their proper slot positions in the rack and that the CPU is wired up and properly connected.

2. Trace incoming power. Visually trace incoming power to the CPU and I/O rack. Verify that all electrical connections and grounding techniques conform to the electrical code.

3. Check all termination screws. This check will ensure that all termination screws are securely tightened and that there is no danger of a wire coming loose upon start-up.

4. Verify that the system is properly fused. This step is critical when commissioning a PLC system. If any fuses are incorrectly sized, severe damage to the system could result in an overcurrent condition. (Refer to your manufacturer's specifications for proper fuse requirements for CPU, power supply, and I/O modules.)

5. Check all hardwired components, i.e., Stop/Start stations, motor magnetics, etc., to ensure that all terminations at field components are correct. Also, verify that all field devices have addresses corresponding to the I/O documentation chart.

6. It is also good practice during field checkout to erase the RAM memory in the CPU. This will help prevent outputs inadvertently becoming energized by any test programs entered without your knowledge. In situations where programs have been permanently entered using EPROM, it is necessary to remove the EPROM chips before performing a system start-up.

Field checkout is generally carried out in two distinct stages:

1. Pre-checkout
2. System checkout

Pre-checkout. After installation of the I/O rack and power supply cables, the internal wiring on the rack is tested and the I/O modules are individually tested. In many cases, the testing of I/O racks and modules is accomplished using a *test trolley*. A typical test trolley consists of a processor, one or two I/O racks, and a test program. The test program sequentially turns on outputs which are wired to the inputs. The next step in the pre-checkout of a PLC system involves applying power to the CPU and I/O system. The CPU should be in the **offline** condition when performing this test. Most PLCs refer to this test as putting the CPU in PROGRAM mode. When the CPU is powered up, there should be some type of pilot light on the CPU to indicate its condition. Allen-Bradley has a green pilot light, which is ON if the CPU is functioning properly and a red pilot light, which is energized in the event of a CPU failure.

Test each input and verify its operation on the I/O module. The pilot light on the module should become energized when the field device closes, and de-energized when the field device opens. If there is an emergency stop circuit hardwired into the PLC, it should be tested to verify that power is interrupted at the I/O system when the emergency stop is pressed.

System checkout. After the field wiring to the PLC system is completed, the field devices and wiring are verified using schematic wiring diagrams. During the functional checkout of the system, the leads from rotating machinery are

5-8 PLC MAINTENANCE

A PLC's CPU is designed to minimize the need for maintenance. However, because the processor contains printed circuit boards, it is necessary to keep the processor clean of dust and dirt particles that can accumulate inside the CPU. Older CPUs have fan and filter systems that require periodic cleaning to provide reliable operation. Newer CPUs are rack-mounted modules that are not designed to be taken apart for maintenance. When installing a PLC in an environment where large quantities of dust and dirt particles are present, the CPU and I/O system should be installed inside an enclosure, such as an MCC cabinet. In many instances, the enclosure should be cooled by a fan which must have proper filtering for the enclosure to isolate possible contaminants. It is therefore necessary to inspect any filters which are part of an enclosure's cooling system to provide clean air for the CPU and I/O modules.

Periodic maintenance of a PLC system also includes checking the condition of the Lithium battery, which backs up the RAM memory in the CPU. Most CPUs have a status indicator which shows whether the battery's voltage is sufficient to back up the memory stored in the PLC. Manufacturers such as AEG Modicon provide auxiliary contacts associated with the Lithium battery. These contacts can be entered in a ladder logic program so that if the battery is about to fail, the contacts will energize a warning system to inform maintenance personnel of a potential system failure.

Some companies have regularly scheduled PLC system maintenance, which includes changing the battery backup every 12 months regardless of the battery's condition. Because a Lithium battery has a typical lifespan of two years, this type of preventative maintenance will minimize the chance of a battery causing failure in the PLC system.

Any terminating screws should also be periodically checked in the event that vibration has caused the screws to loosen. Industries which have large revolving equipment are especially prone to vibration, and it is not unusual for terminal screws to work themselves loose over extended periods of time. Actual I/O modules and related plugs and sockets should also be regularly checked to make sure that the connections are good and the modules are securely installed. This is particularly important when the PLC is in an environment where constant vibration occurs.

Many companies have become so dependent on their PLC systems that the plants simply cannot function without their PLCs in operation. In these situations, it is critical that **down-time** be kept to an absolute minimum. In many situations, the person maintaining a PLC system is expected to correct a fault almost as quickly as it occurs. Although this is rarely possible, there are some steps which can be taken to reduce down-time. One step involves keeping a modest inventory of spare parts. As a general rule of thumb, at least 10 percent of each type of

disconnected from devices such as motor starters and circuit-breakers. The starters are then operated by the PLC without running the rotating equipment. The main document used for this dry run is the specific control logic diagram for the process system. After entering the control program into the PLC, if possible, obtain a printout copy of the program. This printout is useful, although not essential, for checking the original control program against the program entered into the machine. Check each instruction in the program against the original to verify that no errors in entering the program have occurred. These errors include improper addressing of inputs and outputs, as well as register values such as preset quantities for timers, counters, and analog inputs and outputs.

I/O module should be kept as spare. For example, if your system has less than 10 I/O of a particular type, keep at least one card as a spare.

It is also good practice to keep one spare main board for the CPU. Although CPUs rarely fail, if one should malfunction, it may take weeks to obtain a replacement. Because many PLC failures are caused by problems with I/O cards, it is often faster to simply replace the suspect module, get the machine up and running, and then inspect the damaged I/O card under less stressful conditions. Semiconductor devices such as triacs and SCRs can be checked with an ohmmeter to determine if they are damaged. In most cases, the semiconductor device must first be removed from the module's printed circuit board to obtain an accurate reading with an ohmmeter.

If a module is going to be replaced, it must be replaced with exactly the same type of module. Some PLCs allow modules to be replaced while the system is powered up, where other manufacturers insist that the system be shut off before replacing a module. The manufacturers specification sheet for the module will usually state whether the module can be replaced in a powered-up condition. If a new module is installed and the fuse immediately blows, chances are that the module itself is not the problem, and perhaps an output device, such as a solenoid or motor magnetic, is shorted out.

5-9   PLC TROUBLESHOOTING

As with any electromechanical device, there are basic troubleshooting techniques which must be followed to ensure reliable results. These techniques involve using a careful, systematic approach when dealing with problems. Safety is of primary importance when troubleshooting any type of industrial equipment. When a PLC is controlling equipment that may become energized during the troubleshooting procedure, it is very important that this equipment be either locked out or tagged to inform other people in the plant that the equipment is under test. Once all safety precautions have been observed, the next step is to analyze what exactly is malfunctioning in the system.

In situations where you are not familiar with the actual operation of the PLC that you are troubleshooting, it is very helpful to obtain as much information as possible about the system. This information can be obtained by technicians or tradespeople who are usually involved in day-to-day PLC operation. It is also possible to obtain a basic understanding of a system by reviewing any documentation which is available for both the program stored in the system, as well as the PLC manufacturer's specification sheets.

Always start with the simplest potential problem and work from there. It is not necessary to completely dismantle a PLC system only to find that the problem was a blown fuse. Do a complete visual inspection of the PLC and all related equipment. Check for blown fuses, loose connections, or any other obvious source of malfunction. Verify that all control circuits have adequate power, and that all switches are set in their proper positions. Check that the documentation for the program is the same as the program entered into the PLC's memory. If any undocumented changes have been made to the program, it is possible that one of these alterations is causing the problem.

Use the troubleshooting features available on the PLC itself. Most systems will have diagnostic tests which can be initiated via the keyboard on the programming terminal. If possible, perform a CPU diagnostic test using the programming terminal and determine if the CPU is the cause of the problem. The CPU diagnostic test will usually check for failed ICs such as ROM or RAM memory chips, as well as testing the actual CPU's IC. Many PLCs will also perform a diagnostic on the CPU's power supply to verify that adequate power is being supplied to the processor.

Check the STATUS indicators on the CPU. These indicators provide a visual readout of conditions such as DC power supply, memory failure, I/O fault, and battery backup. Indicators on a CPU can be somewhat less elaborate, depending on the manufacturer. If any pilot light shown on the CPU indicates a faulty condition, it should be checked. I/O modules also contain fault indicators which will display a blown fuse condition, as well as indicating whether an I/O location is presently in an energized or de-energized state.

The programming terminal also provides access to the FORCE instruction, which is a fairly standard instruction on most PLCs. By using the FORCE key, it is possible to test the input and output status of any devices interfaced at the I/O rack. For example, forcing a solenoid valve ON will immediately tell you whether the solenoid is functional when the program is bypassed. If it is, the problem must be related to the software, and not the hardware. If the output fails to respond when forced, it is either the actual output module causing the problem, or the solenoid itself is malfunctioning. Because FORCE commands must be executed when a system is fully powered up, it is necessary to use extreme caution when performing this type of test. However, the FORCE instruction is a very useful troubleshooting tool and is highly recommended for locating problems related to a PLC.

The most common location of any fault in a PLC system is the I/O module. However, it is not always easy to determine the exact cause of a fault in the I/O system. Many of the problems attributed to PLC I/O systems are actually problems of the sensors and actuators connected to the I/O. Another contributing factor is the integrity of the wiring between devices connected to the I/O. Many of the newer series PLCs have automatic or semiautomatic means by which faults or failures in the I/O system can be detected and reported. This type of capability in a PLC-based system is often referred to as a *diagnostic system*.

Diagnostic systems are based on the detection of faults within an application without regard to how a solution to the problem may be accomplished. This type of system will generally have the ability to detect faults in the I/O chain from a communications parity error, failed I/O module, failed I/O rack or power supply, or a loss of I/O communication in the chain. A good diagnostic system is a form of artificial intelligence because it reaches a conclusion based on known facts introduced to its detection system. Decisions made by diagnostic systems are typically reported in a variety of ways from indicator lights to diagnostic messages generated on display terminals.

The primary advantage of diagnostic systems in PLC-based control is that not only are the actual PLC-related problems reported to the CPU, but also the

TABLE 5-4 Diagnostic Statistics

Fault Type/Source	Fault Distribution	Faults Currently Reported	Potentially Detectable
CPU Parity error, processor, etc.	5%	100%	100%
I/O-power supply, I/O module failure	15%	20%	95%
Wiring-broken wire, shorted wire	5%	0%	70%
Actuators-example starter	30%	0%	60-90%
70% short-circuit/O.L.			
20% coil			
10% other			
Sensors-limit switch:	45%	0%	10%
90% mechanical			
10% broken wire			
	100%	8%	45-54%

(Courtesy of General Electric Co.)

operating condition of the field-wired devices are reported. This is very important because approximately 50% of all PLC system failures are caused by actuators and sensors. In fact, the PLC itself is responsible for less than 20% of all system faults. Table 5-4 illustrates recent statistics from a study done by General Electric concerning control system diagnostics.

Figure 5-11 shows a **flowchart** used for troubleshooting PLC systems. A flowchart is a graphical representation of a problem in which symbols are used to represent questions asked and action taken. In Figure 5-11, the questions asked are indicated by diamond-shaped symbols and the action taken is shown by rectangular symbols. The initial problem, system failure, is represented by an oval-shaped symbol. After consulting with the system operator, the first decision to be made is whether the PLC has completely failed, or is partially shut down. From this first decision, the questions asked and actions taken are broken down into more specific areas.

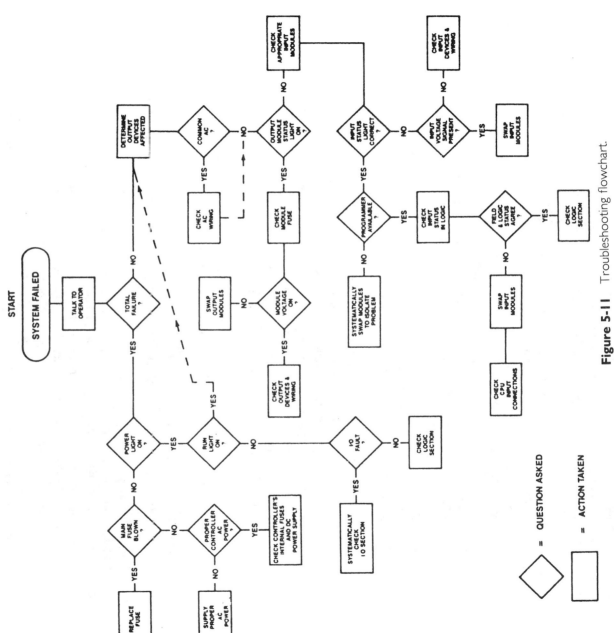

Figure 5-11 Troubleshooting flowchart.

This section discusses the major causes of PLC failure, an architecture that increases reliability, the physical layout of PLCs with respect to synchronization and system restoration procedures, and some basic software considerations.

The four major categories of PLC failure are

1. I/O failure
2. Microprocessor failure
3. Bit error (i.e., one register has an erroneous value for one or more bits)
4. Software design

As mentioned in Chapter 2, a PLC consists of a CPU, memory, and two I/O ports. If an I/O port fails, there is no direct way to determine whether the port failed or the PLC failed. Also, if two PLCs are connected to a single I/O port, a failure of the I/O port would disable the entire system. Therefore, the PLC and its I/O ports should be made *redundant* to minimize the possibility of failure. Although duplicating PLC functions is costly in terms of initial installation costs, it can prove to be tremendously advantageous in preventing down-time.

A microprocessor failure is termed *catastrophic* because it can cause major system malfunctions. PLCs are generally provided with self-diagnostic systems to prevent the microprocessor from issuing further instructions when a failure is detected. When using multiple CPUs, they should be connected together so that the action of one CPU disconnecting itself from the system does not affect system hardware.

The third type of error, called bit error, occurs when the data stored in a bit of memory are erroneous. If a bit error takes place, there are two possibilities:

1. A 0 was transmitted when the bit should have been 1.
2. A 1 was transmitted when the bit should have been 0.

The odds of two PLCs making the same bit error, except where high levels of electrical interference are present, is extremely small.

Using redundant software further helps in reducing the odds of system failure. Once a program has been developed and debugged, the second PLC simply uses a copy. The initial software is designed by considering various possible hardware states. Every possible combination of failure must be identified so that the correct procedures can be determined. Restorative procedures are also developed by considering the hardware states.

The concept of redundancy in process control has been used for many years in systems where down-time is of critical importance. Depending on system design, redundant, or "hot backup" components, can include two CPUs and what is known as a *Redundant Processing Unit (RPU)*. The RPU basically synchronizes the two CPUs so that in the event of system failure, the RPU rapidly switches control from the master CPU to the standby CPU. Figure 5-12 shows a diagram of an RPU system controlling two CPUs and providing access to an optional redundant I/O system. This system functions in the following manner:

1. Prior to system failure, the master CPU is in control, with the standby CPU constantly updated with I/O and register data from the RPU and master CPU.
2. If the RPU detects a fault from the master CPU, within one to three scan cycles, the RPU transfers control to the standby CPU.
3. If the RPU detects an I/O fault, the I/O system is switched over to the

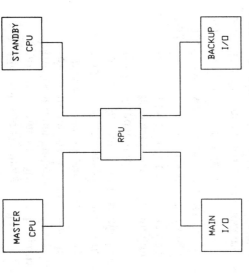

Figure 5-12 RPU controlling main and backup CPU and I/O.

redundant I/O chain. This transfer also requires approximately one to three scan cycles.

4. In the event of either processor or I/O failure, the RPU will also signal the operator that a failure has occurred in either or both systems.

REVIEW QUESTIONS

5-1. What type of information is usually available from the manufacturer regarding PLC installation?

5-2. What are three considerations when designing a system layout?

5-3. What is the best location for a PLC enclosure?
   (a) As close as possible to the machine or process to be controlled
   (b) As far away as possible from the machine or process to be controlled
   (c) In the control room
   (d) Close to the incoming power

5-4. The maximum operating temperature of a PLC inside an enclosure is
   (a) 60° C.
   (b) 50° C.
   (c) 70° C.
   (d) 40° C.

5-5. To allow for maximum convection cooling, how should all PLC components be installed?

5-6. Generally, system grounding conductors are
   (a) #4 AWG.
   (b) #10 AWG.
   (c) #8 AWG.
   (d) #6 AWG.

5-7. Protective ground wires must have a resistance value of less than
   (a) 0.1 Ω.
   (b) 1.0 Ω.
   (c) 10.0 Ω.
   (d) 0.5 Ω.

5-8. List three precautions that should be taken in the design stage to minimize the possibility of electrical interference in a PLC system.

5-9. Electrostatic Discharge (ESD) is caused by
  (a) environments with high humidity levels.
  (b) local radar stations.
  (c) environments with low humidity levels.
  (d) high levels of atmospheric contaminants.

5-10. Radiated electromagnetic interference is caused by
  (a) environments with high humidity levels.
  (b) local radar stations.
  (c) environments with low humidity levels.
  (d) high levels of atmospheric contaminants.

5-11. What is the primary cause of cross-talk interference?

5-12. Name two methods of surge suppression.

5-13. What is a system abstract?

5-14. I/O placement and wiring documents should be updated
  (a) whenever a system modification takes place.
  (b) during specified maintenance periods.
  (c) upon completion of a project.
  (d) during system documentation.

5-15. A field device is to be connected to an analog input module. The field voltage has a 0–20 V range and can supply a current of 10 mA maximum. The analog input module has a voltage range of 0–10 V. Determine the voltage divider required for the analog input module.

5-16. A field device with a current range of 0–100 mA is to be connected to an analog input module with a 0–20 mA input range. Determine the ohmic value of the parallel resistor required for the current divider network. Assume $V_f = 10$ V.

5-17. Determine the power-handling requirements of the resistors in the voltage divider network in Question 5-15.

5-18. What is leakage current and how can it be corrected?

5-19. Parallel communication cables are used in PLC installations where
  (a) the most economical installation is required.
  (b) transmission speed is not a factor.
  (c) environmental conditions are extreme.
  (d) high communication speed is essential.

5-20. Twisted shielded cables should have
  (a) twelve twists per foot.
  (b) the shield terminated at both ends of the conductor.
  (c) twenty-four twists per foot.
  (d) twelve twists per meter.

5-21. What are the two general stages of a field checkout procedure?

5-22. If a module fuse blows repeatedly, what is a probable cause?
  (a) The fuse rating is incorrect.
  (b) The output device may be short-circuited.
  (c) The module's output current is being exceeded.
  (d) All of the above.

5-23. 80% of all PLC faults are caused by
  (a) faulty power supplies.
  (b) malfunctioning microprocessors.
  (c) software failure.
  (d) input devices.

5-24. What is redundant PLC architecture?

5-25. A single output device has failed while the remainder of the PLC system is functioning normally. The indicator light on the output module indicates that a signal is being sent to the output point where the device is connected. You would now:

(a) Trace the circuit back through the logic to locate the inputs.
(b) Use a programming terminal to call up the rung that controls the output to see if the output coil is ON.
(c) Check the point where the output device's field wiring is connected to the output rack.
(d) Check the input modules for short-circuit conditions.

5-26. An entire PLC system appears to have failed. After checking the controller, you notice the power light on the front panel is not lit. However, the controller appears to be receiving its rated AC power. The most likely cause is that

(a) the battery in the backup system is weak.
(b) the processor has failed.
(c) the bus cable between the I/O racks and CPU requires replacement.
(d) the power supply has failed.

5-27. What is the purpose of an RPU?

Relay Logic

Upon completion of this chapter, you will be able to

▼ Understand the operation of relay coils.

▼ Draw the schematic symbols for relay coils and contacts.

▼ List the eight basic types of contact arrangements.

▼ Define the terms "pole," "break," and "throw."

▼ Explain the function of overload protection.

▼ Draw a truth table.

▼ List three typical outputs used in relay logic systems.

▼ Describe the basic operation of a relay timer.

▼ Recognize the schematic symbols for relay timers.

▼ Draw a line diagram.

6-1 RELAYS

To understand the ladder logic used in PLCs, it is necessary to have a thorough knowledge of relay logic. A relay is basically a switch that can be actuated from a remote position. Relays use one or more pairs of contacts to make or break electric circuits. For many years, relay logic was the standard method of controlling industrial electronic systems. The principle of relay logic is based on magnetically operated relays which energize and de-energize associated contacts, as shown in Figure 6-1. A relay is actuated, or energized, by completing the circuit branch that contains the electromagnetic relay coil. When electric current passes through

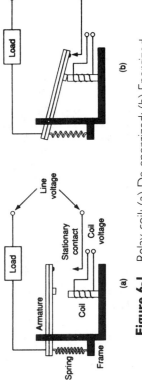

Figure 6-1 Relay coil: (a) De-energized; (b) Energized.

(a)

Armature
Spring
Frame
Coil
Load
Line voltage
Stationary contact
Coil voltage

(b)

Load
Coil voltage
Line voltage

CR

(a)

(b)

(c)

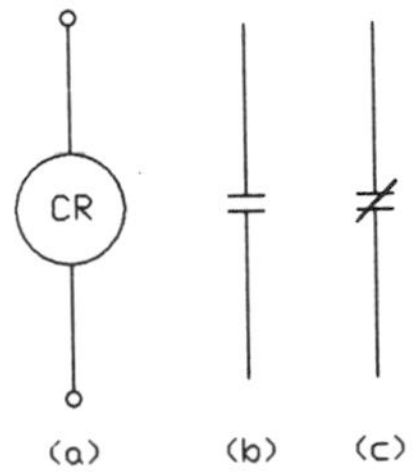

Figure 6-2 (a) Relay coil; (b) Normally open contacts; (c) Normally closed contacts.

a coil, the contacts associated with the coil change to their opposite resting state. For example, a set of contacts that are open when a coil is de-energized will close up on energization.

The schematic symbol for a relay is shown in Figure 6-2. A relay coil is represented by a circle, as in Figure 6-2(a). The CR signifies a Control Relay. If more than one CR is used in a circuit, subscripts such as CR_1 and CR_2 are generally shown on the schematic diagram. These subscripts are also used with contacts to distinguish between two or more CRs. In other words, CR_1 would operate any associated contacts labelled CR_1. Figure 6-2(b) shows a normally open set of contacts that are identified by a pair of parallel lines. The normally closed contacts shown in Figure 6-2(c) are designated by parallel lines intersected by a diagonal line.

There are eight basic types of contact arrangements in relay logic. They are

1. Single-Pole (SP)
2. Double-Pole (DP)
3. Single-Throw (ST)
4. Double-Throw (DT)
5. Normally Open (NO)
6. Normally Closed (NC)
7. Single-Break (SB)
8. Double-Break (DB).

The terms *pole*, *break*, and *throw* are used to describe how a contact arrangement operates. Pole is used to describe the number of completely isolated circuits that are allowed to pass through a switch at a given time. A single-pole switch only allows the current from one circuit to pass through, while a three-pole switch conducts current from three different circuits. A three-pole switch will engage or interrupt the flow of current by opening or closing three sets of contacts at exactly the same instant. The mechanical interconnection between poles is shown on a schematic by a dashed line that connects the poles together.

The term "throw" is used to describe the total number of individual circuits that each pole is capable of controlling. In other words, it is quite common to have a single pole controlling more than one circuit. If there were two possible paths for the current to take, and the switch was fed from only one circuit, depending on the position of the switch, the switch would be considered to be a single-pole (SP), double-throw (DT).

The number of separate contacts required by a switch to either open or close an individual circuit is referred to as the *break*. If flow of current is interrupted at two points by a switch, it is called a double-break (DB) switch. If power is interrupted at only one point by the switch, it is referred to as a single-break (SB) configuration. Figure 6-3 shows different arrangements and types of relay contacts.

6-2 OVERLOAD PROTECTION

The overload protection device used in most relay logic circuits consists of a heater coil and a set of normally closed (NC) contacts. The heater coils are placed in series with the device being controlled, such as a motor which "senses" the current flowing through it. If the load on the motor becomes excessive, the current flowing to the motor will heat up the coils. The heater coils will then open and cause NC contacts to also open.

NC contacts are usually placed in series with the Stop button of a control circuit. The overload protection is capable of disengaging power in both the power circuit and control circuit. Once the heater coil has cooled down, the NC contacts return to their normal condition and the motor is ready to be restarted. The schematic symbols for an overload coil and contact are shown in Figure 6-4.

Figure 6-4 An overload heater coil and its normally closed contacts.

6-3 INPUT DEVICES

For a relay system to function properly, there must be some type of control device used in the circuit. The simplest form of control device is the manual pushbutton. Pushbuttons are used to start, stop, and change operations in a relay system. A pushbutton may consist of one or more contact blocks. A contact block is the actual switching mechanism in a pushbutton station. Figure 6-5 shows the three standard sets of contact configurations available. Virtually any type of switching arrangement is possible by using combinations of NO/NC, NO, or NC contacts.

Another standard control device used in conventional relay systems is a selector switch. A selector switch usually has a set of normally open (NO) contacts and a set of normally closed (NC) contacts. Three-position selector switches are

Figure 6-3 Types of contacts: (a) Single-pole, single-throw, single-break; (b) Single-pole, single-throw, double-break; (c) Single-pole, double-throw, single-break; (d) Single-pole, double-throw, double-break; (e) Double-pole, single-throw, single-break; (f) Double-pole, single-throw, double-break; (g) Double-pole, double-throw, single-break.

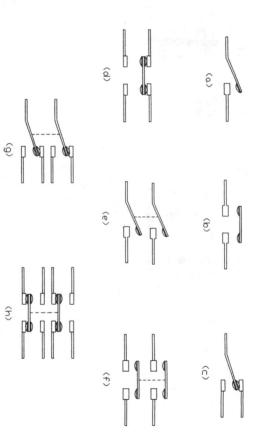

(a)   (b)   (c)

Figure 6-5 Pushbutton schematic symbols: (a) Normally open; (b) Normally closed; (c) Normally open/normally closed.

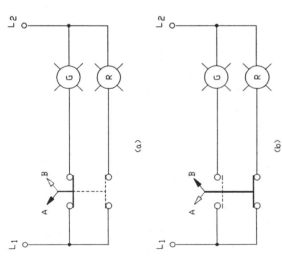

(a)

(b)

Figure 6-6 Two-position selector switch.

also quite common. Selector switches are used to select one of several possible circuit connections.

The switch itself can be in the form of a lever, knob, or key arrangement. Figure 6-6(a) shows a two-position selector switch. In Position A, the NC contacts are used in the circuit and the green pilot lamp is in the energized state. When the selector switch is moved to Position B, as in Figure 6-6(b), the red pilot light becomes energized and the green light is OFF.

The three-position selector switch is very popular in control circuits because it provides the added flexibility of having one position where no contacts are closed. This configuration is commonly referred to as a hand/off/auto switch. Figure 6-7 illustrates the three possible contact states for this type of switching mechanism. Figure 6-7(a) shows the hand position. The contacts are in their normal state; that is, the NC contacts are closed, and the NO contacts are open. Figure 6-7(b) shows the OFF position. The NC contacts are held open, and the NO contacts are unchanged. Figure 6-7(c) shows the auto position. The state of both sets of contacts is changed. The NC contacts are held open and the NO contacts are held closed.

Relay logic diagrams generally show selector switch contact positions, as indicated in Figure 6-7. However, it is also possible to illustrate the operation and position of selector switch contacts by use of a truth table. **A truth table** is a table showing all possible input combinations of a circuit. The table may use a 1 or an X to indicate a contact closure. Figure 6-8 shows the switch positions and truth table for a three-position selector switch.

Another type of control device commonly used in industry is the **limit switch.** The limit switch is used to change mechanical motion into an electrical signal. The limit switch accomplishes this conversion by using a lever of some sort to

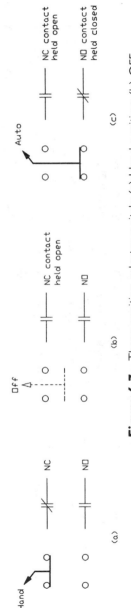

(a)

(b)

(c)

Figure 6-7 Three-position selector switch: (a) Hand position; (b) OFF position; (c) Auto position.

Figure 6-8 Three-position selector switch and truth table.

Contacts		
Position	A	B
Hand	X	
Off		
Auto		X

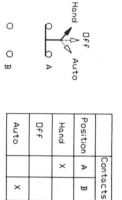

Figure 6-9 Limit switches: (a) Normally open; (b) Normally closed; (c) Normally open, held closed; (d) Normally closed, held open.

force a set of contacts either open or closed inside the switch itself. Limit switches have the same contact configurations as pushbuttons: NO, NC, and combinations of both NO and NC contacts. The standard limit switch usually has one set of NO and one set of NC contacts. The schematic symbols used to represent limit switch contacts and operations are shown in Figure 6-9.

Pressure switches are used to control the pressure of fluids such as air, water, or oil. When a change in pressure is detected, a pressure switch opens or closes a set of contacts. Pressure switches are very common on equipment such as air compressors, where the compressor is started or shut off by a pressure switch responding to a change in tank pressure. Figure 6-10 shows the schematic symbols used to represent NO and NC pressure switches.

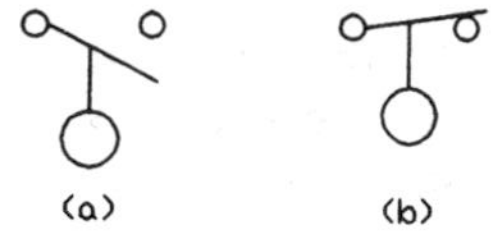

Float switches are used to detect the level of a liquid. A float switch can be used for either a pump or sump operation, depending on whether the NO or NC contacts of the float switch are used. When the NO contacts of a float are used, and the liquid level begins to rise, the contacts will close and a pump motor will be activated. The motor will remain ON until the level falls to an acceptable level. The schematic representation of a float switch is shown in Figure 6-11.

If the NC contacts of a float switch are used in series with a pump motor, the circuit is intended to maintain a specific level of liquid. The NC contacts keep the motor energized until the liquid level rises to a point where the float switch opens the contacts. The motor is then shut OFF until the level begins to fall. As the liquid level is lowered, the contacts eventually reclose and the motor is again energized until the liquid level re-opens the NC contacts.

Temperature control is used to maintain the desired temperature ranges of air, gases, liquids, and solids. Temperature control may be used to either maintain a specific temperature, or to prevent overtemperature conditions from occurring. The schematic symbols for a temperature-actuated switch are shown in Figure 6-12.

6-4 OUTPUT DEVICES

Standard outputs on a relay logic schematic are generally represented by either control relays, motor magnetics, solenoids, or pilot lights. In the case of motor magnetics, overloads are usually included on the diagram and are shown as 1, 2, or 3 NC contacts in series with the motor. In many cases, a single NC contact with the description *ALL OLs* is sufficient to represent any type of motor or motor starter, regardless of whether it is a single-phase or three-phase load. The circuit shown in Figure 6-13 illustrates four basic output devices, as well as the symbol for overloads of either a single-phase or polyphase motor.

Figure 6-10 Pressure switch: (a) Normally open; (b) Normally closed.

Figure 6-11 Float switch: (a) Normally open; (b) Normally closed.

Figure 6-12 Temperature switch: (a) Normally open; (b) Normally closed.

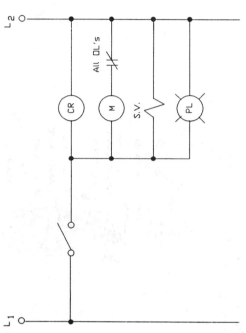

Figure 6-13 Standard outputs used on relay logic diagrams.

6-5 SEAL-IN CIRCUITS

Seal-in, or hold-in circuits, are very common in both relay logic and PLC logic. Essentially, a seal-in circuit is a method of maintaining current flow after a momentary switch has been pressed and released. In these types of circuits, the seal-in contact is usually in parallel with the momentary device.

Figure 6-14 shows a typical application for a seal-in circuit. To start the motor, the operator would press the Start button, sending a momentary signal to the CR. The CR is energized and its associated contacts close. The contact in parallel with the Start button closes, and current is now supplied to the CR via contact CR. The instant the Stop button is pressed, the circuit path is broken and the CR is de-energized. This causes the contacts to return to their NO state, and the motor M cannot be restarted until the Start button is pressed.

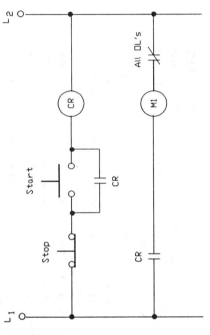

Figure 6-14 Seal-in circuit.

6-6 TIME-DELAY RELAYS

A *Time-Delay Relay* (TDR) is a device that provides a delayed switching action between the time an event is initiated and the time that the event is actually performed. There are several types of TDRs: electropneumatic, electromechanical, and electronic. One type of electropneumatic TDR is a *dashpot* time delay relay, and it consists of a relay that has a plunger connected to a dashpot. A dashpot is a device that utilizes either a gas (such as air) or liquid to absorb energy and retard the moving parts to produce a time delay.

Figure 6-15 shows the internal components of a diaphragm-operated electropneumatic timer. When the coil is energized, the solenoid plunger applies a force on the diaphragm within the sealed air cylinder. When the diaphragm has travelled a certain distance, it actuates a switch connected to the relay contacts. After power has been removed from the solenoid, a one-way exhaust valve provides a quick method of resetting the device.

TDRs use timing coils and timing contacts, or legs, to enable or disable various control circuitry. When the timer coil is energized, the timing legs will either open or close after a predetermined time interval. Relay timers can be divided into two general classifications: on-delay and off-delay. When the contacts of a timer change state after the coil is energized for a period of time, it is called a *Time-Delay ON* (TDON) relay. If the contacts open or close after the coil is de-energized for a period of time, it is called a *Time-Delay OFF* (TDOFF) relay. When timing legs or contacts are shown on a relay logic schematic, they may be either instantaneous or time-delayed in operation. If the contacts change state after a timed interval, they are usually identified by the abbreviations TO and TC. TO represents Time Opening and TC stands for Time Closing. Figure 6-16(a) shows the schematic symbol for an NC TDON timing leg. The symbol for an NO TDON leg is shown in Figure 6-16(b). Figure 6-16(c) illustrates an NC TDOFF timing leg, and the symbol for an NO TDOFF leg is shown in Figure 6-16(d).

Figure 6-17(a) shows the time-delay ON symbols for an NC TO and Figure 6-17(b) shows an NO TC operation. In Figure 6-17(c), the NC TC for an OFF delay-timer is shown. Figure 6-17(d) illustrates the symbol for an NO TO for an OFF delay-timer.

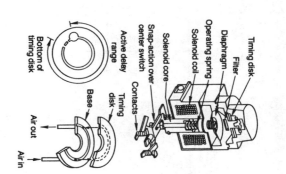

Figure 6-15 Electropneumatic timer. (Courtesy of Machine Design.)

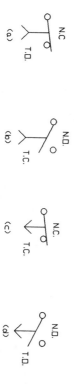

Figure 6-16 Timing legs: (a) Normally closed time opening ON-delay; (b) Normally open time closing ON-delay; (c) Normally closed time closing OFF-delay; (d) Normally open time opening OFF-delay.

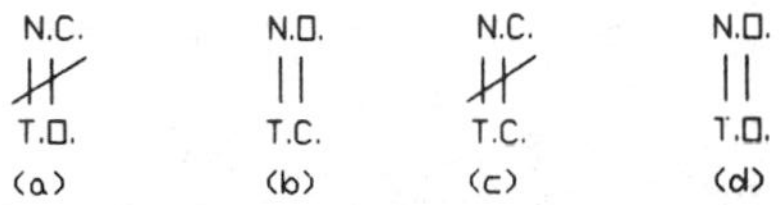

N.C.	N.O.	N.C.	N.O.
T.D.	T.C.	T.C.	T.D.
(a)	(b)	(c)	(d)

Figure 6-17 Timing contacts: (a) Normally closed time opening ON-delay; (b) Normally open time closing ON-delay; (c) Normally closed time closing OFF-delay; (d) Normally open time opening OFF-delay.

An example of a circuit containing both instantaneous and time-delay switch closures is shown in Figure 6-18. When the Start button is pressed, the TR1 coil becomes energized and the TR1 holding contact in parallel with the Start button immediately seals in. After a time delay of a preset value, the timing leg TR1 seals in and motor M1 becomes energized.

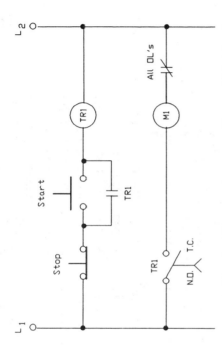

Figure 6-18 Stop/Start station controlling an ON-delay timer.

The circuit shown in Figure 6-19 illustrates the time-delay OFF function. When the Stop button is pressed, the timing leg appears as shown, in the NO position. As soon as the Start button is pressed, the TR1 holding contact seals in, and the timing leg also closes. In other words, as soon as Start is pressed, the motor starts running. After a time delay of a preset value, the timing leg opens and motor M1 becomes de-energized.

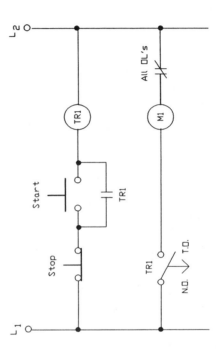

Figure 6-19 Stop/Start station controlling an OFF-delay timer.

Whenever timing circuits are used in control systems, it is occasionally necessary to graphically represent the time intervals. *Timing graphs* are frequently used to indicate how a timer affects a load during a timing sequence. Figure 6-20 shows an example of a load circuit timing graph. When the waveshape rises, the timing leg is closed and power is applied to the load. When the waveshape falls, the timing leg is opened and power to the load is interrupted.

6-7 LINE DIAGRAMS

In relay logic terminology, the circuit of Figure 6-19 would be referred to as a line diagram. There are some basic rules for line diagrams, such as

1. The two vertical lines which connect all devices on the line diagram are labelled L_1 and L_2. The space between L_1 and L_2 represents the voltage of the control circuit.

2. Output devices are always connected to L_2. Any overloads that are to be included must be shown between the output device and L_2; otherwise, the output device must be the last component before L_2.

3. Control devices are always shown between L_1 and the output device. Control devices may be connected either in series or in parallel with each other.

4. Each rung, or line, of a line diagram should be numbered.

Figure 6-21 shows a motor control schematic that uses relay logic to limit the current to a motor's armature as the motor is brought up to speed. This type of starter uses current limit contacts that remain open as long as a minimum value of current flows through them. If the current falls below this preset value, the contacts close. This type of contact is known as a *series-lockout contact*.

When the Start button is pressed, relay coil M becomes energized and causes the two M contacts to close. The motor begins operating as current flows through the starting resistor and series relay 1SR. The 1SR coil is a fast-acting relay, so its NC contact is opened before coil 1A becomes energized. Therefore, the motor starts with maximum resistance in series with the armature. When the current through the armature falls back to a normal operating value, coil 1SR is no longer operational, and contact 1SR returns to its NC state. Relay coil 1A now becomes

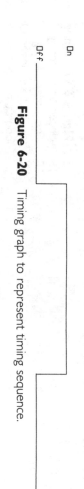

On

Off

Figure 6-20 Timing graph to represent timing sequence.

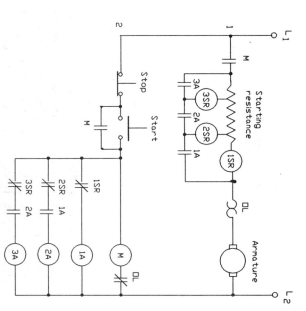

Figure 6-21 Current-limit acceleration starter with series relays.

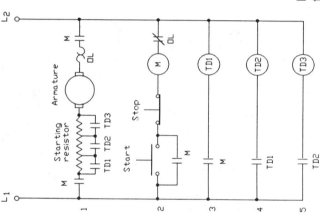

Figure 6-22 Motor-starting circuit using time-delay relays.

energized, removing a portion of the starting resistance and energizing relay 2SR. Because relay 1A's contacts are closed, when the current through coil 2SR falls below a certain value, 2SR will drop out, enabling relay 2A. The cycle then repeats until the starting resistor is removed from the circuit entirely.

Figure 6-22 shows an example of a line diagram using time-delay relays. This circuit is also used for starting a motor with reduced voltage. In this circuit, the resistance, in series with the armature, is gradually reduced during a specified time interval. When the Start button is pressed, coil M becomes energized. This action instantaneously closes the four associated contacts marked M. The two M contacts in series with the motor are now closed, so the motor begins to accelerate with maximum resistance connected in series with the armature. The M contact, in series with the coil marked TD1, is also closed. When coil TD1 times out, the TD1 contacts close, and a portion of the starting resistor is removed from the circuit. Coil TD2 also begins to time out, and when the TD2 contacts close, more resistance is removed from the armature circuit. Coil TD3 becomes energized and after a certain time interval, its contacts also close. All resistance has now been removed from the circuit and the motor operates at full speed. When the Stop button is pressed, coils M, TD1 TD2, and TD3 become de-energized and all the contacts return to their NO states.

REVIEW QUESTIONS

6-1. What is a relay?

6-2. List the eight basic types of contact arrangements used in relay logic.

6-3. Mechanical interconnection between poles is represented by
(a) a solid line.
(b) a normally closed contact.
(c) a normally open contact.
(d) a dashed line.

6-4. The term "throw" is used to describe
(a) the number of separate contacts required by a switch to either open or close each individual circuit.
(b) the total number of individual circuits that each pole is capable of controlling.
(c) the mechanical interconnection between poles.
(d) the number of completely isolated circuits that are allowed to pass through a switch at a given time.

6-5. Explain the purpose of overload protection in relay logic circuits.

6-6. What is a heater coil?

6-7. Overload contacts are shown on relay diagrams
(a) as normally closed contacts in parallel with the load.
(b) as normally open contacts in parallel with the load.
(c) as normally closed contacts in series with the load.
(d) as normally open contacts in series with the load.

6-8. Name the two circuits that the overload protection is capable of interrupting power to.

6-9. List the three contact configurations for a pushbutton.

6-10. Describe the operation of a hand/off/auto selector switch.

6-11. What is a truth table?

6-12. A typical limit switch
(a) has two sets of normally closed contacts.
(b) has one set of normally open and one set of normally closed contacts.
(c) has two sets of normally open contacts.
(d) has one set of normally open contacts.

6-13. What is the difference between a pressure switch and a float switch?

6-14. List four standard output devices used in relay logic circuits.

6-15. Describe a typical application for a seal-in circuit.

6-16. What is a time-delay relay?

6-17. Name the three types of time-delay relays.

6-18. What is a dashpot?

6-19. A timing leg
(a) closes instantly when a coil is energized.
(b) opens instantly when a coil is energized.
(c) will open or close after a specific length of time.
(d) functions independently of the timing coil.

6-20. List the four configurations for timing legs.

6-21. What is a timing graph?

6-22. Name four basic rules for line diagrams.

6-23. Describe the operation of a series-lockout contact.

7

Ladder Logic

Upon completion of this chapter, you will be able to

▶ Define ladder logic.
▶ Explain the purpose of I/O addresses.
▶ Understand softwiring, branches, and rungs.
▶ Write a ladder logic program.
▶ Define the terms "examine on" and "examine off."
▶ Explain the purpose of a latching relay instruction.
▶ Differentiate between an internal output and an actual I/O output.
▶ Understand controller scan.
▶ Name two programming restrictions.
▶ Define "nesting."
▶ Explain why safety circuitry is important in ladder logic systems.
▶ List three types of I/O addressing.

7-1 INTRODUCTION

Ladder logic is a term used to describe the format of schematic diagrams to be entered into a PLC. Ladder logic programming uses two basic types of ladder language elements: *relay logic instructions* and *data transfer instructions*. This chapter shall examine the application of discrete relay logic instructions. The relay logic instruction set indicates the ability of the ladder language to replace control circuits originally designed for relay networks with a control system based on a PLC. Data transfer instructions increase the versatility of the ladder language

7-2 LADDER LOGIC CIRCUITS

program by introducing the computer characteristics of the PLC to the control system. The data transformation instruction set takes the PLC beyond the ability to simply replace a relay system and allows it to function as a process controller.

A ladder logic circuit is an electrical network consisting of lines or rungs in which each line or rung must have continuity to enable the output device. A ladder network consists of a number of rungs, with each rung controlling an output. This output is controlled by a combination of input or output conditions. The conditions that represent the inputs are connected in series, parallel, or series-parallel to obtain the logic required to drive the output. The ladder network forms an electrical schematic diagram for the control of input and output devices. Unlike a relay logic diagram, a ladder network does not represent physical connections. Ladder networks form schematics that are *softwired* within a PLC. Input and output devices are hardwired to the input and output modules of a PLC, but this wiring has no bearing on the interconnections formed by the ladder logic circuit.

Ladder logic was developed based on relay logic and therefore many similarities exist between the two logic systems. The main difference between ladder logic and relay logic is that in relay logic, actual device symbols are shown on the diagram. In ladder logic, only contacts and coils are used to represent input and output devices. For example, the circuit shown in Figure 7-1(a) is a relay logic diagram with a Stop/Start station and a CR operating a solenoid. In this circuit, when CR1 is OFF, the solenoid is energized. If the same diagram were

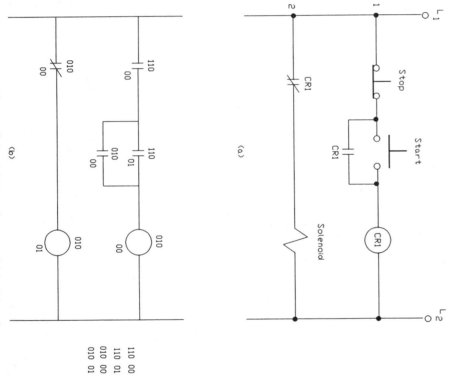

Figure 7-1   (a) Line diagram; (b) Ladder diagram.

110 00 = Stop
110 01 = Start
010 00 = CR1
010 01 = Solenoid

to be drawn in ladder logic, it would appear as shown in Figure 7-1(b). In this circuit, the input and output devices are now represented by numbers. These numbers are referred to as **addresses.** The addresses shown in Figure 7-1(b) are typical of an Allen-Bradley PLC.

Some basic points regarding ladder logic diagrams are as follows:

1. All devices that represent resistive or inductive loads to the circuit are shown at the right of the diagram.

2. All devices that represent make or break electrical contacts are shown at the left of the diagram.

3. Devices connected in parallel with other devices are often called **branches.** Each complete horizontal line of a ladder diagram is typically referred to as a **rung.**

4. Electrical devices are shown in their normal conditions. An NC contact would be shown as normally closed, and a NO contact would appear as a normally open device. All contacts associated with a device will change state when the device is energized.

5. Devices which perform a stop function are usually connected in series, while devices that perform a start function are connected in parallel.

7-3 WRITING A LADDER LOGIC DIAGRAM

In many cases, it is possible to prepare a ladder diagram directly from the narrative description of a control event sequence. In general, the following suggestions apply to writing ladder logic diagrams:

1. Define the process to be controlled.

2. Draw a sketch of the operation process. Make sure all of the components of the system are present in the drawing.

3. Determine the sequence of operations to be performed. List the sequence of operational steps in as much detail as possible. Write out the sequence in sentences, or put them in table form.

4. Write the ladder logic diagram from the sequence of operations.

▶ *EXAMPLE 7-1*

A workpiece is loaded on a conveyor belt and operates between two limits of travel. When limit switch LS2 is activated, the conveyor moves forward. When limit switch LS1 is activated, the conveyor changes direction. Pressing the Start button causes the motor to run in the forward direction, and pressing the Stop button stops the motor.

Solution

Example 7-1 is a reciprocating motion problem. Figure 7-2 is an illustration of the conveyor belt and control devices.

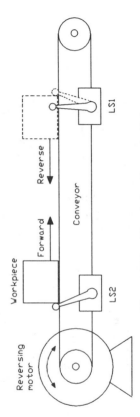

Figure 7-2 Circuit for Example 7-1.

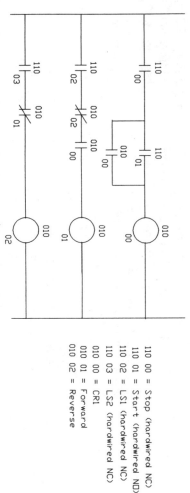

Figure 7-3 Ladder logic circuit for Example 7-1.

110 00 = Stop (hardwired NC)
110 01 = Start (hardwired NO)
110 02 = LS1 (hardwired NC)
110 03 = LS2 (hardwired NC)
010 00 = CR1
010 01 = Forward
010 02 = Reverse

The sequence of operations is as follows:

1. When the Start button is pressed, control relay CR1 is energized, and the conveyor moves in a forward direction.
2. When the workpiece makes contact with limit switch LS1, the motor is reversed and the conveyor moves in the opposite direction.
3. When the workpiece makes contact with limit switch LS2, the motor returns to the forward direction.
4. The Stop button stops the motor, regardless of which direction it is turning.

Figure 7-3 shows the equivalent ladder logic circuit for Example 7-1.

7-4 I/O INSTRUCTIONS

In the circuit shown in Figure 7-3, the Stop button and limit switches are shown as NO contacts, although they are actually hardwired in the closed position. In almost all cases, an NC input device is entered as NO. When a CPU is reading, or scanning, the I/O rack, and it detects a device which is hardwired NC in the field, it will instruct the PLC to change the state of the contact in the program. Allen-Bradley refers to this operation as EXAMINE ON and EXAMINE OFF. Virtually all PLCs will do this when they sense a closed input device.

The NO, or EXAMINE ON, instruction is programmed to test for an ON condition from a reference address. During the execution of a program, the processor *examines* the reference address of an instruction for an ON condition. If the reference address contains a logic 1(ON), the processor will automatically *close* the NO contact to provide power flow. If the reference address contains a logic 0(OFF), the processor will not change the state of the NO contact.

In Figure 7-3, the output contacts associated with Forward and Reverse motor magnetics are shown in exactly the same format that they would be if drawn in relay logic form. If an output contact is meant to be normally closed, it is entered into the PLC as an NC contact. The following rule of thumb is used for entering contacts in a PLC:

All inputs are usually entered as normally open, and the field closure will take care of itself. All outputs are entered as they appear.

There are some cases where an input must be entered as normally closed, but these instances are rare and the above rule of thumb is true for most situations for practically all types of PLCs.

The NC, or EXAMINE OFF, instruction is programmed whenever a test for an OFF condition is required from a reference address. When a processor examines a reference address for an OFF condition, if the NC contact has a logic

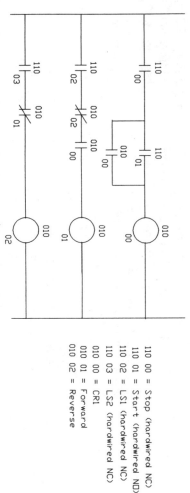

0(OFF) status, the instruction will continue to provide logic continuity through the rung. If the NC contact address has a logic 1(ON) status, the instruction will open the NC contacts and interrupt power flow on the rung.

In most ladder logic circuits, an output coil is the last device to be entered on a line. It is not possible to enter overloads to the right of a coil, as is the case with relay logic. If overloads are required on a ladder logic program, they must be entered before the coil, and they must be entered as NO contacts because an overload is an input device.

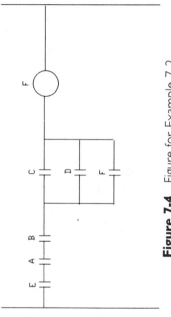

Figure 7-4 Figure for Example 7-2.

▶ **EXAMPLE 7-2**

Draw a ladder logic diagram showing two Stop pushbuttons and two Start pushbuttons controlling one motor. Include the overload contacts in your diagram and use the following I/O addresses: $Stop_1$ = A, $Stop_2$ = B, $Start_1$ = C, $Start_2$ = D, Overload = E, Motor = F.

Solution

Figure 7-4 shows the equivalent ladder logic circuit. The Stop buttons are entered as NO contacts and are connected in series with each other. Because the overload is hardwired as NC, it is also entered as an NO input instruction. The two Start buttons are connected in parallel with the holding contact from motor F.

Most PLCs have outputs known as latching relays. A **latching relay** is an output instruction that maintains an energized or de-energized state after power to the output has been removed. Unlike a normal output coil, which is not always energized at power up (when power is applied to the PLC), a latched coil will usually return to the state it was in before power was removed.

A latch coil is also referred to as a *retentive coil*. On most PLCs, a latched coil will remain in its latched state, even when the rung changes state. In other words, if the rung containing the latched coil is de-energized, the latched coil may remain energized. The unlatch coil is the only programmed method of resetting a latched output coil. The unlatch coil instruction is programmed to reset a latched output of the same reference address. Figure 7-5 shows the ladder logic symbols for latch and unlatch output instructions.

Latched coils are frequently used in ladder logic programs where it is imperative that the output devices are always in their proper states during certain stages of control processes. These types of circuits are known as **fail-safe** circuits. For example, a latched or retentive coil may used to ensure that venting fans and blower motors are always on before a manufacturing process can begin. Fail-safe

Figure 7-5 (a) Latch coil; (b) Unlatch coil.

circuits can also be used to turn off outputs in the event of a system malfunction. Figure 7-6 shows a typical application of a latch/unlatch instruction using an Allen-Bradley PLC. In this circuit, contacts 110 00 and 110 01 represent momentary pushbuttons. If 110 00 is pressed, output 010 00 becomes energized and remains energized after the input returns to its NO state. The only way output 010 00 can be turned off is by pressing pushbutton 110 01. Note that both the latch and unlatch instructions have the same reference address.

Figure 7-6 Latch/unlatch ladder logic circuit.

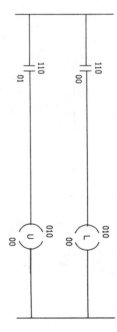

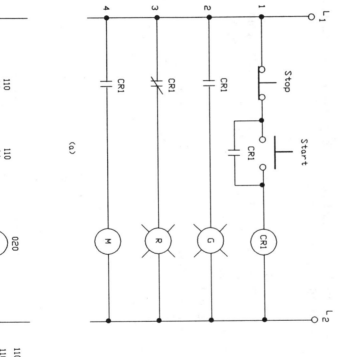

(a)

(b)

110 00 = Stop
110 01 = Start
020 00 = CR1
010 00 = Green P.L.
010 01 = Red P.L.
010 02 = Motor

Figure 7-7 (a) Relay logic circuit with control relay; (b) Ladder logic with internal output.

Figure 7-8 De-energize coil controlled by contact.

Latch and unlatch commands are also termed *set* and *reset*, respectively. The ladder logic circuit shown in Figure 7-6 is the equivalent of a flip-flop in a digital circuit. A flip-flop is a digital circuit, or device, containing active elements, capable of assuming either one of two stable states at a given time. As mentioned in Chapter 2, flip-flops are primarily used as memory storage devices; each flip-flop holds one binary digit of information.

Internal outputs are coils that are used in ladder logic programs, but are not accessible at I/O racks. These output instructions are also known as *software coils* and *dummy relays*. The advantage of using internal outputs is that there are many situations where an output instruction is required in a program, but no physical connection to a "real world" device is needed. Because I/O modules and racks are expensive, it is best to minimize output card requirements whenever practical. By eliminating hardwired control relays, installation and maintenance of those particular outputs are nonexistent.

The relay logic circuit of Figure 7-7(a) and its equivalent ladder logic circuit in Figure 7-7(b) illustrate an internal coil. In this circuit, a Stop/Start station controls relay CR1. When CR1 is energized, the green pilot light (G) turns ON, the red pilot light (R) turns OFF, and motor M starts running. Although control relay CR1 in Figure 7-7(a) is an output device, it is not directly energizing the pilot lights or the motor. In the circuit of Figure 7-7(b), Allen-Bradley I/O addressing is used, and the CR1 is represented by output 020 00. Because 020 00 is an address that is not accessible by the I/O rack, it is considered an internal coil.

Another output instruction used by many PLCs is the *de-energize coil*. This type of coil is programmed to control either an internal output or an output device connected to the I/O rack. Figure 7-8 shows the symbol for a de-energize coil. In this circuit, if contact A is closed, the output coil B will turn OFF. Conversely, if the input contact is open, the output is ON. Any contacts controlled by this type of coil function normally. That is, if the output is de-energized, NO contacts will open and NC contacts will close.

▶ *EXAMPLE 7-3*

Figure 7-9 shows how one limit switch is used to control two output devices. Redraw the circuit in ladder logic form without using an NC contact.

Solution

In Figure 7-9, when limit switch A is open, output C is ON and B is OFF. Figure 7-10 is an equivalent circuit because it performs the same function as Figure 7-9. When contact A is closed, output B turns ON and the de-energize coil turns OFF.

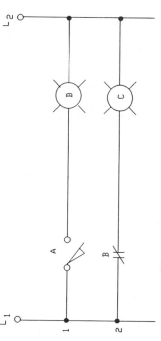

Figure 7-9 Figure for Example 7-3.

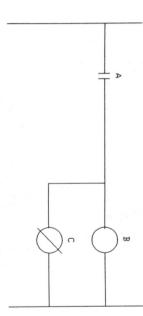

Figure 7-10 Solution to Example 7-3.

Figure 7-11 Transitional contacts: (a) OFF-ON; (b) ON-OFF.

A **Transitional contact** is designed to provide a one-shot pulse when the referenced trigger signal makes a transition; either from ON-to-OFF or OFF-to-ON. The symbols for a transitional contact are shown in Figure 7-11. Essentially, these contacts are different from regular contacts in that they will only stay open or closed in the program for one scan each time they are energized. These types of contacts are generally used in sequencer and math functions.

Figure 7-11(a) shows the ladder logic symbol for an OFF-ON transitional contact. This contact will close for exactly one program scan whenever the trigger signal goes from OFF-to-ON.

An ON-OFF transitional contact is shown in Figure 7-11(b). This instruction is programmed to provide a one-shot pulse when the referenced trigger signal makes an ON-to-OFF transition. The ON-OFF transitional contact will allow logic continuity for one program scan and then it opens.

7-5 CONTROLLER SCAN

The means employed by the CPU to "read" a ladder logic program is called a **scan**. There are two basic scan patterns that different PLC manufacturers use to accomplish the scan function. The logic may be solved by either columns or rungs. Figure 7-12 shows the scan by column method used by AEG Modicon. Using this system, the processor "looks" at the first contact at the top left corner and reads the first column from the top to the end of the column. Next, it reads the second column from the top to the end, then the third, etc. When the first network is scanned, the processor proceeds to the second until the entire program has been read; the cycle then repeats. Scanning is how the CPU determines the status of input and output devices in the program.

The scan by rung method used by Allen-Bradley is shown in Figure 7-13. In this type of system, the processor examines input and output instructions in a left-to-right direction moving down one rung at a time. When programming certain circuits using ladder logic, it is necessary to know how your PLC scans the user program.

A full scan of ladder logic includes not only the reading of the actual program, but also the updating of memory locations and accessing of peripheral devices such as programming terminals. The PLC will scan a program regardless of whether there is a programming terminal connected or not. In reality, the machine is simply checking bits of information stored in memory locations. However, it is reading those bits in a manner which is identical to a left-to-right or top-to-bottom format on a ladder logic diagram.

The time required for a typical PLC to scan 128 inputs and outputs is approximately 1 millisecond. As mentioned in Chapter 2, the scan time for a ladder logic program is also dependent on the types of instructions entered. For example, a sequencer or math function will take longer to process than a discrete input due to the larger memory requirements of these types of instructions.

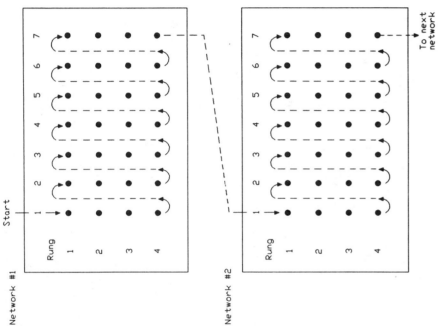

Figure 7-12 Scanning by column.

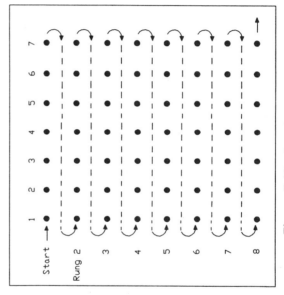

Figure 7-13 Scanning by rung.

7-6 PROGRAMMING RESTRICTIONS

When writing programs in ladder logic form, there are some restrictions that must be kept in mind. For example, the circuit shown in Figure 7-14 is a conventional relay logic circuit where current will flow from L_1 to L_2 as long as there is a path.

Figure 7-14 Relay logic circuit with "reverse power" flow.

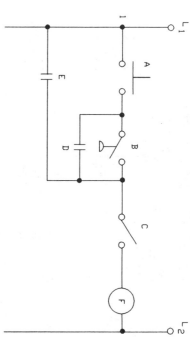

In this circuit, it makes no difference which combination of devices is closed. As long as a path is established between the two points of potential difference, current will flow between the two points. The following combination of device closures cause output F to be energized:

A,B,C   A,D,C   E,C   E,D,B,C

If the same circuit were redrawn in ladder logic form, as shown in Figure 7-15, only three of the four combinations discussed previously would cause output F to be energized. If contacts E,D,B,C were closed, coil F would not be ON. The reason for this is that in any PLC, the direction of "power flow" is left-to-right only. A PLC will never energize an output if the contact closure requires "power flow" in a right-to-left direction.

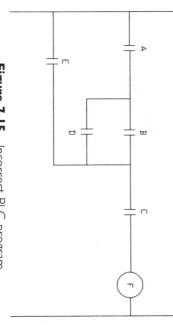

Figure 7-15 Incorrect PLC program.

For the circuit shown in Figure 7-14 to function in the same manner on a PLC, it must be drawn in a manner similar to that shown in Figure 7-16. In this circuit, the reverse power flow condition is eliminated. Some manufacturers refer

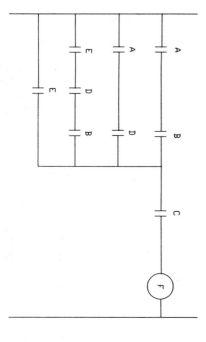

Figure 7-16 Correct PLC program.

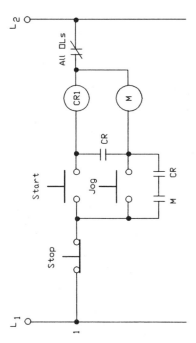

Figure 7-17 Relay circuit with vertical contact.

to this as a schematic scan direction limitation, and it can be expressed by the following statement:

PLCs will scan in a left-to-right direction only, never right-to-left.

When working with relay logic schematics, it is not unusual to see vertical contacts shown on a diagram. These contacts are often used to represent master control relay functions. In PLCs, there is no such thing as a vertical contact. No PLC manufacturer has currently included vertical contact programming, so it is necessary to modify any relay logic program which contains vertical contacts so that it can be run on a PLC. Figure 7-17 shows a standard relay schematic containing vertical contacts.

To modify a program to be run on a PLC, refer to Figure 7-18. In the circuit of Figure 7-18, the ladder logic program is written in such a way that the vertical contacts are no longer required and the program will still operate in exactly the same manner as the circuit of Figure 7-17.

▶ *EXAMPLE 7-4* Rewrite the circuit of Figure 7-19 in ladder logic form, eliminating the vertical contact.

Solution

To draw an equivalent circuit for Figure 7-19, it is necessary to first determine the operating criteria for the circuit. For example, when switches A and B

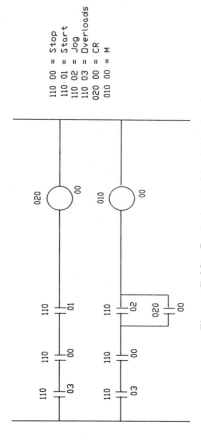

Figure 7-18 Equivalent ladder logic circuit.

are closed, outputs D and E are both ON. When inputs A and C are closed, only output E is energized. The equivalent ladder logic circuit is shown in Figure 7-20.

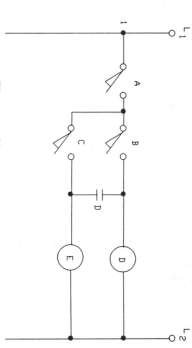

Figure 7-19 Figure for Example 7-4.

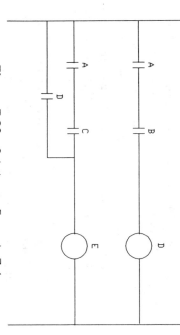

Figure 7-20 Solution to Example 7-4.

Some PLCs, particularly the Allen-Bradley PLC2, have a programming limitation which is referred to as **nesting**. The term nesting is loosely defined as a ladder logic condition when a "branch within a branch" exists. The relay logic circuit shown in Figure 7-21 is an example of a circuit that cannot be converted directly to ladder logic and entered into an Allen-Bradley PLC2.

The circuit shown in Figure 7-22 is the modified program from Figure 7-21, which an Allen-Bradley PLC will accept. In many cases, the simplest method of eliminating nesting is to duplicate contacts. For example, the circuit of Figure

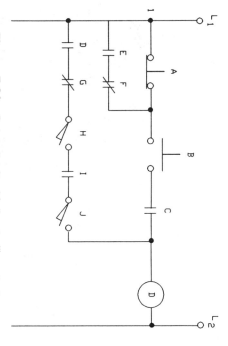

Figure 7-21 Relay circuit with "nested" contacts.

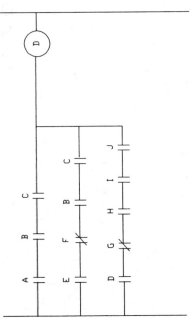

Figure 7-22 Equivalent ladder logic program.

7-21 has a nesting problem due to contacts E and F being connected between switches A and B. By duplicating switch B and contact C in Figure 7-22, the nesting problem has been eliminated.

▶ *EXAMPLE 7-5*

Convert the nested program of Figure 7-23 to a circuit that will function on any PLC system.

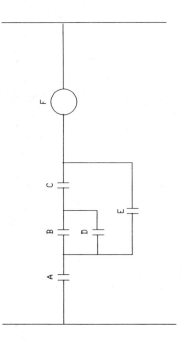

Figure 7-23 Figure for Example 7-5.

Solution

Contact D is the cause of the nesting problem on Figure 7-23. This nest can be eliminated by duplicating contact C, as shown in Figure 7-24.

All PLCs have limits as to the number of contacts that can be seen on one line at a time. Typically, the maximum number of contacts per line is between 12 and 15. The number of lines that can be displayed on a programming screen is limited to usually about seven rungs. The number of rungs that can be entered into a PLC memory is usually limited only by the PLC's actual memory.

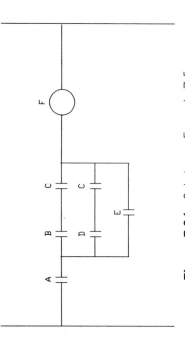

Figure 7-24 Solution to Example 7-5.

PLCs are extremely powerful machines that have capabilities which far exceed any conventional relay logic system. For this reason, it is extremely important that safety considerations are taken into account when either installing a PLC or writing a ladder logic program. To determine how safe a PLC system is, it is necessary to identify components that are potentially dangerous to anyone who may come in contact with the PLC. Any person who may be involved with loading or unloading materials from a PLC-controlled system, making adjustments during production, changing or adjusting tools controlled by the PLC, removing jammed materials, or modifying an existing program while the machine is operating, runs the risk of being injured when working around the PLC.

It is important to remember that a PLC is still a machine, and machinery will break down regardless of how thoroughly it is maintained. For example, virtually all output modules use thyristors to control power flow from the module. Thyristors such as SCRs and triacs are extremely reliable, but, if used constantly over a period of time, or in extreme temperatures, can break down. When a semiconductor is destroyed, it may either become short-circuited or open-circuited. This type of event is commonly referred to as *random failure*, and it occurs when a semiconductor is destroyed for no apparent reason. Fortunately this occurrence is rare, but when writing a program for a PLC, it is the type of situation where some type of protection circuitry should be considered.

Another cause of safety problems with PLC systems is the effect of electromagnetic or electrostatic interference. If an output coil is in the de-energized state, a binary 0 is stored somewhere in the RAM memory. If the RAM memory chip is subjected to electromagnetic or electrostatic interference, it is possible for this binary 0 to change to a 1, and vice versa. This change could result in an output turning ON or OFF seemingly by itself.

To minimize the risk of interface failure and electromagnetic/electrostatic interference, the proper installation of filtering devices and shielded cables should be used.

Most PLCs also come equipped with a **FORCE** instruction which is a very useful tool for troubleshooting programs. However, it is also an extremely dangerous instruction if used incorrectly. The FORCE key will override a conventional Stop button wired to the PLC, making it impossible to turn OFF an output that is forced ON. If, for example, a motor has been forced to the ON state, the only way the motor can be shut OFF is by physically removing power to the motor, i.e., opening the disconnect switch, or by forcing the motor OFF at the PLC's programming terminal.

In addition to shielding and filtering, there are some safety functions that can be incorporated into a PLC system to minimize the risks of equipment failure and operator error. One such precaution is the installation of hardwired Master Control Relays (MCR). In conventional relay logic systems, an **MCR** is often used to control power to the entire system or to specific rungs. A hardwired MCR can be incorporated so that if an emergency Stop is pressed, the MCR will work independent of the PLC and remove power to either the PLC output modules, or to any associated equipment that should be shut down. Using this method, in the event of a PLC failure, it is still possible to shut down a system without depending on the PLC. Usually, if a hardwired MCR is controlling a PLC, it will remove power only to the I/O system, allowing the CPU to continue to function. The hardwired MCR is not to be confused with the MCR instruction available on most PLCs. This MCR instruction for PLCs will be discussed later in this book.

Figure 7-25 shows a schematic of two hardwired MCRs controlling both the input and output modules of a PLC system. To start the system, the enable input

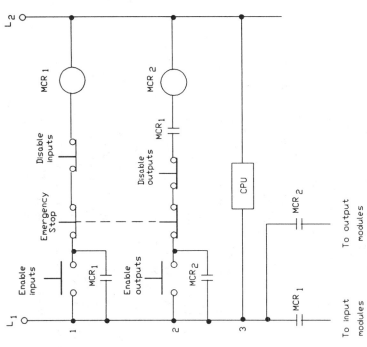

Figure 7-25 Safety circuit using two hardwired MCRs.

button and the enable output button are pressed. If the emergency Stop button is pressed, both the input and output modules will become de-energized. Pressing either the disable input button or the disable output button will result in the respective modules becoming de-energized. An interlock between the two MCRs is included so that the enable input button must be pressed before the enable output button will provide power to the output modules. The CPU retains power throughout this process.

Another potential hazard when working with PLCs is the use of latched output. This type of output is ideal for storing error functions, i.e., keeping track of which output failed at what time.

Latched coils can also be very dangerous when used with hardwired outputs. If a latched output is used to control a machine process and the inputs to the machine change state, the latch coil could remain energized regardless of the input conditions. For this reason, all outputs that cause mechanical motion should be programmed with non-retentive outputs.

7-8 I/O ADDRESSING

I/O addressing is defined as the method of determining where a particular input or output device is located in a PLC's memory. Addressing also takes into account the relationship between a memory location and a physical location on the I/O rack. All coils and contacts have addresses, as well as timers, counters, math functions, registers, etc. Each PLC manufacturer uses a slightly different method of addressing. Some use a combination of letters and numbers, while others use strictly numerical addressing. In this section, we will look at the I/O addressing of three of the more common PLCs used in industry: Allen-Bradley, Texas Instruments, and AEG Modicon.

Allen-Bradley

A typical Allen-Bradley PLC uses five digits to address input or output instructions. Figure 7-26(a) shows an example of an input address, and Figure 7-26(b) is an example of an output address. The first digit specifies whether the address is an input or output function. If the first digit is zero, the address is an input instruction. The second digit indicates the position of the module in the I/O rack. The I/O rack is capable of holding eight modules, which are labelled in the octal numbering system as 0 through 7.

The fourth and fifth digits indicate the address in the module itself. Allen-Bradley modules can contain up to 16 inputs or outputs on a single module, so in octal form, the addresses for the fourth and fifth digits are as follows: 00, 01, 02, 03, 04, 05, 06, 07, 10, 11, 12, 13, 14, 15, 16, 17.

Allen-Bradley timers and counters have addresses based on their locations in the data table. Because the data table is variable in size, the addressing of timers and counters will depend on how the memory of the PLC is configured. Timer and counter instructions use only three digits, and the first digit is always zero. The second and third digits contain information regarding the memory location of the timer or counter in the data table.

The addressing of timers and counters begins immediately after the last rack number in the I/O system. For example, if two racks are accessible, the second digit of a counter or timer will have its lowest number as 3. The size of the PLC's memory will determine how high this second digit goes. Typically, on a two-rack system, the second digit of a timer or counter will vary from 3 through 7. The third digit will vary from 0 through 7.

Internal coils on most Allen-Bradley PLCs can be addressed with any location that is not accessible at the I/O rack. The second digit of an internal coil can be any number from 3 through 7 if the PLC is accessing two I/O racks.

The data table for an Allen-Bradley PLC contains input and output image tables for the system. I/O reference addresses are derived from these image tables. The PLC also stores any data associated with the control program in the data table. For example, the presets and addresses of timers and counters are stored in this area. Figure 7-27 shows the I/O addressing for an Allen-Bradley PLC2-30 data table.

Texas Instruments

Most TI I/O addressing systems use X, Y, and C to label discrete inputs and outputs. An input is designated as an X, an output accessible at the I/O rack is labelled Y, and an internal coil is identified by the letter "C". A typical Texas Instruments I/O rack holds eight modules, and each module contains eight input or output locations. Therefore, one TI rack holds 8 × 8, or 64 I/O points. Figure 7-28 shows the addressing of two racks, or bases, on a standard Texas Instruments 500 series PLC. The top right corner of the first rack is always addressed as I/O point #1. If module #1 is an input module, the first eight addresses will be X1 through X8. If the first module is an output card, the first eight addresses will be Y1 through Y8.

Timers and counters on a typical Texas Instruments PLC are addressed simply from 1 to 128. Each timer and counter must have an individual address. In other words, you cannot have Timer #1 and Counter #1 in the same program. Because timers and counters share the same locations in the data table, each must be addressed individually.

Figure 7-26 Allen-Bradley I/O addressing.

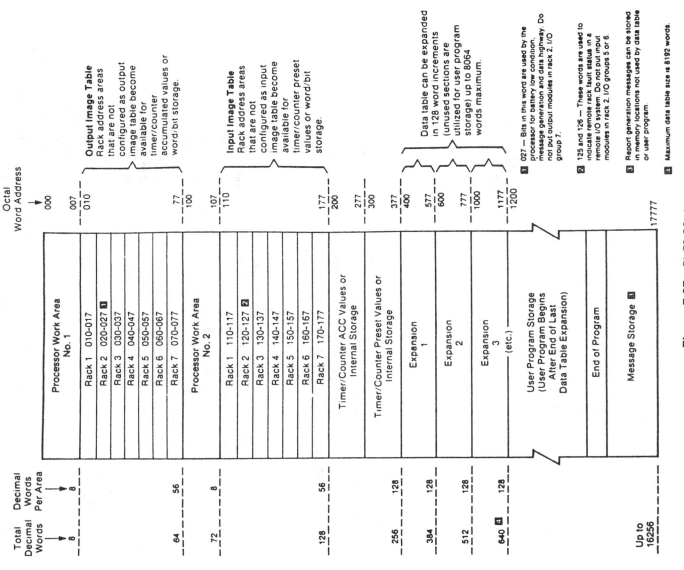

Figure 7-27 PLC2-30 data table.

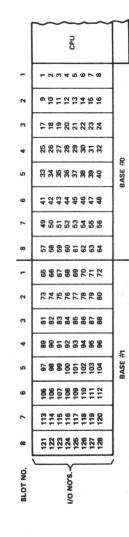

Figure 7-28 TI I/O numbering system.

Most TI PLCs have up to 128 internal coils available for use in programs. These coils are addressed from C1 through C128.

AEG Modicon

The early series of Modicon PLCs, such as the 484, use four digits for addressing. The first digit of a contact indicates whether the device is an input/output or a function of a sequencer. If the first digit is a 1, the contact is an input; a 0 indicates an output; and a 2 indicates that the contact is controlled by a sequencer. The last three digits can vary from 001 through 256. Larger Modicon systems, such as the 584, 884, and 984 processors, use five digits for addressing. Unlike Allen-Bradley, Modicon PLCs do not identify racks and modules in the I/O address because Modicon uses the decimal numbering system for addressing. Figure 7-29 shows the I/O numbering system for the Modicon 484 PLC. Each module contains either four or eight inputs or outputs. The modules are grouped in *housings*, and each housing holds a maximum of 32 inputs or outputs.

Modicon 484 timers and counters also use four-digit addressing. The first digit of a timer or counter is 4, and the last three digits vary from 001 to 254, depending on the size of the memory. The 584 and 884 Modicon PLCs use five-digit addressing for timers and counters.

Internal coils in a Modicon 484 system have addresses which range from 0258 to 0512. Internal coil 0257 can be used in a program to monitor the lithium battery voltage. This coil will remain energized as long as the battery has sufficient voltage to back up the RAM memory.

Module Number (Top of Bottom)	Circuit Number	CHANNEL ONE							
		Housing One Output	Housing One Input	Housing Two Output	Housing Two Input	Housing Three Output	Housing Three Input	Housing Four Output	Housing Four Input
1	1	0001	1001	0033	1033	0065	1065	0097	1097
	2	0002	1002	0034	1034	0066	1066	0098	1098
	3	0003	1003	0035	1035	0067	1067	0099	1099
	4	0004	1004	0036	1036	0068	1068	0100	1100
2	1	0005	1005	0037	1037	0069	1069	0101	1101
	2	0006	1006	0038	1038	0070	1070	0102	1102
	3	0007	1007	0039	1039	0071	1071	0103	1103
	4	0008	1008	0040	1040	0072	1072	0104	1104
3	1	0009	1009	0041	1041	0073	1073	0105	1105
	2	0010	1010	0042	1042	0074	1074	0106	1106
	3	0011	1011	0043	1043	0075	1075	0107	1107
	4	0012	1012	0044	1044	0076	1076	0108	1108
4	1	0013	1013	0045	1045	0077	1077	0109	1109
	2	0014	1014	0046	1046	0078	1078	0110	1110
	3	0015	1015	0047	1047	0079	1079	0111	1111
	4	0016	1016	0048	1048	0080	1080	0112	1112
5	1	0017	1017	0049	1049	0081	1081	0113	1113
	2	0018	1018	0050	1050	0082	1082	0114	1114
	3	0019	1019	0051	1051	0083	1083	0115	1115
	4	0020	1020	0052	1052	0084	1084	0116	1116
6	1	0021	1021	0053	1053	0085	1085	0117	1117
	2	0022	1022	0054	1054	0086	1086	0118	1118
	3	0023	1023	0055	1055	0087	1087	0119	1119
	4	0024	1024	0056	1056	0088	1088	0120	1120
7	1	0025	1025	0057	1057	0089	1089	0121	1121
	2	0026	1026	0058	1058	0090	1090	0122	1122
	3	0027	1027	0059	1059	0091	1091	0123	1123
	4	0028	1028	0060	1060	0092	1092	0124	1124
8	1	0029	1029	0061	1061	0093	1093	0125	1125
	2	0030	1030	0062	1062	0094	1094	0126	1126
	3	0031	1031	0063	1063	0095	1095	0127	1127
	4	0032	1032	0064	1064	0096	1096	0128	1128

Figure 7-29 Modicon 484 I/O numbering system.

7-1. Define ladder logic.

7-2. What are the two types of ladder language elements?

7-3. An output in a ladder logic program is controlled by
(a) input instructions.
(b). output instructions.
(c). input and output instructions.
(d). all of the above.

7-4. What does the term "softwired" refer to?

7-5. What is the main difference between ladder logic and relay logic?

7-6. Explain the meaning of the term "address" in ladder logic circuits.

7-7. Devices connected in parallel with other devices are typically called
(a) rungs.
(b) networks.
(c) coils.
(d) branches.

7-8. Each complete horizontal line of a ladder diagram is generally referred to as a
(a) rung.
(b) branch.
(c) input.
(d) output.

7-9. The term "examine ON" refers to
(a) a normally closed (NC) instruction.
(b) a normally open (NO) instruction.
(c) the status of the CPU.
(d) all of the above.

7-10. The last element to be entered on a ladder logic rung is a
(a) coil.
(b) contact.
(c) overload.
(d) examine OFF instruction.

7-11. A latching relay is an output that
(a) shuts off upon energization.
(b) cannot be programmed with a PLC.
(c) is also known as a "reset" instruction.
(d) maintains an energized or de-energized state after power is removed.

7-12. What is a fail-safe circuit?

7-13. Internal outputs are
(a) accessible at the I/O rack.
(b) not accessible at the I/O rack.
(c) not practical in PLC circuits.
(d) also known as hardware coils.

7-14. List two advantages of using internal outputs.

7-15. What is a transitional contact?

7-16. Name the two types of controller scan.

7-17. How long does it take a typical PLC to scan 128 inputs and outputs?
(a) 5 ms
(b) 3 ms
(c) 1 ms
(d) 2 ms

7-18. List three common programming restrictions.

7-19. "Nesting" is defined as

    (a) scanning in a left-to-right direction.

    (b) scanning in a top-to-bottom direction.

    (c) exceeding the maximum number of contacts per rung.

    (d) creating a branch within a branch.

7-20. Define the term "random failure".

7-21. What is the purpose of a hardwired MCR?

7-22. The first digit in an Allen-Bradley I/O address determines

    (a) whether the device is an input or output.

    (b) the rack number.

    (c) the module number.

    (d) the I/O position in the module.

7-23. The second digit in an Allen-Bradley I/O address determines

    (a) whether the device is an input or output.

    (b) the rack number.

    (c) the module number.

    (d) the I/O position in the module.

7-24. The third digit in an Allen-Bradley I/O address determines

    (a) whether the device is an input or output.

    (b) the rack number.

    (c) the module number.

    (d) the I/O position in the module.

7-25. What is a data table?

8

Timers

Upon completion of this chapter, you will be able to

▶ Name two types of relay logic timers.

▶ List the five basic types of PLC timers.

▶ Describe the function of a time-driven circuit.

▶ Differentiate between an ON-delay and an OFF-delay instruction.

▶ Write a ladder logic program using timers.

▶ Understand retentive timers.

▶ Explain the purpose of cascading timers.

▶ Define "reciprocating" timers.

8-1 INTRODUCTION

Two logic devices that allow automatic control systems to activate output devices during specific stages in a process operation are **timers** and **counters.** This chapter shall examine the operating functions of timing circuits, as well as their applications in industry. In both traditional relay logic and PLC systems, timers are used to delay starting cycles, control intervals, repeat operational cycles, and provide reset capabilities upon the completion of cycles.

In relay logic circuits, timers are generally electronic or electromechanical devices that, upon energization, will change the state of a set or sets of contacts. There are two basic types of relay logic timers, **digital** and **analog.** A digital timer is designed to count pulses generated by an electronic clock circuit. Analog timers respond to physical quantities or changes. For example, a *dashpot timer* provides

8-2 TYPES OF PLC TIMERS

a time delay by controlling how rapidly air or a liquid is allowed to pass into or out of a container through an opening of fixed diameter.

One of the advantages of using a PLC for timing circuit applications is that the entire timing function occurs "inside" the controller. The timer does not physically exist, it is a programmed instruction that is designed to function in exactly the same way as its predecessor, the relay logic timer. PLC timers are extremely powerful software instructions that allow a programmer to easily modify PLC programs to suit a wide variety of tasks.

As with any ladder diagram instruction, timers and counters are based on relay logic equipment. The Allen-Bradley timer looks very similar to a conventional relay timer schematic, while companies such as Westinghouse, Texas Instruments and AEG Modicon use timers that resemble "boxes" in ladder logic circuits.

Most PLC timers display two quantities on their associated terminal screens: the *preset time* and *accumulated time*. The preset time represents the time duration for the timing circuit. For example, if a time delay of 10 seconds is required, the timer will have a preset of 10 seconds. The accumulated time represents the amount of time that has elapsed from when the timing coil became energized. Once the timing rung has continuity, the timer counts in time-based intervals and times down until the preset value and accumulated value are equal. The intervals that the timers time out at are generally referred to as the **decrement** or **resolution** of the timers. These values are typically in 1-ms, 0.01-s, 0.1-s, or 1-second intervals. Allen-Bradley and Modicon timers have maximum preset values of 999 seconds.

The five basic types of PLC timers are

Timer ON-delay energize
Timer ON-delay de-energize
Timer OFF-delay energize
Timer OFF-delay de-energize
Retentive timer

The timer ON-delay energize instruction is the equivalent of the TDON or TDOFF devices used in relay logic circuits. It is also known as an *ON-delay (TON)* instruction. If the contacts associated with a timer close after the timing coil has been energized, it is referred to as a timer ON-delay energize. If the contacts open after the timing coil has been energized for a time interval, it is called a timer ON-delay de-energize. Figure 8-1 shows the timing graphs for timer ON-delay energize and timer OFF-delay energize circuits. The time delay is the preset value entered into the timer. The timer's control input is initially OFF. When the input is closed, the timing cycle begins. For example, if a timer in the circuit has a preset of 10 seconds, after a 10-second delay, the timer ON-delay energize contacts close and power is supplied to an output device connected via these contacts. When the timer times out, the timer ON-delay de-energize contacts open, and power is removed from any load connected through the timer contacts.

Figure 8-2 shows timing graphs for an OFF-delay timer circuit. Assuming a preset of 10 seconds, if the timing coil input contacts open, the time delay is initiated. After a 10-second delay, the associated contacts change state. The OFF-delay energize contacts close and power is supplied to the device being controlled. The OFF-delay de-energize contacts open, and power is removed from the controlled load.

ON-delay and OFF-delay timers are generally capable of executing more

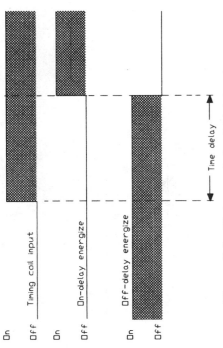

On
Off — Timing coil input

On
Off — On-delay energize

On
Off — Off-delay energize

|← Time delay →|

Figure 8-1 Timing graph for ON-delay timer.

than one type of control function. For example, if a device is required to be energized immediately upon the beginning of a timing cycle, an instantaneous contact would be required. This type of timer would then be capable of performing both time delay and instantaneous operations. Allen-Bradley refers to these contacts as *enabled* and *timed* contact instructions.

Most PLCs also have an instruction capable of retaining the accumulated value even if system power is lost to the controller. This timer is called a *Retentive ON-delay Timer (RTO)*. The main difference between a retentive ON-delay timer (RTO) and a Time delay ON (TON) timer is that the accumulated value of the RTO is not reset to zero when the rung is de-energized. The only way to reset an RTO is to use a *Reset (RTR)* instruction. If the input contact to an RTR instruction is closed, the RTR instruction will reset the accumulated value of any retentive timer instruction with the same reference address.

Allen-Bradley Timers

The timer shown in Figure 8-3 is an Allen-Bradley timer with its associated contacts. The letters TON indicate that this timer performs a time delay ON operation. If this were a time delay OFF instruction, the letters TOF would be displayed inside the coil. The number 050 represents the timer's address in CPU memory.

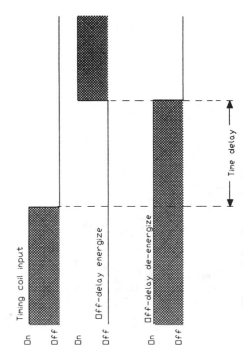

On
Off — Timing coil input

On
Off — Off-delay energize

On
Off — Off-delay de-energize

|← Time delay →|

Figure 8-2 Timing graph for OFF-delay timer.

The number immediately below the letters TON indicate the timed base. This base is a multiplier in units of either 1.0, 0.1, or 0.01. In other words, the value entered here will cause the timer to time out in increments of 1 second, 1/10 of a second, or 1 millisecond. Because the number 1.0 is shown in Figure 8-3, the timer times out in 1-second increments.

The letters PR represent the Preset value. The number 10 has been entered into the preset, so the timer will energize an output after 10 × 1.0, or 10 seconds. The letters AC represent the Accumulative value. This is the amount of time that has elapsed since contact 11004 was closed. When PC = AC the timer times out.

The rung below the timer in Figure 8-3 contains contact 050 17. The number 17 represents what is known as the **instantaneous** bit. This contact will immediately become energized when contact 110 04 is closed. Therefore, when 110 04 closes, output 010 01 becomes energized. The rung containing contact 050 15 is the rung that is affected by the timer. The number 15 represents what Allen-Bradley calls the *time delay* bit. In Figure 8-3, 10 seconds after contact 110 04 closes, contact 050 15 becomes energized and output 010 02 turns ON. In addition to enabling the timing function, contact 110 04 also acts as a reset instruction when opened. If 110 04 is opened at any point during the timing cycle, the accumulated value of the timer is reset to zero.

Allen-Bradley timing circuits also have a control bit called the **timed base.** This contact will turn ON and OFF at the rate of the timing intervals. In other words, if the decrement of the timer is in 1-second intervals, this contact will open and close at 1-second intervals. The reference address for the timed base control bit is 16.

An example of an Allen-Bradley time delay OFF circuit is shown in Figure 8-4. In this circuit, timer 051 has a preset of 20 s and a decrement of 1.0 s. The

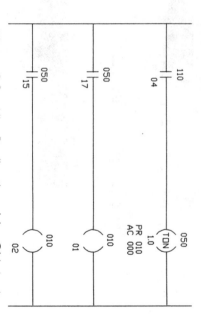

Figure 8-3   Allen-Bradley time delay ON circuit.

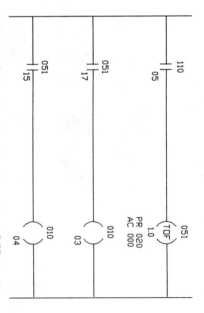

Figure 8-4   Allen-Bradley time delay OFF circuit.

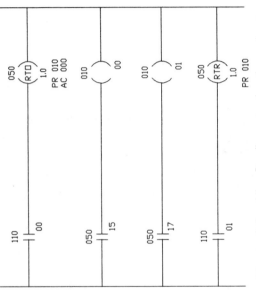

Figure 8-5 Allen-Bradley retentive timer circuit.

control input for the TOF instruction is labelled 110 05. When contact 110 05 is closed, bits 15 and 17 are set to 1 and outputs 010 03 and 010 04 are energized. When input 110 05 is *open*, the timer begins to accumulate time. Bit 17 opens and 010 03 goes OFF. Bit 15 remains closed until 20 s has elapsed, and then 010 04 goes OFF. The TOF instruction is reset by reclosing input 110 05.

In addition to conventional ON-delay and OFF-delay timers, Allen-Bradley PLCs also have retentive timer instructions. Figure 8-5 shows a circuit with a retentive timer. When contact 110 00 is closed, contact 050 17 immediately becomes energized and coil 010 00 turns ON. After the timer has timed out, the time delay bit, 050 15, becomes energized and coil 010 01 turns ON. If contact 110 00 is opened at any point during or after the timing cycle, the RTO remains latched in the energized state. The accumulated value of the RTO can only be reset by closing contact 110 01. This activates the reset instruction, causing the timer to reset and the time delay and instantaneous bits to re-open.

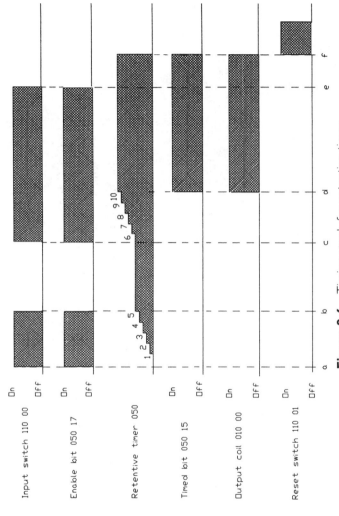

Figure 8-6 Timing graph for retentive timer.

Figure 8-6 shows a timing graph for the circuit shown in Figure 8-5. The shaded portions of the graph represent the conducting times of the various devices. The input switch, 110 00, is shown as being ON between points a and b, and between points c and f. The enable bit, 050 17, is also ON during these times because bit 17 is the instantaneous bit. When the input switch is closed, the timer begins timing. After five seconds, the input switch is opened and the accumulative value of the timer remains at 5 s. When the input switch is opened and the accumulative value of the timer remains at 5 s. When the preset value equals the accumulated value, the timed bit 050 15 is energized, and output 010 00 is turned ON. At point e, the input switch is again turned OFF, and the enable bit and output 010 01 are turned OFF. The opening of 110 00 has no effect on the retentive timer coil or the timed bit instruction. When the reset switch, 110 01, is closed, the timer is reset and the timed bit is turned OFF.

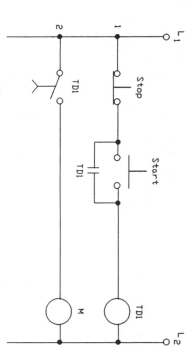

Figure 8-7 Circuit for Example 8-1.

Solution

The circuit shown in Figure 8-8 is the equivalent ladder logic circuit. The holding contact is labelled 050 17, and the time delay leg is identified as 050 15.

Convert the relay logic circuit shown in Figure 8-7 to a ladder logic circuit using the following Allen-Bradley I/O addresses: Stop button = 110 00, Start button = 110 01, Timer TD1 = 050, Motor M = 010 00

AEG Modicon Timers

The AEG Modicon PLC has a timer available in increments of either 1.0, 0.1, or 0.001 seconds. The preset value of this type of timer can be set between 0001 to 0999, which means that the maximum preset value of a Modicon timer is 999 seconds. Modicon timers contain both time delay ON and time delay OFF functions, allowing the operator the choice of using either or both functions from any given timer.

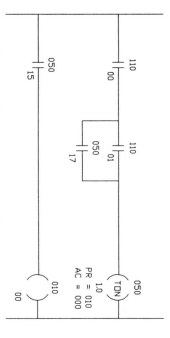

Figure 8-8 Equivalent ladder logic circuit.

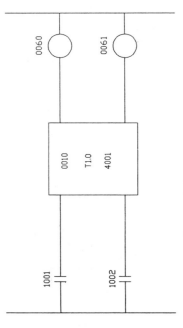

Figure 8-9 Modicon timer.

Modicon PLCs use either four or five digits for I/O addressing. If the first digit is 1, it represents an input device; if the first digit is 0, it is an output; and, if the first digit is 4, it designates the **register** where the timer is stored. A register is a memory location within the CPU allocated for the storage of numerical data.

Figure 8-9 shows a Modicon timer with output 0060 representing the time delay ON coil, and output 0061 representing the time delay OFF coil. The statement in the middle of the timer box, T1.0, tells us that the timer selected will time out in 1-second increments. The number 0010 indicates the preset value selected, and the number 4001 represents the address of the timer. Contact 1001 represents the *set* function and contact 1002 represents the *reset* function. When 1001 and 1002 are closed, the timer begins timing out. After a delay of 10 seconds, output 0060 becomes energized and output 0061 becomes de-energized. Therefore, output 0060 is a Normally Open Time Closing (NOTC) operation, and 0061 is a Normally Closed Time Opening (NCTO) instruction. To reset the timer, contact 1002 must open. Essentially, control input 1001 acts as a *latch control*, due to the fact that when 1001 opens, the accumulative value of the timer is not lost, it is retained. The timer simply stops timing until 1001 is reclosed.

Timing graphs for the input and output devices of Figure 8-9 are shown in Figure 8-10. When 1001 and 1002 are closed, the timing cycle begins. After a 10-second delay, output 0060 becomes energized and any associated contacts change state. When the set input opens, output 0060 remains ON and the accumulated data are stored. The accumulated value is only erased when the reset contact, 1002, is opened.

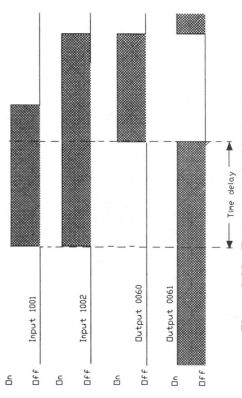

Figure 8-10 Timing graphs for Modicon timer.

If the retentive timing function is not required in a Modicon ladder circuit, it is possible to control the operation of the timer by a single input. Figure 8-11 shows a practical method of accomplishing this. Rather than duplicate contact 1001, the lower input is branched for the upper input line.

One fundamental difference between Modicon timers and those used by Allen-Bradley is that Modicon timers do not directly display the accumulated value. To display the accumulated value of a timer or counter, you must move the cursor on the CRT to the GET area. On the P190 programmer, the GET area is in the lower section of the screen. Once the cursor is properly positioned, enter the timer number and press the GET key. The accumulative value will now be displayed.

Texas Instruments Timers

Figure 8-12 shows the ladder diagram of a Texas Instruments timer. Texas Instruments uses X and Y to identify input and output devices. This type of timer requires both contacts, in this case X1 and X2, to be closed in order to initiate the timing function. The timer shown in Figure 8-12 has a preset value of 10 seconds. The letter C represents the accumulative, or *Current value* of the timer. When the timer begins timing, C = P. When C is equal to zero, the output associated with the timer is energized. When the timer is selected from the menu line of the programming terminal, the operator has a choice of selecting a timer function that can be selected is a preset of 3,276.7 seconds for the 0.1-s decrement, or 32.767 seconds for the 0.001-s decrement.

Contact X1 in Figure 8-12 represents the freeze/enable contact. This contact must be closed to initiate timing. If X1 is opened during the timing cycle, the current value of the timer is frozen. If X1 is reclosed, the timer continues to time

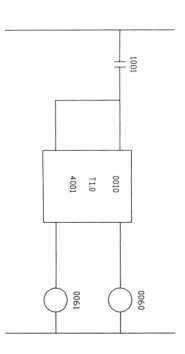

Figure 8-11 Modicon timer with single input.

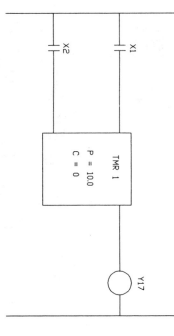

Figure 8-12 Texas Instruments timer.

out from the value that the current count was at when timing was interrupted. In other words, X1 acts as a "retentive" control input. For example, if the timer began timing out from the 10-second preset value and X1 was opened 5 seconds later, the timer would continue to time out from the 5-second point when X1 was reclosed. Contact X2 is referred to as the reset/enable function. If X2 is opened at any point during the timing function, the current value is reset to the preset value. In other words, opening X2 clears the current value.

8-3 CASCADING TIMERS

In situations where it is necessary to extend the timing operation beyond the preset value of a timer, two or more timers may be connected in a cascading configuration, as shown in Figure 8-13. Cascading is defined as using the output of one timer to initialize the timing function of a second timer. If, for example, you are working with a Modicon PLC and you require a timer that will time out for 30 minutes, more than one timer would be required. The maximum time that can be accumulated using a Modicon timer is 999 seconds. To achieve a timing sequence of 1,800 seconds, one timer would be set at 999 seconds and the other at 801 seconds, as illustrated in Figure 8-13. With this circuit, when timer 1 times out, the second timer is energized, and after timer 2 times out, output 0001 becomes energized.

A cascading function of a Texas Instruments timer is shown in Figure 8-14. When contacts X1 and X2 are closed, output Y17 will become energized 3,600 seconds, or one hour, later. Because only one timer may be entered on a line in a TI system, control relay C1 is used to initialize timer #2. If contact X2 opens

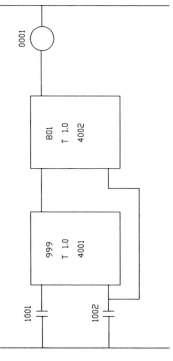

Figure 8-13 Modicon cascading timer circuit.

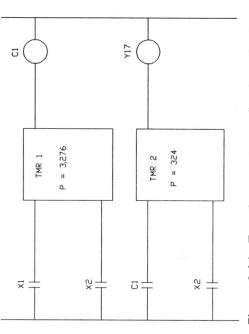

Figure 8-14 Texas Instruments cascading timer circuit.

at any point during the timing cycle, both timers will be reset. X2 directly resets timer 1, while timer 2 is reset by the action of the control relay becoming de-energized and opening its associated contacts.

An example of a cascading timer using an Allen-Bradley PLC is shown in Figure 8-15. The PLC-2 system has a maximum preset of 999 seconds, so two or more timers must be cascaded to achieve a time duration greater than this value. In the Figure 8-15 circuit, output 010 00 will become energized after 1,800 seconds, or one-half hour, after contact 110 00 is closed. Contacts 030 15 and 031 15 are the time delay bits. These contacts close when their respective timers have completed their timing cycles.

The circuit shown in Figure 8-16 is a relay logic schematic of reduced voltage starting for a three-phase motor. This circuit utilizes cascading timers to gradually bring a motor up to full speed. As each timer times out, a set of contacts are closed, and resistance is removed from the starting circuit via contacts 1A, 2A, 3A, 4A, and 5A.

The circuit of Figure 8-16 has two modes of operation: manual and automatic. When the manual mode is selected, the MCR coil and CR1 are energized. The MCR contacts seal in and bypass the float switches (FS1 - FS6) in the circuit. When CR1 is energized, the M coil turns ON and the motor begins to rotate with maximum starting resistance. The M coil energizes timing coil T1 and after a time delay, the time leg T1 closes energizing coil CR2. When CR2 turns ON, it closes the CR2 contact, which energizes coil 1A. Consequently, the 1A contacts seal in and part of the circuit resistance is dropped out. Coil 1A also initiates the second timer, T2, which functions in the same manner as T1. This cycle continues until all the timers have timed out and the motor runs at maximum speed with all resistors out of the circuit.

When the automatic mode is selected and float switch FS1 closed, the CR1 coil is energized and timer T1 times out. When the time leg T1 closes the output coil, CR2 will not energize until float switch FS2 is closed. When FS2 closes, CR2 is energized and the resistors controlled by coil 1A are dropped out of the circuit.

Convert the relay logic circuit shown in Figure 8-16 into an equivalent Allen-Bradley ladder logic circuit using the following I/O addresses:

MFS	= 110	00	MCR = 020	00
Manual/Off = 110	01	CR1	= 020	01
Auto/Off	= 110	02	CR2	= 020	02
FS1	= 110	03	CR3	= 020	03
FS2	= 110	04	CR4	= 020	04

Figure 8-15 Allen-Bradley cascading timers.

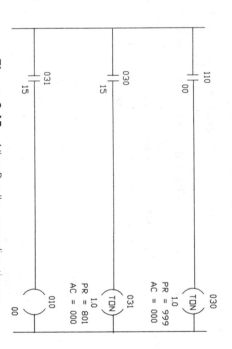

FS3	= 110 05	CR5	= 020 05
FS4	= 110 06	CR6	= 020 06
FS5	= 110 07	M	= 010 00
FS6	= 112 00	1A	= 010 01
OLs	= 112 01	2A	= 010 02
		3A	= 010 03
T1	= 050	4A	= 010 04
T2	= 051	5A	= 010 05
T3	= 052		
T4	= 053		
T5	= 054		

(Assume a preset value of 5 s for each timer.)

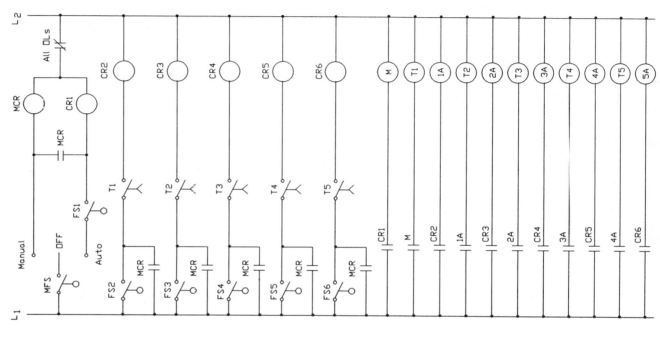

Figure 8-16 Circuit for Example 8-2.

Sec. 8-3 / Cascading Timers

▲

EXAMPLE 8-3

Convert the relay logic circuit shown in Figure 8-18 into a ladder logic circuit using the following Modicon I/O addresses:

1001 = OL   0060 = M
1002 = Stop   0061 = TD1 contacts

Solution

The equivalent ladder logic circuit using an Allen-Bradley PLC is shown in Figure 8-17. Note that the MCR vertical contact shown in Figure 8-16 has been replaced with an equivalent horizontal control circuit because vertical contacts cannot be entered in a PLC.

Figure 8-17 Equivalent Allen-Bradley ladder logic circuit for Example 8-2.

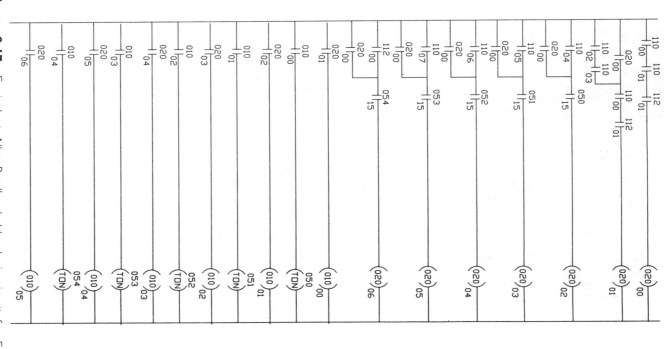

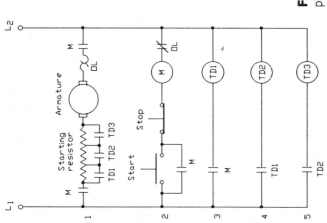

Figure 8-18 Relay logic circuit for Example 8-3.

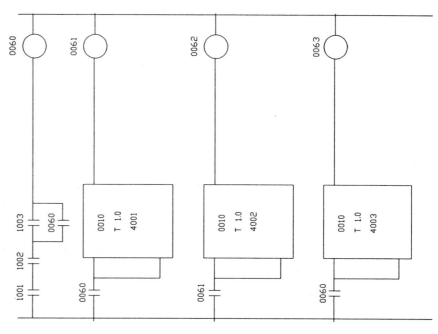

Figure 8-19 Modicon ladder logic circuit for Example 8-3.

8-4 RECIPROCATING TIMERS

Reciprocating timers are defined as timing functions where the output of one timer is used to reset the input of a second timer. These types of timers are used in situations where a constant cycling of an output is required. For example, if a flashing light is required in the event of a control system failure, a program with reciprocating timers could be used to create the flashing output function.

Figure 8-20 is an example of a reciprocating timer using an Allen-Bradley PLC. When contact 110 01 is closed, timer 050 begins its timing cycle. After three seconds, bit 050 15 becomes energized, and both timer 051 and coil 050 00 become energized. 050 00 is activated from the instantaneous bit of 051. After three seconds, timer 051 opens timing bit 051 15, and resets timer 050. When 050 turns OFF, timer 051 becomes de-energized, as does coil 010 00. This causes 051 15 to reclose and the timing function of 050 repeats. The reciprocating function of timers 050 and 051 cause output 010 00 to flash ON and OFF at three-second intervals.

Figure 8-21 illustrates a Texas Instruments program to create a flashing output for coil Y17. When contact X1 is closed, after a delay of three seconds, output Y17 becomes energized. When Y17 turns ON, the associated contacts change state, and the timing function of timer 2 begins. After three seconds, coil C1 becomes energized and timer 1 is reset. When timer 1 is reset, it immediately opens contacts Y17 and resets timer 2. Therefore, coil C1 is only ON for approximately one scan, so it is very difficult to see this coil become energized. Output Y17 will flash ON and OFF at three-second intervals as long as contact X1 remains closed.

A typical application for a PLC circuit combining both cascading and reciprocating functions would be the control of traffic signals. An advanced green may be established by using reciprocating timers, while the transition from green to yellow to red would be accomplished by a cascading timer circuit. Example 8-4 illustrates this type of problem.

(Assume a timer preset of 10 s.)

Solution

Figure 8-19 shows the equivalent ladder logic circuit using Modicon I/O addressing.

1003 = Start	0062 = TD2 contacts
4001 = TD1	0063 = TD3 contacts
4002 = TD2	
4003 = TD3	

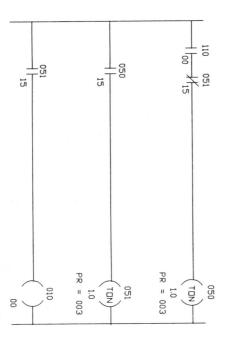

Figure 8-20 Allen-Bradley reciprocating timer circuit.

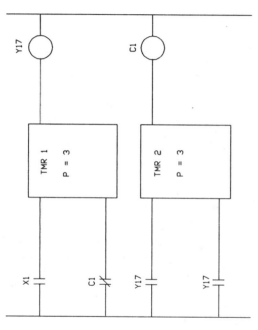

Figure 8-21 Texas Instruments reciprocating timer circuit.

▶ *EXAMPLE 8-4*

Two sets of traffic lights are required. One controls traffic in a north/south direction, the other controls traffic in an east/west direction.

The north lights have an advanced green that flashes at one-second intervals for ten seconds. It then changes to solid green for 20 seconds, yellow for five seconds, and red for 25 seconds. The south lights have no advanced green, so the south light is red for 35 seconds.

The east/west traffic lights have no advanced green. The green is ON for 20 seconds, yellow for five seconds, and red for 35 seconds.

Use the following Allen-Bradley I/O addresses for this circuit:

110   00 = Stop/Start switch
010   00 = Green north light
010   01 = Green south light
010   02 = Yellow north/south light
010   03 = Red north light
010   04 = Red south light
010   05 = Green east/west light
010   06 = Yellow east/west light
010   07 = Red east/west light

Solution

Figure 8-22(a) is a sketch of the traffic intersection. The advanced green is shown on the north side of the intersection and the flow of traffic for that light is indicated by the dashed lines. Figure 8-22(b) shows the graph for the timing sequence.

The ladder logic circuit for Example 8-4 is shown in Figure 8-23.

The following example illustrates how timers can be used in process control systems to energize and de-energize output devices. The mixing circuit of Figure 8-24 shows a sequential control system that controls three different processes; fill, agitate, and drain, with a single timing function.

▶ *EXAMPLE 8-5*

In Figure 8-24, when the start button is pressed, solenoid A is energized and a batch of liquid enters the mixing tank. Float switch FS1 detects the upper limit of the liquid level and FS2 detects the lower limit. As the tank begins to fill, FS2 closes. When the tank is full, switch FS1 shuts off solenoid A and starts the

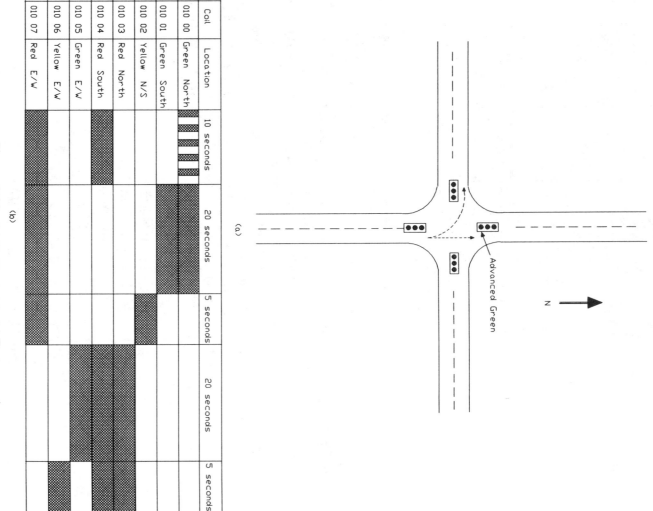

Figure 8-22 (a) Traffic sketch; (b) Timing graph.

Coil	Location	10 seconds	20 seconds	5 seconds	20 seconds	5 seconds
010 00	Green North					
010 01	Green South					
010 02	Yellow N/S					
010 03	Red North					
010 04	Red South					
010 05	Green E/W					
010 06	Yellow E/W					
010 07	Red E/W					

agitator to mix the liquid. The agitator mixes the liquid for 30 seconds and shuts off. When the agitator turns off, solenoid B is energized to drain the liquid. After the tank has been emptied, float switch FS2 opens and solenoid B shuts off.

Write a ladder logic program using Allen-Bradley I/O addressing to solve this problem.

Solution

The ladder logic circuit for Example 8-5 is shown in Figure 8-25. In this circuit, both the normally-open and normally-closed sets of contacts for float switch FS1 are used. When the start button is pressed, control relay 020 00 is energized and solenoid A turns on. As the tank fills, FS2 (110 03) closes. When the tank is full, FS1 (110 02) changes state. This shuts off solenoid A, starts timer 050, and energizes the agitate motor (010 01). After 30 seconds, the contacts associated

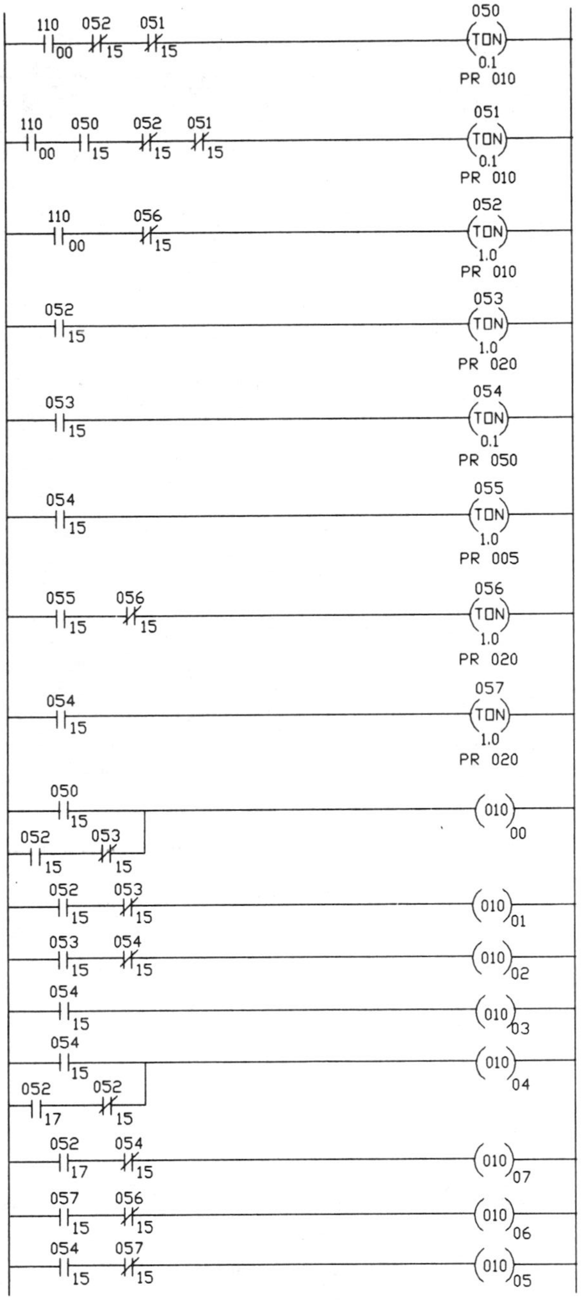

Figure 8-23 Ladder logic circuit for Example 8-4.

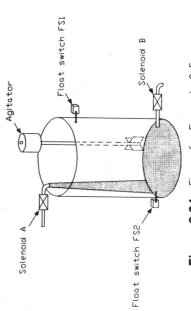

Figure 8-24 Figure for Example 8-5.

Agitator

Float switch FS1

Solenoid B

Solenoid A

Float switch FS2

with the timer (050 15) change state, causing the agitate motor to shut off and solenoid B to energize. As the liquid begins to drain, FS1 returns to its normal resting state. When the tank is completely empty, FS2 re-opens and the drain valve (010 02) is shut off.

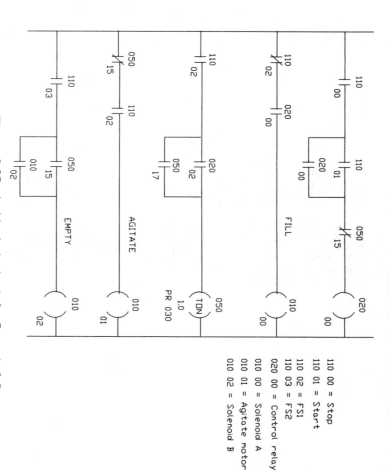

Figure 8-25 Ladder logic circuit for Example 8-5.

110 00 = Stop
110 01 = Start
110 02 = FS1
110 03 = FS2
020 00 = Control relay
010 00 = Solenoid A
010 01 = Agitate motor
010 02 = Solenoid B

REVIEW QUESTIONS

8-1. Name the two basic types of relay logic timers.

8-2. What is the most common timing function using a PLC?

8-3. List the typical decrement values of a timer.

8-4. What are the two quantities that most PLC timers display?

8-5. List the four basic types of PLC timers.

8-6. What is the purpose of an RTO timer?

8-7. Modicon PLCs use what term to define where data are stored?

8-8. The TON timing instruction is similar to which relay logic device?

    (a) TDON or TDOFF
    (b) RTO
    (c) RTR
    (d) TDON only

8-9. Describe the function of the enabled and timed contact instructions.

8-10. Contact 1001 in Figure 8-26 performs what function?

8-11. A retentive timer

    (a) has an accumulated value that is reset to zero when the rung is de-energized.

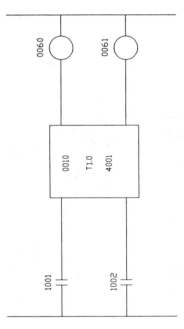

Figure 8-26 Figure for Question 8.10.

(b) has an accumulated value that is not reset when the rung is de-energized.

(c) has an accumulated value that is reset to zero when the rung is energized.

(d) has an accumulated value that is not reset when the rung is energized.

8-12. What is the purpose of an RTR instruction?

8-13. The "timed base" control bit performs what function?

8-14. Convert the circuit shown in Figure 8-27 to a ladder logic circuit using the following Modicon I/O addresses: 1001 = Stop, 1002 = Start, 4001 = TD1, and 0060 = M.

8-15. The main difference between Modicon timers and Allen-Bradley timers is

(a) maximum preset.

(b) Allen-Bradley does not directly display accumulated values.

(c) Modicon does not directly display accumulated values.

(d) one does not require a reset instruction.

8-16. What is the purpose of cascading timers?

8-17. Convert the relay logic circuit shown in Figure 8-28 to a ladder logic circuit using the following Allen-Bradley I/O addresses: 110 00 = OL, 110 01 = Stop, 110 02 = Start, 050 = TD1, 051 = TD2, and 052 = TD3. Assume a timer preset of 10 s.

8-18. Describe one application of reciprocating timers.

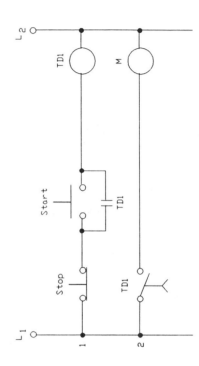

Figure 8-27 Figure for Question 8.14.

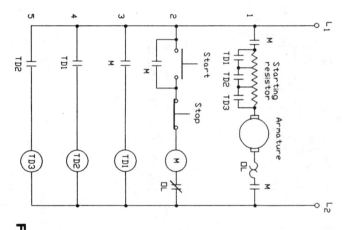

Figure 8-28 Figure for Question 8.17.

9

Counters

Upon completion of this chapter, you will be able to

▶ Name two types of mechanical counters.

▶ Define the two basic types of PLC counters.

▶ Explain the terms "underflow" and "overflow."

▶ Describe the function of an event-driven circuit.

▶ Design an up/down counter.

▶ Define "cascading" counters.

▶ Explain the advantages of combining timers and counters.

9-1 INTRODUCTION

Many situations arise in industry where there is a need for both simple and complex counting systems. Counters are used for tasks such as keeping track of the number of items passing by on a conveyor, counting the length of material being manufactured, or counting the number of revolutions made by a rotating machine. Traditional relay logic counters are mechanical devices that are generally either stroke type or mechanical revolution types. Figure 9-1 shows the two basic types of mechanical counters. Both of these counters require physical contact with the material being counted. In Figure 9-1(a), the counter uses a stroke arm to increment the count register. Figure 9-1(b) uses a friction wheel of a specific size which increments the register after rotating a certain number of times.

127

9-2 TYPES OF PLC COUNTERS

There are two basic types of PLC counters: *up-counters* and *down-counters*. When an up-counter has reached its preset value, it will energize an output device and any associated contacts will change state. A typical down-counter will count down to zero and energize an output.

Depending on the input device used, PLC counters can perform simple counting instructions similar to the counters shown in Figure 9-1. However, PLC counters are also easily adapted to non-physical counting requirements by simply changing the input device. For example, if a count pulse were to be generated from a beam of light, or from physical proximity, a PLC counter would require only a voltage signal from the transducer wired to the input module. Then, each time the transducer supplied a voltage pulse, the accumulated count would either increase or decrease.

Regardless of the manufacturer, all PLC counters require some type of reset instruction to clear the counter's accumulated value. Allen-Bradley uses a separate coil (CTR), while others, such as Modicon, use an input contact to perform the reset function. A typical maximum preset for a PLC counter is 999, although some companies, such as Texas Instruments, have maximum presets of 32,767. If the preset value is exceeded, some controllers provide an **overflow** instruction. The overflow is basically a contact that changes state if the accumulated count of an up-counter exceeds the maximum preset. If the accumulated value of a down-counter falls below zero, an instruction known as the *underflow* bit becomes energized.

Counters can be triggered by either a leading or trailing input pulse, although the vast majority are based on positive-edge transition. A leading-edge input causes the counter to increment or decrement when the input contact goes from an open to closed state. In other words, every time the input contact closes, the accumulated value of the counter changes. Figure 9-2 shows an example of a

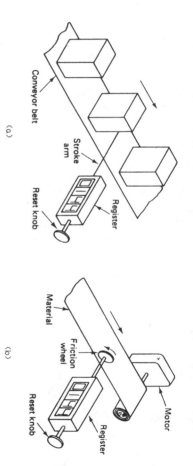

Figure 9-1 (a) Stroke register counter; (b) Mechanical revolution counter.

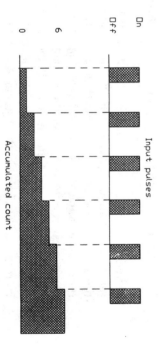

Figure 9-2 Positive-edge trigger counter input.

leading-edge input pulse and its effect on the accumulated value of a counter. Six input pulses of fixed duration are shown in Figure 9-2. In the OFF state, the input voltage is 0 V. When the input device switches ON, 5 V is applied at the input module and the current count increases by 1.

The input pulse supplied to the counter is often referred to as an *event*. This term is often used in process control to describe the change in a process, or change in the operation of machinery, when some event takes place. Consequently, counter circuits are classified as "event-driven" instructions. The timer circuits discussed in Chapter 8 would be considered "time-driven" instructions because they initiate or terminate an operation after a certain time interval.

Allen-Bradley Counters

Figure 9-3 shows an Allen-Bradley counter and its associated contacts. The letters "CTU" in the coil on the top rung indicate that this is an up-counter, which means that the count function is operative when the counter counts up to a preset value. The letters "PR" and "AC" indicate the Preset and Accumulative values, respectively. The counter shown in Figure 9-3 is located in address 070 of the CPU's memory, and has a preset value of 999 selected. The accumulative value of the counter is shown at 200. Every time contact 110 00 opens and closes, the accumulative value increments by 1.

When the preset and accumulative values are equal, the contact identified by bit 15 becomes energized. In the circuit of Figure 9-3, this contact is labelled 070 15. Therefore, when AC = PR output 010 02 is ON. As was the case with the Allen-Bradley timer, bit 17 is the instantaneous bit. Any contact associated with this address will become energized as soon as the counter rung becomes energized. In the circuit shown in Figure 9-3, every time 110 00 opens and closes, 070 17 also opens and closes. Contact 070 14 represents what Allen-Bradley calls the "overflow bit." This contact will become energized if the accumulative count exceeds the preset count.

Allen-Bradley PLCs require a separate coil function to reset the counter. This coil is identified as CTR. In Figure 9-3, when contact 110 01 is closed, the up-counter at address 070 is cleared of its accumulative value.

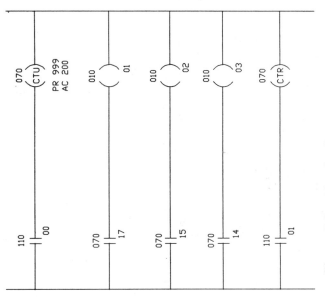

Figure 9-3 Allen-Bradley up-counter circuit.

The down-counter function of the Allen-Bradley PLC is programmed using the CTD coil key. The main difference between the CTU and CTD functions is that every time the contact ahead of the CTD is opened and closed, the accumulative value decrements by one, instead of incrementing. When the accumulative value is equal to zero, bit 15 becomes energized. The CTD instruction uses bit 16 as the instantaneous bit, and bit 14 is called the "underflow bit."

Figure 9-4 shows an example of an Allen-Bradley down-counter. In this circuit, each time contact 110 00 closes and reopens, the counter-accumulated value is decremented by one. Contact 050 16 closes each time the down-counter is enabled. Contact 050 14 indicates when the counter is decremented below 000. When the preset and accumulated values are equal, or when the accumulated value is greater than the preset value, contact 050 15 will be closed and output 010 02 will be energized. If contact 110 01 is closed, the accumulated value is reset to 000 and will decrement to 999 when the next input pulse is applied, followed by 998 on the second pulse, and so on.

Unlike some PLCs, Allen-Bradley controllers do not have an up/down counter instruction. Instead, it is necessary to combine an up-counter and a down-counter to create a circuit that is capable of both incrementing and decrementing the accumulated value. An example of an Allen-Bradley up/down counter circuit is shown in Figure 9-5. In this circuit, the CTU and CTD instructions both have the same address. Consequently, whenever input 110 00 closes, the accumulated value increases by one; when input 110 01 closes, the accumulated value decreases by one.

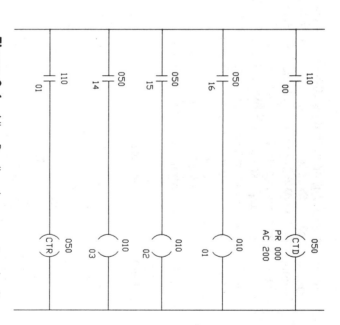

Figure 9-4 Allen-Bradley down-counter circuit.

A counting circuit is required to keep track of the number of cars entering and leaving a parking lot with a capacity of 500 cars. Contact 110 00 counts the cars entering the lot, and 110 01 counts the cars leaving. When there are 500 cars in the lot, output 010 00 energizes a "FULL" sign. When there are less than 500 cars, output 010 01 energizes a "VACANCY" sign. Input 110 02 is a key switch kept in the closed position by the parking lot attendant. Write a ladder logic program that will accomplish this scenario.

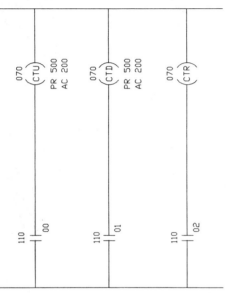

Figure 9-5 Allen-Bradley up/down counter circuit.

Solution

Figure 9-6 is a sketch of the parking lot and the input and output devices required.

Figure 9-7 shows the ladder logic circuit for Example 9-1. If the parking lot is designed to hold 500 cars, the preset for the up and down counts would be 500. Contact 110 00 is a limit switch to count the cars entering the lot, and input 110 01 detects the cars leaving. Output 010 00 energizes a FULL sign, and output 010 01 energizes a VACANCY sign. When there are between 0 and 499 cars in the lot, counter 050 is not activated, so contacts 050 15 are in their normal resting states. When the accumulated count reaches 500, contact 050 15 changes state, causing 010 00 to become energized, and 010 01 to become de-energized. Input 110 02 is used to reset both the up and down counts.

Modicon Counters

An example of a Modicon counter is shown in Figure 9-8. The value shown at the top of the box, 0010, is the preset count. Input 1001 is the up-count input, and input 1002 is the reset input. Contact 1002 is shown as an NC instruction. When this contact opens, the accumulated value of the counter is reset. When the accumulated count equals the preset count, output 0005 becomes energized and 0006 becomes de-energized. Address 4001 is the memory location of the counter in the PLC's data table. The maximum count that can be achieved using a Modicon counter is either 999 or 9999. As was the case with Modicon timers,

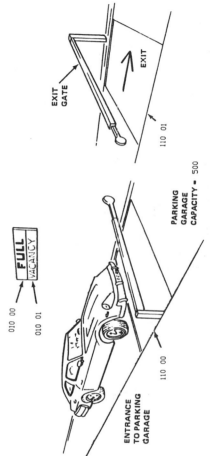

Figure 9-6 Figure for Example 9-1.

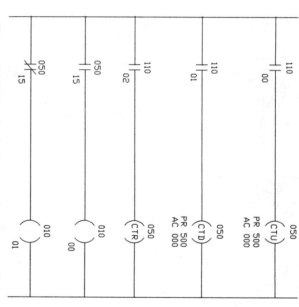

Figure 9-7 Ladder logic circuit for Example 9-1.

the accumulated count is not displayed in the box area. Instead, you must enter the counter's number and use the GET key to obtain a visual display of the accumulated value.

Figure 9-9 shows an example of a Modicon down-counter. In this circuit, the current count decrements each time input 10020 is closed and re-opened. Output 00060 will be energized and 00061 de-energized after contact 10020 has opened and closed ten times. Input 10021 is the reset instruction.

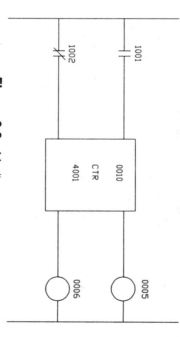

Figure 9-8 Modicon up-counter.

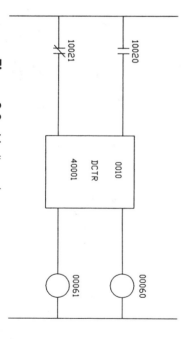

Figure 9-9 Modicon down-counter.

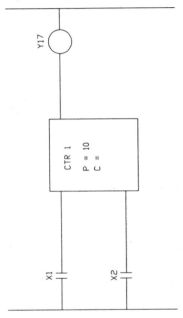

Figure 9-10 Texas Instruments up-counter.

Texas Instruments Counters

An example of a Texas Instruments counter is shown in Figure 9-10. This type of counter has a maximum preset value of 32,767. The two contacts, X1 and X2, represent the up-count increment and the reset/enable function, respectively. When the current count equals the preset count, output Y17 becomes energized.

A Texas Instruments up/down counter is shown in Figure 9-11. This box function has three input contacts and can directly control up to two outputs. In the circuit of Figure 9-11, contact X1 is the up-count input, X2 is the down-count input, and X3 is the reset/enable input. The UDC contains a "Z flag", which is an instruction to control either an internal coil, such as C1, or any Y output coil. When the current count is equal to zero, any coil designated by the Z flag will be energized. In Figure 9-11, when C=0, coil C1 will be energized and output Y18 will turn OFF. Output Y17 becomes energized under two conditions: when the counter counts down to zero, and when the counter counts up to its preset value. In the circuit shown in Figure 9-11, when C=0, Y17 is ON, C1 is ON, and Y18 is OFF. When C equals between 1 and 9, Y17 is OFF, C1 is OFF, and Y18 is ON. When C=10, Y17 is ON, C1 is OFF, and Y18 is ON.

The circuit shown in Figure 9-12 illustrates how Example 9-1 would be implemented using a Texas Instruments up/down counter. Contact X1 would count the cars entering, X2 would count the cars leaving, and X3 would be the reset instruction. Output Y17 would energize the FULL sign and Y18 would energize the VACANCY sign. Y18 is shown as a normally energized coil, meaning that whenever Y17 is ON, Y18 will be OFF, and vice versa. Usually output Y17 would be energized when P=C, or when C=0. By placing an NC C1 contact in series with Y17, output Y17 will now only be energized when the current count equals the preset count. This is because coil C1 is designated as the Z flag, which

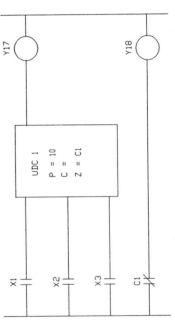

Figure 9-11 Texas Instruments up/down counter circuit.

means coil C1 becomes energized when the current count is zero. Therefore, contact C1 opens when the parking lot is completely empty, coil Y17 goes OFF, and Y18 becomes energized.

Figure 9-12 Texas Instruments circuit for Example 9-1.

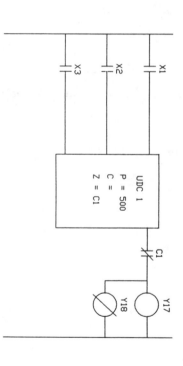

9-3 CASCADING COUNTERS

In situations where it is necessary to extend a counting operation beyond the preset value of the counter, two or more counters may be connected in a **cascading** configuration. Cascading is defined as using the output of one counter to initialize the counting function of a second counter.

Figure 9-13 shows an Allen-Bradley program using cascading counters. In this circuit, output 010 00 will become energized after contact 110 00 has opened and closed 999×2, or 1998 times. Contact 050 14 is the overflow bit for counter 050. This contact will be energized when the accumulated value of counter 050 equals 999. Contact 050 15 can be used instead of bit 14 to make the circuit work in the same manner. The closing of contact 050 14 enables the second counter, and every transition of 110 00 is now recorded in the accumulated count of counter 051. When the accumulated count equals the preset count of 051, output 010 00 becomes energized.

Figure 9-14 shows a Texas Instruments program which provides for a maximum count of 32,767 × 2, or 65,534. Contact X2 is the reset contact and contact X1 is the input count. When the accumulated count of counter 1 reaches 32,767, output C1 becomes energized. This sets up counter 2 to begin counting. After X1 has toggled 65,767 times, output Y17 becomes energized.

Another method of cascading counters is used in situations where an extremely large number must be stored. For example, if we require a counter to

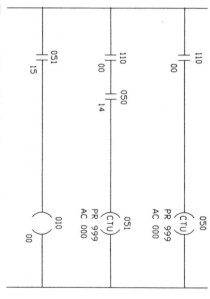

Figure 9-13 Allen-Bradley cascading counter circuit.

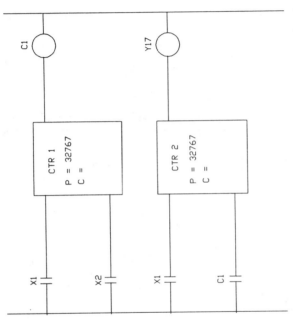

Figure 9-14 Texas Instruments cascading counter circuit.

count up to 250,000, it is possible to achieve this by using only two counters. Figure 9-15 shows how a Modicon counter would be used for such a purpose. Counter 1 has a preset of 500 and counter 2 has a preset of 500. Contact 1002 is the count input and 1003 is the reset input. Whenever counter 1 reaches 500, output 0001 becomes energized and counter 1 is reset. When 0001 becomes energized, counter 2 is pulsed and its current count increases by 1. When 0001 has turned ON and OFF 500 times, output 0002 becomes energized. Therefore, 0002 turns ON after 500×500, or 250,000 transitions of 1002.

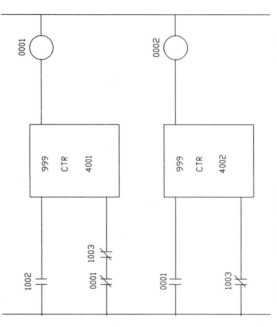

Figure 9-15 Modicon cascading counter circuit.

9-4 COMBINING COUNTER AND TIMER CIRCUITS

There are many industrial applications for PLCs that involve combining both timers and counters to achieve a desired result. For example, if an output is required to be energized after a 24-hour time period has elapsed, the most efficient method would be to use a timer and counter combination. Although this type of problem could be solved by using cascading timers, the program would be considerably longer than if a single counter and timer were used. Figure 9-16 shows how this program could be written using a Modicon PLC. In this circuit, input 1002 is the reset/enable switch. When this contact is closed, the timer begins timing. Every 600 seconds, or 10 minutes, the timer resets itself and provides an input pulse for the counter. In other words, the counter increments by 1 every 10 minutes. After the counter has been pulsed 144 times, output 0002 is energized.

Figure 9-17 shows an example of a manufacturing process requiring both a timer and counter. In this circuit, conveyor 1 is used to stack metal plates onto conveyor 2. A light source and detector provide the input pulse for the PLC counter. The light source is interrupted each time a metal plate passes through it from conveyor 1. When a certain number of plates have been stacked, conveyor 2 is activated for a time period controlled by a timer.

Figure 9-16   Modicon 24-hour clock circuit.

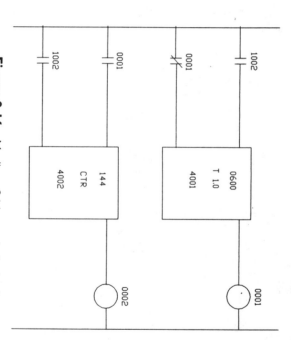

Write the ladder logic program for the circuit shown in Figure 9-17. Use Modicon I/O addressing and include a Stop/Start station. The counter has a preset of 10 s. and the timer a preset of 5 s.

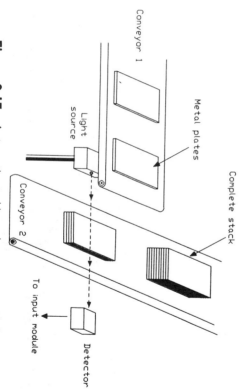

Figure 9-17   Automatic stacking using counter and timer.

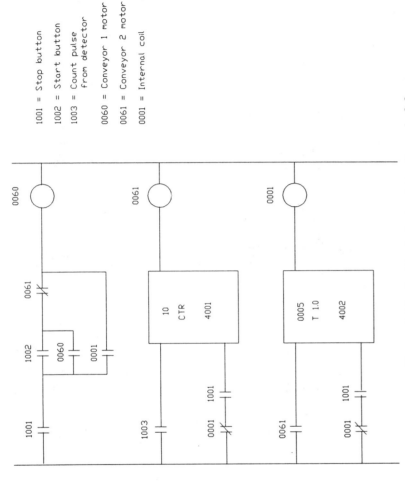

1001 = Stop button

1002 = Start button

1003 = Count pulse from detector

0060 = Conveyor 1 motor

0061 = Conveyor 2 motor

0001 = Internal coil

Figure 9-18 Ladder logic circuit for Example 9-2.

Solution

The ladder logic circuit for Example 9-2 is shown in Figure 9-18. When the Start button is pressed, conveyor 1 begins operating. After 10 plates have been stacked, conveyor 2 starts and conveyor 1 is stopped. After conveyor 2 has been operating for 5 seconds, it stops. The output coil for the timer resets the timer and counter and also provides a momentary pulse to automatically restart conveyor 1.

REVIEW QUESTIONS

9-1. Name the two basic types of relay logic counters.

9-2. List three applications for counter circuits in industry.

9-3. What are the standard types of counters found in most PLCs?

9-4. Define the terms "overflow" and "underflow."

9-5. A positive-edge trigger device produces a pulse when
   (a) the counter is reset.
   (b) the signal goes from high to low.
   (c) the signal goes from low to high.
   (d) the signal goes from either high to low, or vice versa.

9-6. The input pulse supplied to a counter is often referred to as
   (a) a positive edge.
   (b) an event.
   (c) a negative edge.
   (d) a transition.

9-7. What is the purpose of contact 110 02 in the circuit of Figure 9-19?

9-8. The CTD instruction performs what function?

Figure 9-19 Figure for Question 9.7.

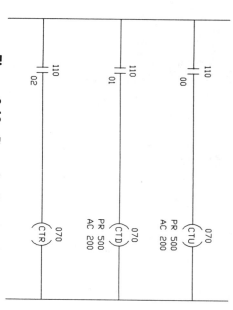

9-9. In a typical up-counter circuit, what happens when the preset count and accumulated count are equal?

9-10. Contact 10020 in Figure 9-20 performs what function?

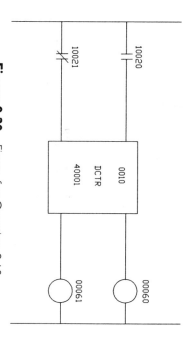

Figure 9-20 Figure for Question 9.10.

9-11. What is the purpose of a Z flag in an up/down counter?

9-12. Describe the function of cascading counters.

9-13. Write a program using Allen-Bradley I/O addressing that will energize an output 24 hours after the input has closed. Use one timer and one counter.

10

MCRs, ZCL, JUMP, and FORCE Instructions

Upon completion of this chapter, you will be able to

► Define "master control relay."
► Explain the purpose of a "zone" of control.
► Describe the function of "zone control latch."
► Understand the purpose of first failure annunciators.
► Differentiate between a jump instruction and a Jump to Subroutine instruction (JSR).
► Explain the advantage of using subroutines.
► Use the FORCE instruction for troubleshooting.

10-1 MASTER CONTROL RELAYS (MCRs)

As mentioned in Chapter 7, master control relays, or MCRs, are used in relay logic circuitry to control power to an entire system or to control power to a portion of a circuit. An example of a conventional relay logic circuit with an MCR is shown in Figure 10-1. In this circuit, the Master Start button overrides the start circuit for motor M. Unless the Master Start is pressed, there is no power flow between L_1 and the Stop/Start circuit for control relay CR1. When the MCR is energized, pilot light PL1 becomes energized, the vertical MCR contact is sealed in, and the Stop/Start station for CR1 is enabled.

The circuit shown in Figure 10-1 could not be entered as it appears into a PLC because the circuit contains a vertical contact. Many relay instructions related to MCRs involve vertical contacts. For this reason, most PLC manufacturers include a separate control relay identified as an MCR. Most PLC MCRs function in a similar manner. That is, when the MCR coil is energized, the circuit functions normally, and when the MCR is de-energized, any outputs below the MCR are OFF. Figure 10-2 shows how the circuit of Figure 10-1 would be entered using an Allen-Bradley PLC.

The circuit shown in Figure 10-3 illustrates how the relay circuit of Figure 10-1 would be implemented on a Texas Instruments PLC.

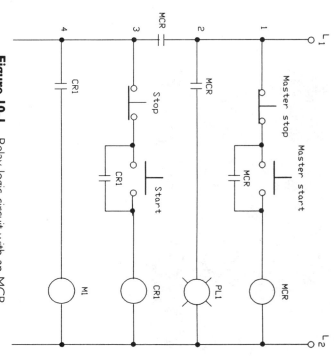

Figure 10-1 Relay logic circuit with an MCR.

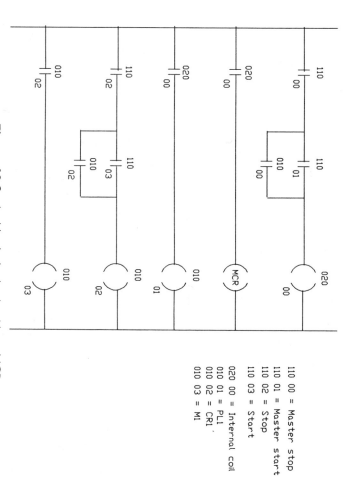

Figure 10-2 Ladder logic circuit with an MCR.

110 00 = Master stop
110 01 = Master start
110 02 = Stop
110 03 = Start

020 00 = Internal coil
010 01 = PL1
010 02 = CR1
010 03 = M1

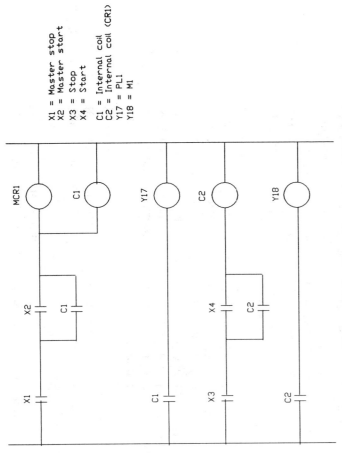

X1 = Master stop
X2 = Master start
X3 = Stop
X4 = Start

C1 = Internal coil
C2 = Internal coil (CR1)
Y17 = PL1
Y18 = M1

Figure 10-3 Texas Instruments MCR circuit.

In addition to controlling power to an entire system, MCRs are also used when only a portion of a program must be isolated. Figure 10-4 shows a conventional relay schematic where the MCR is controlling power to a section of the diagram, while the rest of the relay logic is unaffected by the MCR. In this circuit, when the Start button is pressed, CR1 becomes energized and motor M1 begins operating. When M1 is energized, the MCR coil is also energized, which enables the Stop/Start station for motor M2. In this circuit, M2 is dependent on M1 to

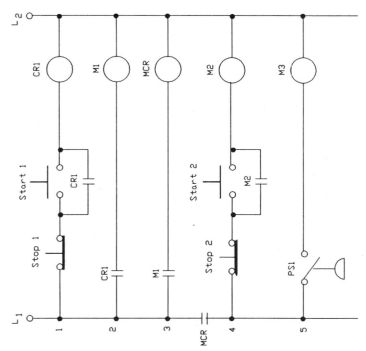

Figure 10-4 Relay logic circuit with partial MCR control.

▲ *EXAMPLE 10-1*

operate. Motor M3 is energized by pressure switch PS1 and is also dependent on the MCR coil to operate.

Determine the equivalent ladder logic program for the circuit shown in Figure 10-4. Use Allen-Bradley I/O addressing.

Solution

The equivalent ladder logic circuit is shown in Figure 10-5.

In some situations, the section of a PLC program which is required to be isolated is between the beginning and the end of the logic circuit. For example, if the circuit of Figure 10-4 required only motor M2 to be isolated and not M3, it would appear as shown in Figure 10-6. In this Allen-Bradley program, a "zone" is established between the two MCR coils. When the MCR is OFF, motor M2 will not function, but motor M3 will still operate if pressure switch PS1 is closed.

Texas Instruments establishes a zone of control for an MCR by using an MCR and an MCR end, MCR(e), instruction. The equivalent circuit of Figure 10-6 is shown in Figure 10-7 using a TI program.

Unlike Allen-Bradley, Texas Instruments MCRs can be "nested" in a program. That is, it is possible to use one MCR zone inside another MCR zone. An example of this is shown in Figure 10-8. The program controls four outputs, and each output has a Stop/Start station. If output Y17 is ON, outputs Y18 and Y19 can operate. If Y17 is OFF, all outputs are OFF. If Y17 is ON and input X5 is open, only outputs Y17 and Y18 are energized.

When using more than one MCR in a TI program, it is necessary to provide an address for the MCR and MCR(e) instructions. A TI 520 CPU provides up to eight MCRs, and the MCR addresses are between 1 and 8. The addressing must be included for each individual MCR to determine the length of zone that each MCR is controlling.

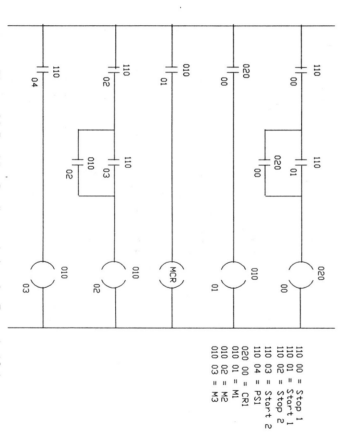

Figure 10-5 Allen-Bradley equivalent for Example 10-1.

110 00	=	Stop 1
110 01	=	Start 1
110 02	=	Stop 2
110 03	=	Start 2
110 04	=	PS1
020 00	=	CR1
010 01	=	M1
010 02	=	M2
010 03	=	M3

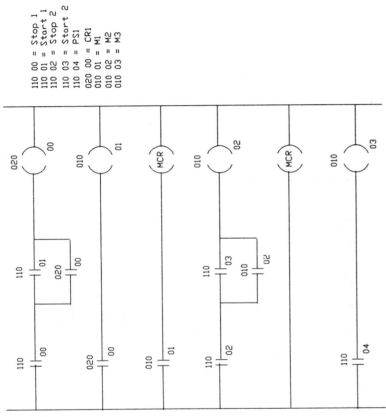

Figure 10-6 Allen-Bradley circuit with MCR zone.

110 00 = Stop 1
110 01 = Start 1
110 02 = Stop 2
110 03 = Start 2
110 04 = PS1
020 00 = CR1
010 01 = M1
010 02 = M2
010 03 = M3

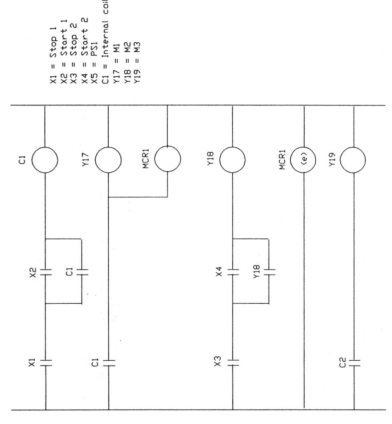

Figure 10-7 Texas Instruments circuit with MCR zone.

X1 = Stop 1
X2 = Start 1
X3 = Stop 2
X4 = Start 2
X5 = PS1
C1 = Internal coil (CR1)
Y17 = M1
Y18 = M2
Y19 = M3

Sec. 10-1 / Master Control Relays (MCRs)

▲
EXAMPLE 10-2

The circuit shown in Figure 10-9 is a grain supply bin with a conveyor system. A hopper valve controls the flow of grain onto the conveyor and a motor drives the conveyor at a fixed speed. If the conveyor motor stops due to system or mechanical failure, the hopper valve must close. Assume that when the hopper valve is energized it is open, and when de-energized, it is closed.

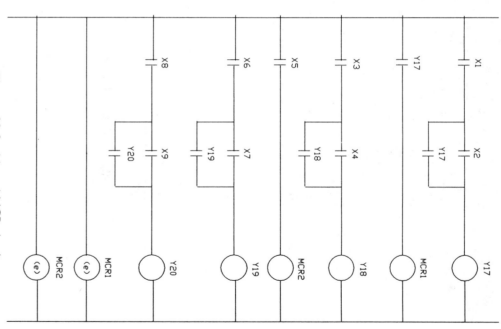

Figure 10-8 Nested MCR circuit.

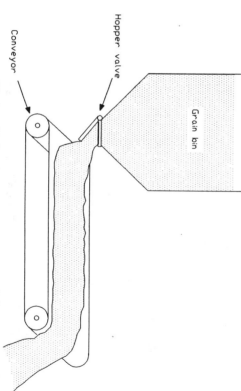

Figure 10-9 Grain bin of Example 10-2.

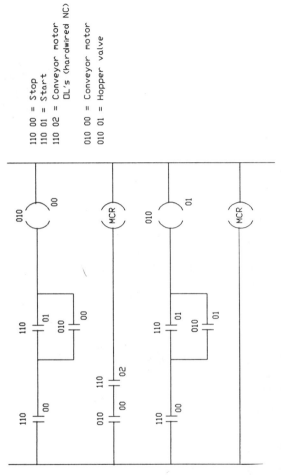

110 00 = Stop
110 01 = Start
110 02 = Conveyor motor
         OL's (hardwired NC)

010 00 = Conveyor motor
010 01 = Hopper valve

Figure 10-10 Circuit for Example 10-2.

Write a program using Allen-Bradley I/O addressing and an MCR to provide fail-safe control of the hopper valve. Include a stop/start station.

Solution

The equivalent ladder logic circuit is shown in Figure 10-10. By establishing an MCR zone around the hopper valve coil, if the conveyor stops for whatever reason, the hopper valve will close.

10-2 ZONE CONTROL LATCH (ZCL)

The Zone Control Latch (ZCL) instruction is used on Allen-Bradley PLCs to "freeze," or latch, the output coil in either an energized or de-energized state. This type of instruction is useful when de-bugging or troubleshooting programs, because it provides a method of determining the particular state of an output at the time of system failure. Figure 10-11 shows a programming example using a ZCL instruction. In this circuit, input 110 00 operates the ZCL instruction. When

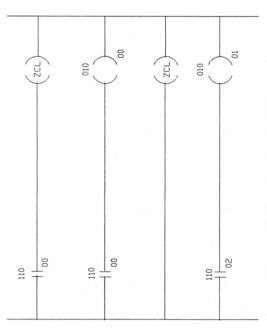

Figure 10-11 Allen-Bradley ZCL circuit.

146

11000 is closed, the circuit functions normally. If 11000 opens, all outputs between the two ZCL coils will be "frozen" in the state they were in when 11000 opened. For example, if output 010 00 was ON when 110 00 opened, it will remain ON, even if input 110 01 is opened. When 110 00 is re-closed, the outputs will be OFF if the input to the coil is OFF, or ON if the input instruction is ON. Output 010 01, which is outside the zone of control, will be unaffected by the operation of the ZCL.

A ZCL instruction can be used with another ZCL instruction, as shown in Figure 10-11, to control a specific portion of a program, or it can be used on its own to control the outputs from the ZCL to the last line of the circuit.

ZCL circuits are very useful in systems employing *first failure annunciators*. A first failure annunciator is a circuit that informs system operators which input device gave a warning signal that resulted in system shut-down. Consider the system shown in Figure 10-12. Three monitoring devices are used: pressure, temperature, and liquid level. If an unsafe condition should occur, certain combinations of these devices could shut down the system. Unfortunately, once a system has been shut down, it may be impossible to determine which combination of devices caused the failure. Consequently, by using a ZCL instruction, it is possible to record which combination of input devices gave the warning and to rectify the problem.

For the system of Figure 10-12, the following three conditions are considered to be unsafe and will activate an alarm, thus shutting down the system:

High level with high temperature
High level with high pressure
High level with high temperature and high pressure

If we assume that the transducers for these three devices produce signals in their high states and no signals in their low states, the relay logic schematic shown in Figure 10-13 represents the states of the devices for the three alarm conditions. For example, if the high level and high temperature inputs are closed, the alarm is activated.

Figure 10-14 shows a ZCL circuit that will indicate which devices caused the system failure. When the alarm is activated, the zone controlled by the ZCL instruction freezes the indicators in the state they were in at the time of system failure. For example, if high liquid level and high pressure caused the failure, outputs 010 01 and 010 03 would be latched ON. Input 110 03 is the reset instruction that would be manually switched by the system operator. The advantage of this type of system is that the input devices can change state after the alarm has latched and the data will still be recorded by the ZCL instruction.

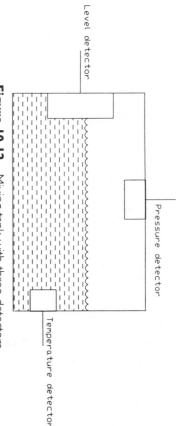

Figure 10-12 Mixing tank with three detectors.

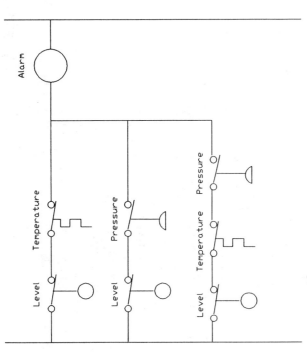

Figure 10-13 Relay logic schematic for alarm conditions.

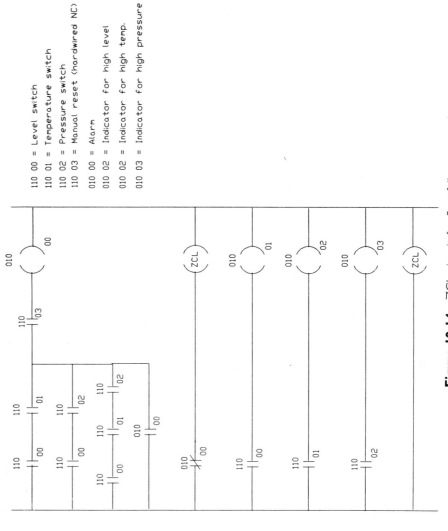

110 00 = Level switch
110 01 = Temperature switch
110 02 = Pressure switch
110 03 = Manual reset (hardwired NC)

010 00 = Alarm
010 02 = Indicator for high level
010 02 = Indicator for high temp.
010 03 = Indicator for high pressure

Figure 10-14 ZCL circuit for first failure annunciator.

Sec. 10-2 / Zone Control Latch (ZCL)

147

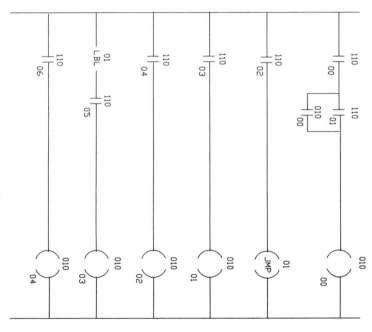

Figure 10-15 Allen-Bradley jump circuit.

On a typical PLC, a JUMP instruction is primarily used to reduce scan time. Some PLC manufacturers provide an output coil known as a SKIP instruction, which is essentially the same as a JUMP coil. By using the SKIP command, it is possible to branch, or skip, to a different portion of a program. The coils skipped over remain in the state they were in during the last scan before the SKIP instruction was enabled.

To understand the JUMP operation on an Allen-Bradley PLC, it is necessary to discuss both the LABEL and Jump to Subroutine (JSR) instructions. As mentioned, the main application of a JUMP instruction is to reduce scan time. Overall scan time is reduced by the fact that the processor skips, or jumps, over designated portions of a program. The area that the processor jumps over is defined by where the JUMP and LABEL instructions are located in the program. If the JUMP coil is energized, all logic between the JUMP and LABEL instructions is bypassed and the processor continues scanning after the LBL instruction.

Most types of Allen-Bradley PLCs have up to eight JUMP coils which are addressed from JMP 00 through JMP 07. JUMP and LABEL instructions must have the same address, i.e., JMP1 and LBL1. The LABEL instruction must also be entered as the first contact on a line. Any contacts and coils that are entered after LBL will not be affected by the jump zone established between JMP and LBL.

Figure 10-15 shows a circuit containing JUMP and LABEL instructions. In this circuit, the Stop/Start station on the first line is not affected by the jump zone. Contacts 110 05, 110 06, and coils 010 03 and 010 04 are also outside the jump zone and are therefore not affected by the JMP and LBL instructions. When contact 110 02 is open, the circuit functions normally. When the JMP coil is OFF, all outputs between JMP and LBL are OFF because the processor is not scanning this zone.

The Jump to Subroutine (JSR) instruction is a coil which instructs the processor to jump from the main program to a subroutine area in the CPU's memory.

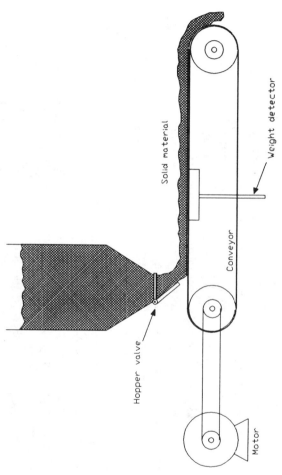

Figure 10-16 Conveyor system with weight detector.

The subroutine area is a portion of the PLC's RAM memory which is allocated for executing programs that are not always required in the main program. The subroutine area is situated between the end of the main program and the beginning of the area allocated for message storage.

Figure 10-16 shows an example of a solid-flow conveyor measuring system. If the weight on the conveyor indicates a certain preset value, an alarm light will begin flashing.

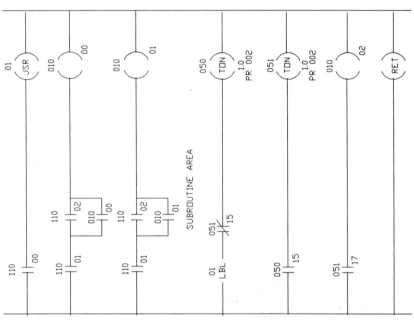

Figure 10-17 Ladder logic circuit with subroutine.

A JSR instruction can be used in a ladder logic program for the system shown in Figure 10-16 to activate the alarm condition for the circuit. Figure 10-17 shows a ladder logic circuit with a flashing alarm as a subroutine. If the weight detector on the conveyor exceeds a certain value, contact 110 00 closes, the JSR is activated, and the processor scan jumps to the subroutine area. The subroutine is continually scanned and the alarm output (010 02) flashes until contact 110 00 is re-opened. When 110 00 is re-opened, the processor will no longer scan the subroutine area. Operation of the main program is not affected by the JSR instruction. The Return instruction RET is used on the last line of the subroutine. Because a PLC may contain up to eight subroutines, the RET instruction is necessary to differentiate between each subroutine.

The advantage of using a subroutine in a program is that it reduces the scan time of a program that is only used under certain operating conditions. Instructions such as sequencers and data transfer consume relatively large amounts of scan time. If these instructions are only used sporadically in a program, it can be advantageous to enter them as subroutine programs.

10-4 FORCE INSTRUCTIONS

Almost all PLCs have an instruction which will allow an output or input to be forced to its ON or OFF state. The FORCE key is a very powerful, and potentially dangerous, troubleshooting tool. By using this instruction, any software protection that was incorporated into a ladder logic program is bypassed.

In situations where rotating equipment is operational, the FORCE instruction can be extremely dangerous. For example, if an electrician is performing routine maintenance on a de-energized motor, the machine may suddenly become energized by someone forcing the motor to turn ON. This is why many employers insist on using hardwired MCRs for the I/O rack. A hardwired MCR will provide a method of physically removing power to the I/O system, thereby insuring that it is impossible to energize any inputs or outputs when the MCR is OFF.

The following steps are taken to force an Allen-Bradley input or output:

1. Select Run/Program mode for the CPU.
2. Move the cursor until it is on the device required to be forced. Contact or coil should now be flashing.
3. Press the FORCE ON key to energize the device, or the FORCE OFF key to de-energize it.
4. Press the INSERT key. The word ON or OFF should now be displayed beneath the coil or contact that you are forcing.
5. To remove the FORCE instruction, press either FORCE ON or FORCE OFF, then press the REMOVE key.

To force a Modicon input or output, take the following steps:

1. Place the cursor on the coil or contact to be forced.
2. Enter the reference number in the assembly area and press GET.
3. Press the DISABLE key. A disable icon now appears in front of the input or output.
4. Press the FORCE key to force the input or output to its ON or OFF state.
5. Press the DISABLE key again to remove the FORCE instruction.

The steps taken to force a Texas Instruments input or output are as follows:

1. Place the cursor on the instruction that you wish to force.

2. Press the FORCE key. The menu line will display X (F6), C (F7), or Y (F8). Select the appropriate function key and enter the address.

3. Menu line now displays ON (F2) or OFF (F3). Select the appropriate function key.

4. To remove a FORCE instruction, press FORCE, and then from menu line, select UNFORCE (F1). Enter the address of the device to unforce.

Some PLCs, such as Allen-Bradley and Texas Instruments, also allow word addresses to be forced. This allows the operator to directly enter decimal or binary numbers into word locations. Forced word locations using Allen-Bradley machines are displayed by pressing SEARCH FORCE ON, or SEARCH FORCE OFF.

Pressing SEARCH, 5, 3, on an Allen-Bradley PLC will display the status of the 16 individual binary digits, or bits, associated with a particular address. Any individual bit may be forced to a 1 or 0 by simply using the horizontal cursor movement keys to move to the desired bit, and entering either 1 or 0. The FORCE ON and INSERT keys should now be pressed.

10-1. What is the purpose of a PLC MCR?

10-2. Define the term "MCR zone."

10-3. Is it possible to nest MCR commands?

10-4. A ZCL instruction
   (a) shuts off outputs when energized.
   (b) shuts off outputs when de-energized.
   (c) latches outputs when energized.
   (d) latches outputs when de-energized.

10-5. List two applications for a ZCL instruction.

10-6. What is a "first failure annunciator?"

10-7. A JUMP instruction
   (a) is similar to an MCR command.
   (b) is similar to a ZCL command.
   (c) is similar to a SKIP command.
   (d) is similar to a JSR command.

10-8. Why would a JUMP coil be used in a PLC program?

10-9. How many JUMP coils does a typical PLC have?

10-10. What is a subroutine?

10-11. A JSR instruction
   (a) freezes outputs in their last states.
   (b) tells the processor to jump forward in a program.
   (c) tells the processor to jump backward in a program.
   (d) establishes a zone of control.

10-12. The LBL and RET instructions
   (a) establish a subroutine area.
   (b) tell the processor to jump to a subroutine area.
   (c) establish a zone of control.
   (d) freeze outputs in their last states.

10-13. Why would a subroutine be used in a ladder logic program?

10-14. What does the FORCE command do?

10-15. What safety precautions must be taken when using the FORCE command?

10-16. Why should a hardwired MCR be incorporated into a PLC system?

Sequencers

Upon completion of this chapter, you will be able to

▼ Understand the operation of a mechanical drum controller.

▼ Describe the basic operation of a PLC sequencer.

▼ Differentiate between time-driven sequencers and event-driven sequencers.

▼ Derive a sequencer chart.

▼ Define the term "matrix."

▼ Explain the purpose of masking.

▼ List three types of sequencers.

11-1   INTRODUCTION

In PLC systems, a sequencer is the equivalent of a mechanical drum controller used in conventional relay logic systems. For this reason, some manufacturers, such as Texas Instruments, refer to the sequencer as a drum controller.

The mechanical drum controller, which is still widely used in industry, is a rotary, manual switching device made up of moving contacts mounted on an insulated rotating shaft. Because there is a set of moving contacts and stationary contacts inside the mechanical controller, as the manual switch is rotated, the moving contacts make and break connections with the stationary contacts. Mechanical drum controllers are mainly used to reverse the direction of a motor's rotation, and to control the speed of a motor. They are particularly common in situations where motors are frequently started, stopped, and reversed. Figure 11-1 shows a typical mechanical drum controller. In this type of device, spring-

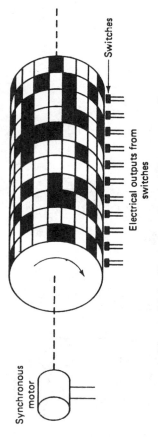

Figure 11-1 Typical mechanical drum controller.

loaded switch contacts are mounted very close to the rotating surface of the drum. The shaded areas of Figure 11-1 represent small protrusions, that when rotated by the synchronous motor into position under the appropriate switch, will energize electrical outputs. The protrusions can be connected to each other so that the duration that each switch is activated can be controlled.

Although the basic operation of sequencers is very similar for each type of PLC on the market, the appearance and programming of each sequencer varies quite substantially. Some sequencers will automatically step from one position to the next, while others require an event to occur before the sequencer moves on to the next position. Sequencers that advance automatically are called *time-driven sequencers*. Sequencers that advance after an event occurring, such as a switch closing, are called *event-driven sequencers*.

11-2 SEQUENCER CHART

A sequencer chart is a table that lists the sequence of operations of certain outputs in a circuit. If a sequencer is event-driven, the chart will also show the input devices required for operation. Figure 11-2 shows a basic three-position switch and sequence chart. This device could be considered an event-driven sequencer because different combinations of contacts are closed at different positions of the switch. A 1 inside the chart represents a closed contact and a 0 represents an open contact. In position 1, contact A is closed; in position 2, no contacts are closed; and, in position 3, only contact B is closed.

The format for a PLC sequencer chart is very similar to that of its mechanical counterpart. These tables both use a **matrix**-style chart format. A matrix is a two-dimensional rectangular array of quantities. A time-driven sequencer chart usually indicates outputs on its horizontal axis and time duration on its vertical axis. An

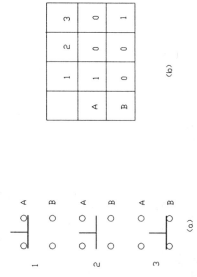

Figure 11-2 (a) Three-position selector switch; (b) Sequencer table.

event-driven sequencer indicates outputs on its horizontal axis and the input, or event, on its vertical axis. A typical PLC chart will use a 1 to represent an energized output and a 0 to indicate a de-energized output. Figure 11-3 shows an example of a time-driven sequencer circuit. The circuit shown in Figure 11-3 is a reduced voltage starting circuit for a three-phase motor. When the start button is pressed, the M contacts close, and the motor starts with maximum resistance. As the motor is brought up to speed, the sets of contacts close until finally, all resistance is removed from the circuit.

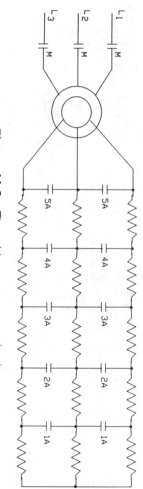

Figure 11-3 Time-driven sequencer circuit.

	Outputs				
Position	1A	2A	3A	4A	5A
1	0	0	0	0	0
2	1	0	0	0	0
3	1	1	0	0	0
4	1	1	1	0	0
5	1	1	1	1	0
6	1	1	1	1	1

Figure 11-4 Sequencer chart for reduced voltage starter.

Event	Water input	Soap release	Hot wax	Air blower
LS1	1	0	0	0
LS2	1	1	0	0
LS3	0	1	0	0
LS4	0	0	1	0
LS5	0	0	0	1
LS6	0	0	0	0

Figure 11-5 Event-driven sequencer chart.

Figure 11-4 shows a sequencer chart for the circuit of Figure 11-3. In Position 1, all outputs are OFF and the associated contacts are open. After a certain time period, the sequencer is incremented to Position 2 and output 1A becomes energized. After another time period has elapsed, the sequencer automatically moves to Position 3 and both outputs 1A and 2A are energized. The cycle continues until at Position 6, all five relay coils are energized.

A sequencer chart for an automatic car wash is shown in Figure 11-5. This type of circuit is considered to be event-driven because a car activates various limit switches as it is pulled by a conveyor chain through the car wash bay. The car wash operates in the following manner:

1. The vehicle pulls up to the car wash and is connected to the conveyor chain.
2. The car is pulled inside the wash bay and limit switch LS1 activates the water input valve.

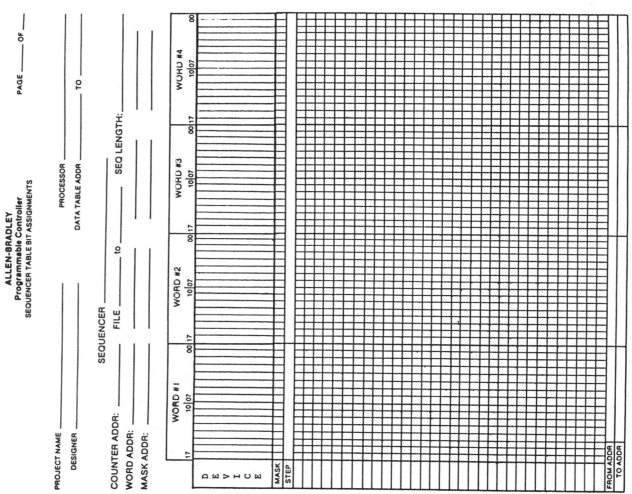

Figure 11-6 Allen-Bradley sequencer chart. (Courtesy of Allen-Bradley.)

3. After being pulled a certain distance, the soap release valve is activated by LS2, which mixes with the water input valve to provide a wash spray.
4. LS3 shuts off the soap valve, and the water input valve remains on to rinse the vehicle.
5. LS4 shuts off the water input valve and activates the hot wax valve.
6. LS5 shuts off the hot wax and starts the air blower motor.
7. LS6 shuts off the air blower. Vehicle exits car wash.

Figure 11-6 shows an example of an Allen-Bradley sequencer chart. This table includes the bit pattern, addresses, step numbers, and I/O locations accessed by the sequencer. This particular chart is for a sequencer capable of accessing 64 I/O locations. The 64 locations are divided into four words, each containing 16 bits. The grid below the device locations in the chart is intended for the bit pattern of the sequencer. In this type of chart, if a square in the grid is shaded, it implies that the device may be active when the sequencer is at that particular step. Whether a device is ON is also determined by the mask, as discussed in Section 11-3.

Many PLC sequencers use a mask to control which outputs are allowed to become active at any given sequence step. A typical PLC sequencer will use a block of 8 or 16 outputs known as a word. The data of the sequencer are stored in a file in the data table. A file is defined as a number of consecutive data table words stored in the data table. Files must be designed so they do not overlap, because overlapping files will overwrite one another. Therefore, the file address chosen for a sequencer should not coincide with other files, counters, timers, etc.

Because all outputs in a word may not be required for a specific process, it is possible to *mask* the outputs that are not needed, allowing these outputs to be used for other applications. In masking, certain bits of a word are set to 0, or, in effect, removed. Essentially, a mask is a type of digital filter. If the mask contains a 1, the data will pass through; if the mask contains a 0, the data are blocked.

Figure 11-7 shows how a mask operates. If the mask contains a 1, the output will become active because data are transferred through the mask to the output file. If the mask contains a 0, data are prevented from being transferred to the

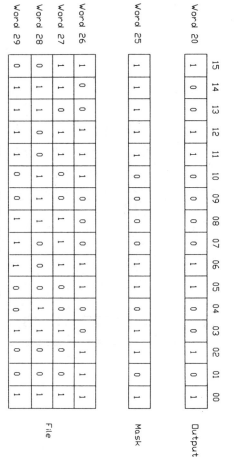

Figure 11-7 Mask operation.

output file. Consequently, a mask can be thought of as a bridge between the sequencer word file and the output word. For each bit of output word that is required to be controlled by the sequencer, the corresponding bit of the mask word must be set to 1. In Figure 11-7, word 26 is transferred from the file to the output word via the mask. Bit 00 indicates a 1 in the output word because the file and mask are both 1. Bit 01 shows a 0 because the mask is set to 0.

11-4 TYPES OF SEQUENCERS

Although each PLC manufacturer has a relatively unique type of sequencer, fortunately there are similarities between machines. A typical PLC sequencer will be up to 999 steps in length, and can access up to 64 outputs. The method used by manufacturers for storing sequencer data in memory is also quite similar. The data configuration for a sequencer is similar to that of a file. Consequently, the data for a sequencer are stored as a pattern of bits in a file.

Data can be entered either by a programming terminal or, on some PLCs by a *sequencer load* instruction. By using a sequencer load command, it is possible to set bit patterns for the sequencer file via input devices such as thumbwheel switches connected to the input rack. Generally, the sequencer load command does not allow masking. The *sequencer input* instruction is also common on PLCs. This sequencer allows input data to be compared against data stored in the sequencer file. Virtually all manufacturers provide some type of *sequencer output* instruction. A typical sequencer output is designed to energize outputs in specific combinations and time durations. The sequencer output instruction is very similar to its mechanical counterpart, the drum controller.

Allen-Bradley Sequencers

An Allen-Bradley sequencer consists of a function block and data table. An example of an Allen-Bradley data table is shown in Figure 11-8. Each step in the data table can be between one and four words wide, depending on how the data table is configured. Because each word is 16 bits, and each bit can represent an output, it is possible to access 64 outputs per step. The sequencer table shown in Figure 11-8 will access two words and eight steps. If this were the data table for a sequencer output, wherever there was a 1 in the word column, the output associated with that bit would be energized. Whenever a 0 would appear in the word column, the output would be OFF. If a sequencer chart were used, the bit pattern in the grid portion of the chart would be the same as the bit pattern shown in the PLC's data table.

STEP	WORD 1		WORD 2	
001	0000000	0001010	0000000	0101010
002	1001010	1011101	0110100	1010100
003	1101011	0110101	1000000	0010100
004	0110110	1010010	1010010	1001111
005	1010010	1100010	0100100	1001111
006	1110000	1110010	1010010	0101011
007	1010111	0101101	1110110	1000001
008	1010110	1010010	0100101	111100

Figure 11-8 Data table.

A sequencer output function block is shown in Figure 11-9. There are six values which can be varied with the sequencer output function. They are

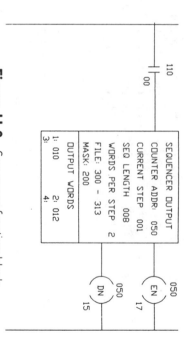

Figure 11-9 Sequencer function block.

COUNTER ADDRESS: Location of counter information stored in the data table.

CURRENT STEP: Step number that is currently being executed. Identifies accumulated value of counter.

SEQ LENGTH: Number of steps programmed in sequencer. Sequencer length may be any value between 1 and 999.

WORDS PER STEP: Number of words used in sequencer data table. This value is typically between 1 and 4, depending on the number of outputs required to be energized.

FILE: Starting address of data table for sequencer.

MASK: Starting address of mask file. Used to control the number of outputs energized at any given time.

OUTPUT WORDS: Sequencer data file destination. Varies between 1 and 4, depending on the number selected in words per step.

In the circuit shown in Figure 11-9, the sequencer length is eight steps and there are two words per step. Each time input 110 00 is toggled, the sequencer advances one step, and all corresponding outputs that have a 1 in the data table are energized, assuming the mask bit is set. If this sequencer has the data table shown in Figure 11-8, the outputs for the first step appear as shown in Figure 11-10.

Word 1 has a starting address of 010, and Word 2 has a starting address of 012, according to the function block of Figure 11-9. This means that the least-significant bit of Word 1, or the extreme right side, is output 010 00; the next bit to the left is 010 01; the next is 010 02, etc. The same applies to Word 2, the extreme right bit is 012 00; the bit to the immediate left is 012 01; etc. In the previous example, bits 010 01, 010 04, 012 01, 012 03, 012 05, and 012 06 are set because they have binary 1s in their respective columns. Therefore, these outputs will be energized when contact 110 00 toggles and the accumulative value of the counter is at Step 1. If the input is toggled again, the output bits which are set in Step 2 for Word 1 and Word 2 will be energized.

Figure 11-10 Outputs for table of Figure 11-8.

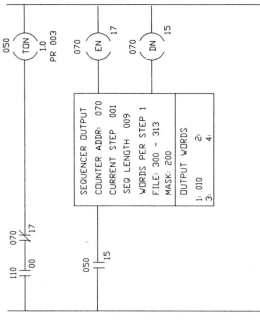

Figure 11-11 Time-driven sequencer.

For an Allen-Bradley sequencer to be automatically incremented through each step, it must have a timer incorporated into its ladder logic program. Figure 11-11 shows a timer with a preset of three seconds, which is used to pulse the input for the sequencer. The instantaneous bit of the sequencer, 070 17, is used to reset the timer after each increment occurs. This circuit automatically increments through the nine steps of the sequencer at three-second intervals.

The data table for the sequencer shown in Figure 11-11 is illustrated in Figure 11-12. The purpose of this circuit is to energize each of eight outputs at three-second intervals. When the sequencer reaches the ninth step, all eight outputs will have been energized for three seconds. The sequencer will continue cycling through these nine steps until contact 110 00 is opened.

The Allen-Bradley sequencer input instruction is used to compare 16 bits of input data to data which are stored in the sequencer's data table. The input data can indicate the state of an input device, such as a combination of input switches. For example, if the statuses of eight input switches are being monitored, if a switch is closed it will appear as a 1 in the data table; if the switch is opened it will appear as a 0 in the data table. When the combination of eight opened and closed switches are equal to the combination of 1s and 0s on a step in the sequencer table, the output of the sequencer becomes energized, or the rung becomes true.

```
SEQUENCER OUTPUT
STEP 001

    FILE 300 - 310

    OUTPUT ADDR. 010

    DATA    00000000 00000001

    MASK ADDR. 200

    DATA    00000000 11111111

    STEP        WORD 1

    001    00000000 00000001
    002    00000000 00000010
    003    00000000 00000100
    004    00000000 00001000
    005    00000000 00010000
    006    00000000 00100000
    007    00000000 01000000
    008    00000000 10000000
    009    00000000 11111111
```

Figure 11-12 Sequencer data table.

The sequencer input instruction contains a step counter that points to the step in the sequencer file which is presently being compared against the input devices.

Figure 11-13 shows a sequencer input function block. Most of the instructions inside the block are very similar to the sequencer output function block, although some slight differences exist. The counter address is the address of the instruction in the accumulated value area of the data table. The current step is the step number which is presently being compared against the input data. Sequencer length is the number of steps being used in the sequencer. The file address is the starting address of the sequencer data table. The input words are the input bits which are being compared against the mask file. The mask address is the starting address of the mask file. When the combination of bits those programmed into each step in the sequencer. When the combination of bits at the input address equals the binary word stored in a step, the sequencer will increment by one step when input 112 00 is pulsed.

Figure 11-14 shows a sequencer input instruction which is programmed in the same rung as a sequencer output instruction. The step counter of the sequencer input is now indexed by the sequencer output instruction because both counters have the same address, 050. This type of programming technique allows input and output sequencers to function in unison, causing a specific output sequence to occur when a specific input sequence takes place.

Allen-Bradley PLCs also have a sequencer load instruction. This instruction is intended to receive up to four words, or 64 bits, of information from input, output, and words stored in registers in memory. The sequencer load instruction allows you to load data into a sequencer table, one step at a time. As the step counter increments, data are loaded until the last step of the sequencer table has been loaded, and the preset count equals the current count. An example of a sequencer load function block is shown in Figure 11-15. This instruction does not use masking. If words are required to be masked, it must be done in conjunction

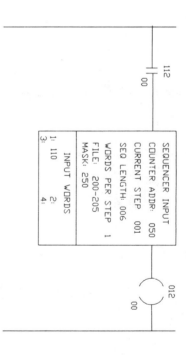

Figure 11-13   Sequencer input function block.

```
          112
         ──┤├──                                         012
           00                                          ─( )─
                                                         00
    ┌─────────────────────────┐
    │    SEQUENCER INPUT       │
    │ COUNTER ADDR:  050       │
    │ CURRENT STEP   001       │
    │ SEQ LENGTH: 006          │
    │ FILE: 200-205            │
    │ WORDS PER STEP 1         │
    │ MASK: 250                │
    ├─────────────────────────┤
    │     INPUT WORDS          │
    │ 1: 110      2:           │
    │ 3:          4:           │
    └─────────────────────────┘
```

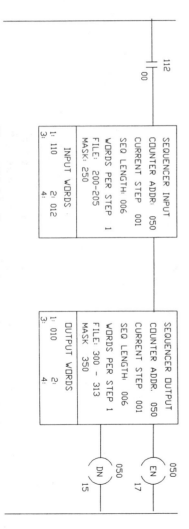

Figure 11-14   Sequencer input and sequencer output.

```
          112
         ──┤├──
           00
    ┌─────────────────────────┐
    │    SEQUENCER INPUT       │    050
    │ COUNTER ADDR:  050       │──┤ EN ├── 17
    │ CURRENT STEP   001       │
    │ SEQ LENGTH: 006          │
    │ FILE: 200-205            │
    │ WORDS PER STEP 1         │
    │ MASK: 250                │
    ├─────────────────────────┤
    │     INPUT WORDS          │
    │ 1: 110      2: 012       │
    │ 3:          4:           │
    └─────────────────────────┘

    ┌─────────────────────────┐
    │    SEQUENCER OUTPUT      │    050
    │ COUNTER ADDR.  050       │──┤ EN ├── 17
    │ CURRENT STEP   001       │
    │ SEQ LENGTH: 006          │
    │ FILE: 300 - 313          │    050
    │ WORDS PER STEP 1         │──( DN )── 15
    │ MASK   350               │
    ├─────────────────────────┤
    │     OUTPUT WORDS         │
    │ 1: 010      2:           │
    │ 3:          4:           │
    └─────────────────────────┘
```

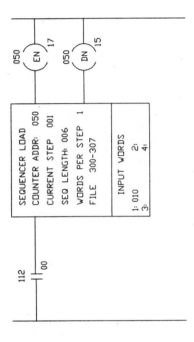

Figure 11-15 Sequencer load function block.

with a sequencer input or sequencer output instruction. The instructions in the function block of the sequencer load are as follows:

COUNTER ADDRESS: Address of instruction in accumulated value area of data table.

CURRENT STEP: Position in sequencer table.

SEQ LENGTH: Number of steps being used in sequencer operation.

WORDS PER STEP: Number of binary words being utilized by sequencer.

FILE: Beginning address of sequencer data table.

INPUT WORDS: Location of data being retrieved by sequencer.

AEG Modicon Sequencers

The function block of a Modicon sequencer, as shown in Figure 11-16, is very similar in appearance to a Modicon counter. This type of sequencer can be programmed for up to 32 steps. In Figure 11-16, the step value selected is 8, as shown at the top of the function block. A typical Modicon PLC accesses up to eight sequencers, and their addresses are as follows:

4051 uses contacts 2101 - 2132
4052 uses contacts 2201 - 2232
4053 uses contacts 2301 - 2332
4054 uses contacts 2401 - 2432
4055 uses contacts 2501 - 2532
4056 uses contacts 2601 - 2632
4057 uses contacts 2701 - 2732
4058 uses contacts 2801 - 2832

In the circuit shown in Figure 11-16, contact 1001 is the stepping contact. Each time 1001 is closed and opened, the sequencer advances by one step. Because register 4051 has been selected, the eight contacts from 2101 to 2108 become energized sequentially as 1001 is pulsed. Output 0005 will become energized when the sequencer counts out the last step. Because normally closed contact 0005 is used on the reset line of the counter, the sequencer will automatically be reset after reaching the last step of the count.

Figure 11-17 illustrates a sequencer function using a Modicon PLC. Eight outputs are required to be energized sequentially, and on the ninth step, all outputs are required to be energized. After nine steps, the circuit is required to be reset

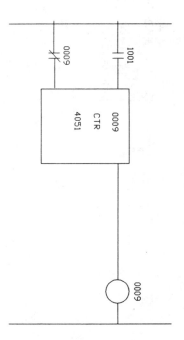

Figure 11-16 Modicon sequencer function block.

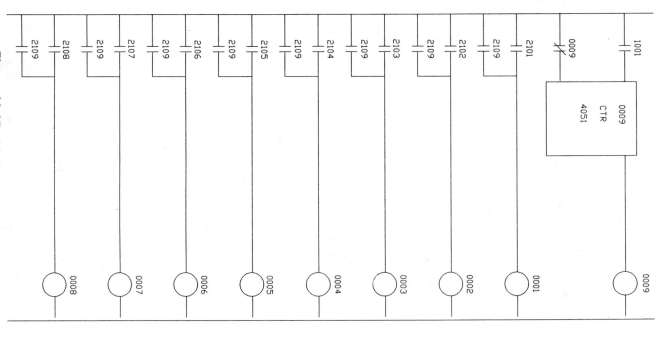

Figure 11-17 Modicon sequencer circuit.

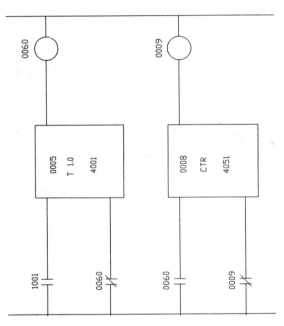

Figure 11-18 Modicon time-driven sequencer.

and must continue again at Step 1. The outputs which will be energized by the sequencer, are labelled 0001 to 0008, respectively.

Figure 11-18 shows an example of a Modicon time-driven sequencer. In this circuit, when contact 1001 is closed, the timer resets itself every five seconds, providing an input pulse for the sequencer function block.

Texas Instruments Sequencers

Figure 11-19 shows a Texas Instruments sequencer which is dependent on time to step through each sequence. The sequencer table itself is set up as a matrix. The outputs accessed by the sequencer are displayed on the top line of the sequencer table. Any time a 1 appears in the column below an output, the output turns ON. Whenever there is a 0 in the column below an output, the output will

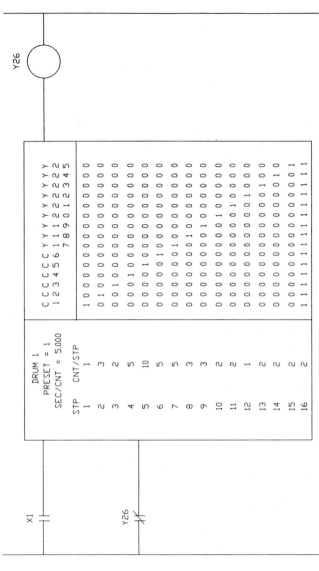

Figure 11-19 Texas Instruments time-driven sequencer.

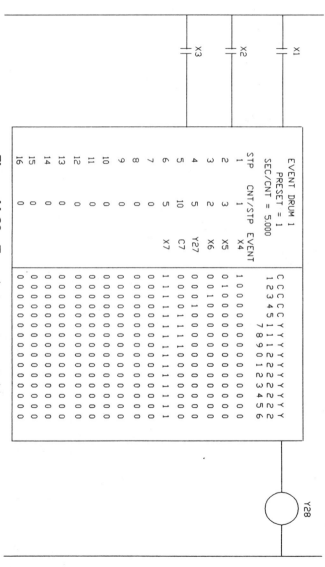

```
EVENT DRUM 1
PRESET = 1
SEC/CNT = 5.000

STP  CNT/STP  EVENT
 1      1      X4     1 0 0 0 0 0 0 0 0 0 0 0 0 0 0
 2      3      X5     0 1 0 0 0 0 0 0 0 0 0 0 0 0 0
 3      2      X6     0 0 1 0 0 0 0 0 0 0 0 0 0 0 0
 4      5      Y27    0 0 0 1 0 0 0 0 0 0 0 0 0 0 0
 5      10     C7     0 0 0 0 1 1 1 0 0 0 0 0 0 0 0
 6      5      X7     0 0 0 0 0 1 1 1 1 1 1 0 0 0 0
 7      0             0 0 0 0 0 0 1 1 1 1 1 1 1 0 0
 8      0             0 0 0 0 0 0 0 1 1 1 1 1 1 1 0
 9      0             0 0 0 0 0 0 0 0 1 1 1 1 1 1 1
10      0             0 0 0 0 0 0 0 0 0 0 0 0 0 0 0
11      0             0 0 0 0 0 0 0 0 0 0 0 0 0 0 0
12      0             0 0 0 0 0 0 0 0 0 0 0 0 0 0 0
13      0             0 0 0 0 0 0 0 0 0 0 0 0 0 0 0
14      0             0 0 0 0 0 0 0 0 0 0 0 0 0 0 0
15      0             0 0 0 0 0 0 0 0 0 0 0 0 0 0 0
16      0             0 0 0 0 0 0 0 0 0 0 0 0 0 0 0

                      C C C C Y Y Y Y Y Y Y Y Y Y Y
                      1 2 3 4 5 1 1 1 2 2 2 2 2 2 2
                                7 8 9 0 1 2 3 4 5 6
```

Figure 11-20   Texas Instruments event-driven sequencer.

be OFF. In Figure 11-19, Step 1 has a 1 below output C1, so when the sequencer begins timing out, it will only energize output C1. When it starts at Step 2, only output C2 is ON. When the sequencer reaches Step 16, all outputs will be energized because there is a 1 below each of the 15 outputs.

The length of time that an output remains energized in Figure 11-19 is determined by the sec/cnt multiplied by the cnt/stp. The seconds per count in this circuit is set at 5.000 seconds. The first step has a counts per step of 1. This means that output coil C1 will be energized for 5 × 1, or 5 seconds. The sequencer remains on Step 2 for 5 × 3, or 15 seconds. This means that output coil C2 will be energized for 15 seconds before the sequencer moves on to Step 3. When the sequencer arrives at Step 5, it will energize all the outputs for a period of 5 × 10, or 50 seconds. When the sequencer has passed through all the steps, the output coil to the right of the sequencer block is energized. In this case, Y26 has a normally closed Y26 contact on the reset/enable line to the sequencer. This means that the sequencer will automatically reset and begin its cycle over again without any manual instruction. The PRESET, which is shown immediately above the sec/cnt value, is the step number at which the sequencer begins. For instance, if the preset were 3, the sequencer would start counting from Step 3 when enable contact X1 was closed.

The TI sequencer shown in Figure 11-20 is referred to as an event drum because it requires an event to occur before it moves on to the next step. This type of sequencer will not automatically move from step to step. Contact X1 is the freeze/enable contact and X3 is the reset/enable contact. X2 is the master event contact. Every time this contact is toggled, the sequencer advances one step. When X1 is closed, Step 1 is energized, but the sequencer will not move on to Step 2 until the event occurs at Step 1. In Figure 11-20, the event at Step 1 is contact X4. This means that the sequencer will remain indefinitely at Step 1 unless either X4 closes, or the master event contact, X2, closes. If either of these contacts close, the sequencer moves on to Step 2 and remains there for 5 × 2, or 10 seconds. The timing cycle for each step does not begin until the input or output in the event column is energized. In Figure 11-20, Step 6 is the last step programmed into the sequencer. When the sequencer has completed its cycle, it will remain at Step 6, with all outputs energized, including output Y28, until the reset contact X3 is opened.

REVIEW QUESTIONS

11-1. What is a mechanical drum controller?

11-2. List two applications of a mechanical drum controller.

11-3. A time-driven sequencer performs what function?

11-4. How is a time-driven sequencer different from an event-driven sequencer?

11-5. What is a sequencer chart?

11-6. Define the term "matrix."

11-7. A mask is
(a) used to automatically advance sequencers.
(b) a method of preventing outputs from being energized.
(c) a table that lists the sequence of operation of certain outputs.
(d) a two-dimensional rectangular array of quantities.

11-8. What is the purpose of a sequencer load instruction?

11-9. Describe a typical application for a sequencer input instruction.

11-10. A sequencer output instruction performs what function?

11-11. How many outputs can a typical Allen-Bradley sequencer access?

11-12. What is meant by the term "words per step?"

11-13. Can a mask instruction be used with a sequencer input?

11-14. How many sequencers can be accessed by a typical Modicon PLC?

Data Transfer

Upon completion of this chapter, you will be able to

▼ Explain the purpose of a "block transfer" instruction.

▼ List three basic types of registers.

▼ Define the term "sign bit."

▼ Understand a register-to-register move.

▼ Differentiate between a table-to-register move.

▼ Define a table-to-table move.

▼ Explain the operation of a register-to-table move and a register-to-table move.

▼ Explain the operation of a shift register.

12-1 INTRODUCTION

Data transfer is the method used by a PLC to move data from one point to another. This can include transferring data from one memory location to another memory location or groups of memory locations, or it can also include the procedure required to move data either to or from an analog I/O module. Data from a single memory location, or register, may be transferred, or, data from a group of locations, or table, may be transferred. Some PLCs, such as those made by Allen-Bradley and Modicon, refer to the transfer of more than one register as a *block transfer*.

The ability of a PLC to perform data transfer operations greatly improves its versatility in process control applications. The register system of data storage used by a PLC is very similar to that of a computer. This chapter shall examine how data are moved from one location in memory to another location.

As mentioned earlier, a register, or word, is a memory location where bits of data are stored. Figure 12-1 shows a basic 16-bit storage register. This type of register represents a location in the PLC's memory where 16 separate bits of data can be stored. The Least-Significant Bit (LSB) is shown at the right side of the register, and the Most-Significant Bit (MSB) at the left. There are many types of registers in a typical PLC: holding registers, I/O registers, shift registers, and FIFO (First-In, First-Out) registers. A **holding register** is used to store data regarding the internal operation of the processor. This register does not directly access the I/O system. Holding registers are mainly used by a PLC to store data when it is processing a program written by a user. The area set aside in the processor's memory for the storage of data for discrete I/O is known as an *input register* or *output register*. In this type of register, each input or output device is represented by one bit.

Figure 12-1 16-bit register.

Depending on the manufacturer, registers are either 4, 8, 16, or 32 bits in length. The data stored in a register are either in *natural binary*, or *Binary Coded Decimal* (BCD). In natural binary, the maximum decimal equivalent of a 16-bit register is 65,535, as shown in Figure 12-2. The contents of a register can be examined by calling up the address via the programming terminal. Although register contents are almost always stored in binary form, it is possible to view the contents of a register using different numbering systems. For example, the contents of a register may be displayed in decimal, octal, or hexadecimal form. The various numbering systems used by PLCs will be discussed later in Chapter 16.

Figure 12-2 Register containing 65,535 in binary.

In some situations, the most-significant bit of a register is used as a sign bit. A *sign bit* is used to indicate whether a number has a negative or positive value. If a register is using a sign bit, the maximum decimal value that can be stored in a 16-bit register is +32767 or −32767. Figure 12-3 shows a 16-bit register using a sign bit. If the MSB is 0, the number is considered positive. If the MSB is 1, the number is negative.

If data are stored in a register using the BCD number system, four bits are

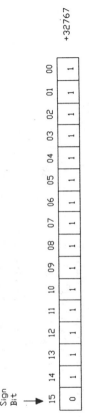

Figure 12-3 16-bit register with sign bit.

used to represent each decimal number. Therefore, only four decimal numbers can be derived from a 16-bit register. The maximum decimal number capable of being stored in a 16-bit BCD-type register would be 9999.

The procedure of storing data in a register is called a **write** operation. Determining the value of the contents in a register is called a **read** operation. When data are transferred from one register to another, they are, essentially, copied from one location to another. In other words, once data transfer has occurred, both the source register and the destination register will contain the same data. If the destination register already contains data, it will be permanently erased when the data transfer occurs. As with data transfer in computer systems, this process is known as writing. In Figure 12-4(a), the source register is shown with combinations of 1s and 0s, while the destination register is cleared, having only 0s. Figure 12-4(b) shows the contents of both registers after data transfer has occurred.

A file, or table, is defined as a group of consecutive registers. Files allow large amounts of data to be scanned quickly and are very useful in programs requiring the transfer, or comparing, of data. Almost all PLC manufacturers display file instructions in block format on the programming terminal screen. These data transfer instructions include register-to-register, file-to-file, file-to-word, word-to-file, matrixes, and shift registers.

12-3 REGISTER-TO-REGISTER MOVES

The transfer of data from one word location to another is called a *register-to-register* move. This type of data transfer instruction is often used for moving the contents of timers and counters from one location to another. Two typical register-to-register move instructions are *GET* and *PUT*. A GET instruction tells the processor which word location to get data from, and the PUT command tells the processor which word location to put these data into. As mentioned in the previous section, the new data will write over any data already stored in the destination address.

Allen-Bradley PLCs utilize GET and PUT instructions for register-to-register moves. Figure 12-5 shows a program which is used to change the preset value of a timer. The timer is programmed with a preset value of 5 seconds. If contact 110 01 is closed, the GET instruction will take the data stored at address 030 and put

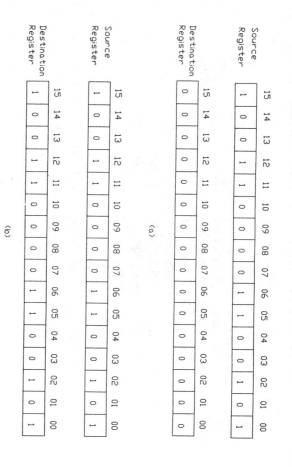

Figure 12-4 (a) Source and destination registers before data transfer; (b) Register contents after data transfer.

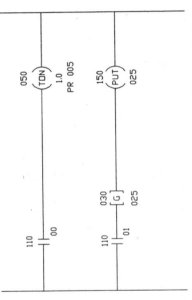

Figure 12-5 Data transfer using GET and PUT.

them at the preset value of timer 050. Because the first digit above the PUT instruction in Figure 12-5 is 1, the data are placed in the preset value of the timer. Therefore, timer 050 now has a preset of 25 seconds. If the first digit were 0, as in 050, the data would be put into the accumulative location of the timer.

▶ *EXAMPLE 12-1*

A single counter is required to perform two different count functions in a manufacturing plant. The first production run requires the counter to count up to 200. After the counter has counted up to 200, the preset value of the counter must be changed so that it will count up to 100 during the second production run. Up-counter 070 is initially programmed with a preset of 0. The input for the counter is a proximity switch, 110 00, which counts the number of items passing by on a conveyor. Output 010 00 is a pilot light that tells the operator when the counter has reached its preset value.

Solution

Figure 12-6 shows an Allen-Bradley ladder logic circuit using GET and PUT instructions. When contact 110 01 is closed, the processor reads the GET instruction, [G], and gets the number 200 from memory location 020. It then immediately reads the PUT instruction and puts the data at location 170, which is the preset address for counter 070. The accumulated address is 070. Consequently, if the number above the PUT instruction was 070, the number 200 would be transferred into the accumulative address of counter 070. If contact 110 01 is opened and 110 02 closed, the number 100 is loaded into the preset value of counter 070. It should be noted that with Allen-Bradley PLCs, a PUT instruction is always preceded by a GET command.

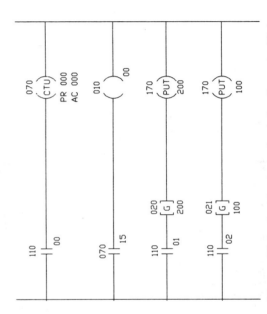

Figure 12-6 Ladder logic circuit for Example 12-1.

Transferring data from a word location to another word location, such as an analog output module, is accomplished with a Texas Instruments PLC by using an LDC instruction. An LDC, or Load Data Constant, is a function block instruction that allows either decimal, binary, or BCD numbers to be loaded into a variety of addresses, including timers, counters, and word locations for I/O modules. The LDC function also contains an integer instruction which allows a number to be identified as a positive or negative value.

Texas Instruments word locations are divided into three main types: WX, WY, and V. A WX location is an input address, WY is an output address, and V is a software memory location. V memory locations are holding registers that are used to store data, but unlike WX and WY locations, V memory addresses are not accessible at the I/O rack. Decimal, binary, and BCD numbers can be directly loaded into a V memory location via a programming terminal. Timers and counters have their current, or accumulative, values stored at TCC word locations, while the preset values of timers and counters are stored at TCP locations.

Figure 12-7 shows a Texas Instruments LDC instruction that is used to load the decimal number 16000 into memory location WY39. WY word locations may also be used as software locations that are not accessible at the I/O rack. For example, WY1 may be used to store data even if its module address is used by a discrete module. Only when a WY address corresponds to a word or analog module is data transferred to a physical location in the I/O rack.

Data are automatically transferred from an analog input module to its corresponding memory location with a Texas Instruments system. For example, if an analog input module is located in slot 6 of an I/O rack, addresses WX41 through WX48 would store any values being converted from voltage levels connected to this module. If a thermocouple was connected at WX41, all voltage levels generated by the thermocouple would be converted to numerical values and stored at memory location WX41.

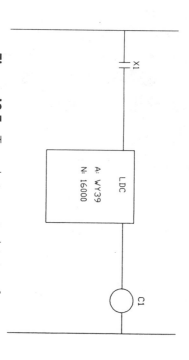

Figure 12-7 Texas Instruments data transfer.

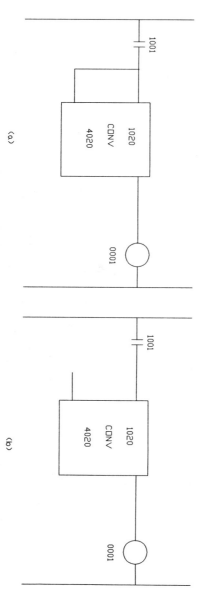

Figure 12-8 Modicon data transfer using CONV: (a) Data stored in binary form; (b) Data stored in BCD form.

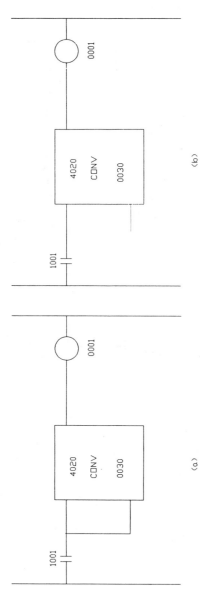

Figure 12-9 Data transfer using a CONV function block: (a) Binary data sent; (b) BCD data sent.

Modicon PLCs use the *CONVERT* or *CONV* instruction for moving data from an input device to a memory location, or from a memory location to an output device. Figure 12-8 shows an example of a CONV function used to input data from an analog card. The data to be input can be either BCD or binary, depending on whether the lower input contact is used. Figure 12-8(a) is a circuit that will store data in binary form, and the configuration of Figure 12-8(b) will store data in BCD form.

Modicon analog output modules also use the CONV function to transfer data from a register to the module. Figure 12-9 shows an example of the data transfer function, where information is sent from the register to the output module. In Figure 12-9(a), the data being sent are binary, and in Figure 12-9(b), the data transmitted are in BCD form.

The CONV function is also used to transfer digital input and output information. For example, if the circuit of Figure 12-9 were connected to a seven-segment display, the data would be transferred from address 4020 to the first 12 consecutive addresses beginning at 0030.

A typical Modicon PLC has two basic types of registers: **input registers** and **holding registers.** Input registers contain data that are directly entered into word locations via input modules. Holding registers are used to store data that can be altered using a programming terminal. Modicon PLCs also use **pointer registers.** These registers contain an address instead of data. In data transfer instructions, a pointer register tells the processor the address where the data are to be either stored or taken from. In other words, the pointer can be either the source address or destination address, depending on the type of instruction. The two commands used by Modicon to transfer data between registers are the Table-to-Register (T-R), and Register-to-Table (R-T).

12-4 TABLE-TO REGISTER MOVES

Most PLCs are capable of performing Table-to-Register (T-R) data transfers. Allen-Bradley refers to this move as a block transfer instruction. Figure 12-10 shows an example of a Modicon function block used for moving data from a table to a register. This type of instruction is used to move data sequentially from a specified data file to a single register. The pointer is used to point to the register being moved at any particular instant. Contact 10001 is used to increment the pointer. Each time contact 10001 is closed and opened, the pointer increments by one. In Figure 12-10, the source address is 40020 and the destination address, or pointer, is 40100. The length of the table is indicated at the bottom of the function block as 00008, so there are eight registers in this particular table. The lower contact, 00060, is the reset input. If this contact is closed, the pointer will

Figure 12-10 Modicon Table-to-Register (T-R) move.

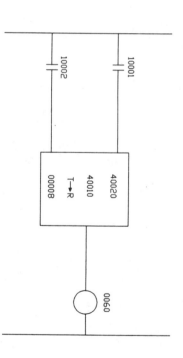

automatically return to its default address, which is 40020. The output coil will energize after the last register has been moved from the table. Because the reset input of this circuit has the same address as the output coil, the function block will be reset after it has stepped through eight registers.

Essentially, the circuit of Figure 12-10 is an event-driven sequencer. Contact 10001 is the event which causes the sequencer outputs to be set by the bit pattern in the address indicated by the pointer. The pointer is initially at address 40020, and each time the input contact changes state, the pointer moves on to the next address in the table. The data from the pointer address are then written into the destination address, which in this case is 40100. Each time the pointer is incremented, the data in the destination address are changed to correspond to the data in the source address.

The speed of a motor is to be varied by using a variable-speed drive and an analog output module. The speed of the motor is dependent on the analog signal supplied by a PLC. The output voltage produced by the module is determined by the binary combination stored in the corresponding register. The data stored in register 40050 will cause the motor to stop. At register 40051, the motor runs at 1/4 speed; 40052 will produce enough analog signal to run the motor at 1/2 speed; and, 40053 will cause the motor to run at full speed. Write a program using a table-to-move instruction and timers to accomplish the following:

1. When the Start button is pressed, the motor runs at 1/4 speed for 20 seconds.
2. After 20 seconds, the motor runs at 1/2 speed.
3. The motor runs at 1/2 speed for 30 seconds and then switches to full speed.
4. The motor runs at full speed for one minute and stops.

Solution

Figure 12-11 shows a circuit that will accomplish the goal. When the Start button is pressed, output 00010 supplies a pulse to output 00017, which increments the pointer to register 400051. The data in register 40051 cause the motor to run at 1/4 speed. Output 00010 also latches the circuit for timer 40001. After 20 seconds, output 00012 is energized, which causes the pointer to be incremented to 400052. The motor is now running at 1/2 speed and timer 40002 begins timing. After 30 seconds, output 00014 turns ON and the pointer is again incremented. Timer 40003 now begins its 60-second timing cycle. When 00017 is energized, the pointer is incremented and reset to 400050. The motor turns OFF and all timers are reset.

With an Allen-Bradley PLC, it is possible to transfer data from a group of memory locations to a register, such as an analog output module address, by using a block transfer write instruction. Figure 12-12 shows an example of a block

▼ EXAMPLE 12-2

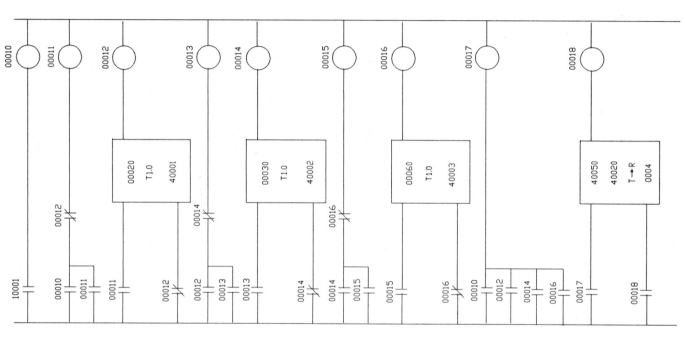

Figure 12-11 Circuit for Example 12-2.

transfer write instruction. The data address is selected as 050, meaning that the first memory location that data are stored in, is at 050, the second is 051, the third is 052, etc. The module address is shown as 131, which means that module 1 in rack 1 at module address 3 has been selected as the destination of binary data to be transferred when contact 112 00 is closed. One word, or 16 bits of data, will be transferred because the block length is chosen as 1. File 300 contains the binary data to be transferred. It is not necessary to use an input contact for any block transfer instruction. If no input contact is used, the data are transferred on every scan instruction.

Data may also be moved from a single word location into a file, or from a file into a single word location with Allen-Bradley PLCs by using the word-to-file and file-to-word instructions. These instructions are externally indexed and do not contain a rate per scan function. The counter can be indexed randomly, by using a GET/PUT instruction, or sequentially, by using another counter.

Figure 12-13 shows an example of a file-to-word instruction. Each time contact 110 00 is closed, the file address is incremented, and the data stored at the file address are transferred to the word location. This function also operates in essentially the same manner as a sequencer.

Word location 010 is also used in Figure 12-13. This address could be an output module location in the I/O rack, and the data being transferred from file locations could be used to energize outputs associated with that module.

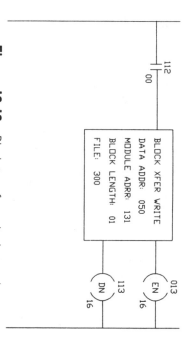

Figure 12-12 Block transfer write instruction.

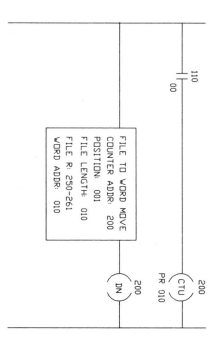

Figure 12-13 A file-to-word move with sequential index.

12-5 REGISTER-TO-TABLE TRANSFERS

A register-to-table transfer moves data sequentially from a single register into a specified section of a table of registers. This can be accomplished with an Allen-Bradley PLC by using a word-to-file transfer. An example of a word-to-file instruction with an additional counter to perform external indexing is shown in Figure 12-14. Each time input 110 00 is closed, the data at word location 112 are incremented by one file address starting at 300. After contact 110 00 has been opened and closed ten times, file addresses 300 through 311 all have exactly the same data. Because word location 112 could be a module location on an I/O rack, the first eight bits of data stored at 112 could represent the status of eight input devices.

Allen-Bradley PLCs receive data obtained from an analog input module by using a block transfer read instruction. Figure 12-15 shows an example of a data transfer read instruction. When contact 112 01 is closed, incoming data from

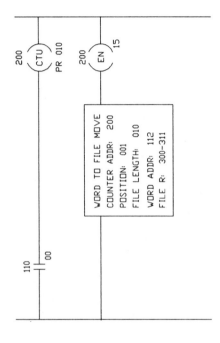

Figure 12-14 A word-to-file move.

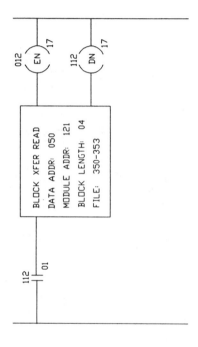

Figure 12-15 A block transfer read instruction.

module address 121 will be stored in the file address beginning at 350. An input contact is not necessary for a block transfer read. If no contact is included, the data stored in the file address are updated on every program scan.

A Modicon register-to-table move is shown in Figure 12-16. The top line of the function block contains the register that supplies data to the processor. The bottom number is the pointer. When contact 10001 is closed, the contents of register 40020 are moved to a table starting with register 40051, one more than the reference number of the pointer register. The second time contact 10001 is closed, the data at 40020 are copied into register 40052. This continues until the pointer value in register 40050 reaches 10. At this point, the middle output, 00060,

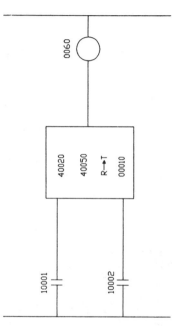

Figure 12-16 A register-to-table move.

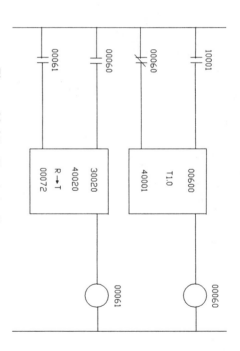

Figure 12-17 Circuit for Example 12-3.

turns ON, indicating the table is full. Closing contact 10002 will reset the pointer value to the beginning of the table and the cycle will repeat. A center contact can also be used with either a table-to-register or register-to-table move. This contact will prevent the pointer from incrementing when the contact is closed.

A temperature reading from a thermocouple is to be read and stored in a separate memory location every 10 minutes for 12 hours. The thermocouple is a transducer that converts temperature to voltage. The voltage signal is then fed into an analog input module. The module converts the analog signal into a digital combination of 16 bits. The address of the I/O connection to the thermocouple is 30020. Design the ladder logic circuit using a Modicon register-to-table instruction.

Solution

The circuit shown in Figure 12-17 will provide a temperature sample every 10 minutes. Because the samples are required to be stored over a 12-hour time period, 72 words are required for the table. The table begins at 40020. The timer is set to cycle at 600-second (10-minute) intervals. Each time the timer is reset, it provides a pulse to the R-T instruction and the pointer increments by 1. When the table is full, output 00061 is energized and the R-T instruction is reset.

12-6 FILE-TO-FILE MOVES

A file-to-file move copies the contents of one file, or table, into another file. With some PLCs, it is possible to specify how many locations are to be transferred during one scan. This is known as the "rate per scan." Data are moved between two tables in an Allen-Bradley PLC by a file-to-file move instruction. This instruction will copy a source file and transfer it to a destination file. The file can be between 1 and 999 words in length. The data, which can be entered into the function block for an Allen-Bradley file-to-file move instruction, are as follows:

COUNTER ADDRESS:	Address of the instruction in the accumulated value area of the data table.
POSITION:	Accumulated value of counter.
FILE LENGTH:	Number of words stored in file.
FILE A:	Source file starting address.
FILE R:	Destination file starting address.
RATE PER SCAN:	Number of data words moved each scan.

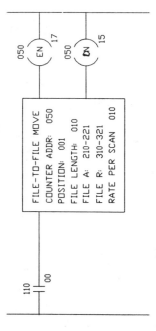

Figure 12-18 A file-to-file move.

ENABLE BIT (EN):   Automatically entered from counter address. Becomes energized when there is power flow to the function block.

DONE BIT (DN):   Automatically entered from counter address. Becomes energized when the file-to-file transfer is complete.

Figure 12-18 shows an example of an Allen-Bradley file-to-file move. When contact 110 00 is closed, the data are transferred from 10 words beginning at file address 210 to the file address beginning at 310. It is also possible to transfer data from input and output modules using a file-to-file move instruction.

File-to-file data transfers are considered to be internally indexed, meaning that the instruction indexes the counter and the number of files being moved is determined by the rate per scan. The three modes of operation for the rate per scan are as follows:

Complete mode: In this mode, rate per scan is equal to file length. Therefore, the entire file is transferred from the source to the destination in one program scan.

Distributed complete mode: This mode is selected when entire files are not required to be moved in one program scan. It is an advantage to use this mode when you are moving large files and the overall scan rate is noticeably slowed when all file information is transferred at once.

Incremental mode: The incremental mode allows data to be transferred one word at a time. In this mode, rate per scan is set at zero.

Modicon PLCs also perform table-to-table, or T-T, data transfers, as shown in Figure 12-19. Closing contact 10001 once will copy ten registers beginning at 40001 into 40050. One register is copied per scan. When the entire contents of

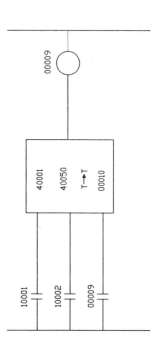

Figure 12-19 A table-to-table move.

the source table are copied, output 00009 is energized. Closing contact 10002 at any point during the data transfer will inhibit the transfer of data as long as the contact remains closed.

Modicon PLCs also have a Block Move instruction, BLKM, that allows the entire contents of a file to be copied in one scan. With the BLKM instruction, no pointer register is used. Figure 12-20 shows an example of a BLKM instruction. When contact 10001 is closed, the contents of the first eight registers beginning at 40001 are copied to the first eight registers beginning at 40050. Output 00060 will turn ON as soon as the transfer is complete.

Figure 12-20 A block transfer instruction.

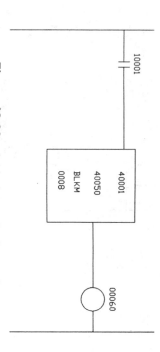

Figure 12-21 shows a three-phase motor with transducers for speed, torque, voltage, current, and power. These data are required to be copied from the memory locations shown to a file beginning at 40001 each time contact 10001 is closed. Write a program using a table-to-table move to accomplish this.

Solution

The ladder logic circuit for Example 12-4 is shown in Figure 12-22. Because there are five input registers, the table length is set at 5.

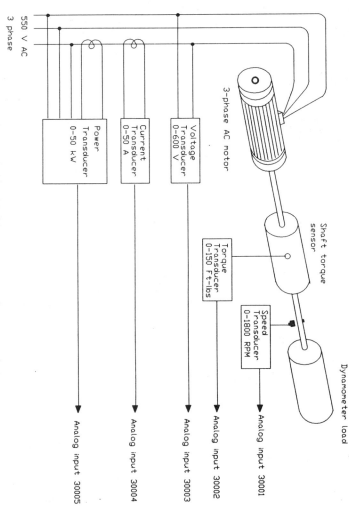

3-phase AC motor

Shaft torque sensor

Dynamometer load

Voltage Transducer 0–600 V

Current Transducer 0–50 A

Power Transducer 0–50 kW

Torque Transducer 0–150 Ft-lbs

Speed Transducer 0–1800 RPM

Analog input 30001

Analog input 30002

Analog input 30003

Analog input 30004

Analog input 30005

550 V AC
3 phase

Figure 12-21 Circuit for Example 12-4.

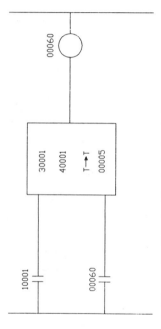

Figure 12-22 Ladder logic circuit for Example 12-4.

12-7 SHIFT REGISTERS

A *shift register* is a register that allows the shifting of bits through a single register, or group of registers. These types of registers are used for temporary storage, changing data from one format to another, sequence control, and timing circuits. When the instruction shifts individual bits of data, they are either shifted to the left or shifted to the right. Consequently, these registers are known as *shift right*, or *shift left* registers. The bit shift left register moves the data bit from the least-significant bit to the most-significant bit. Figure 12-23 shows how a processor shifts a data bit to the left through a 64-bit shift left register.

Figure 12-24 shows an example of a Texas Instruments shift left register instruction. This particular register is a function block format with three inputs. X1 is the shift clock pulse. When X1 is activated, the register shifts all bits one position. Contact X2 determines if a 1 or 0 is inserted in the register. Contact X3 is the reset/enable contact. When this input is opened, the register is cleared. Address Y17 is the starting address of the shift register. A typical bit shift register will consist of 1 to 16 bits. In Figure 12-24, register size is shown as eight bits, so outputs Y17 to Y24 will be controlled by the register. After eight clock pulses have occurred, the number of data bits will exceed the storage capacity of the register.

▶ *EXAMPLE 12-5*

A pass/fail inspection station is used in a conveyor system to keep track of defective parts as they move down the conveyor at an equal distance. A partially-completed part is moved down a conveyor to an inspector before proceeding to the final stages of manufacture. If a part is deemed defective, it is pointless to

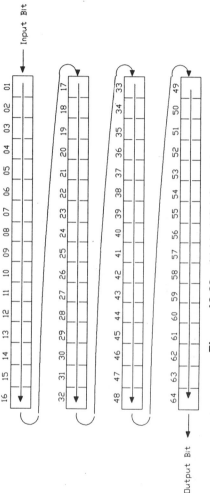

Figure 12-23 64-bit shift left register.

Figure 12-24 Shift register function block.

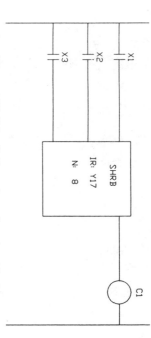

continue building it, so the part is identified as a reject. Before the part arrives at the reject bin, it must pass through five more zones of manufacture. Each station is equipped with a reject lamp to warn the assembler to ignore the part if the lamp is ON. Figure 12-25 shows a sketch of the conveyor circuit. When the workpiece reaches Zone 4, a diverter gate is activated to steer the defective piece into the reject bin.

Write a ladder logic program using a shift register that will accomplish the following:

1. A workpiece enters the inspection zone on the conveyor. The inspector examines the workpiece and presses the reject button if the workpiece fails inspection.

2. When the reject button is pressed, a 1 is applied to the data input line of the shift register.

3. The part proceeds through the inspection zone and activates limit switch X3. This limit switch provides the shift pulse for the register and resets the data input line to 0.

4. Each successive workpiece activating the limit switch will push the data bit one position down the register, energizing the reject lamps and finally the diverter gate.

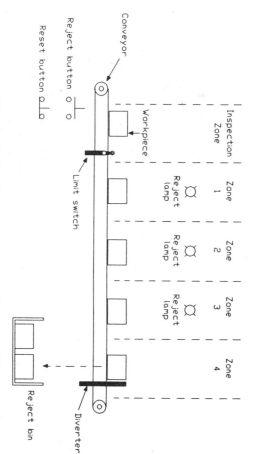

Figure 12-25 Conveyor circuit for Example 12-5.

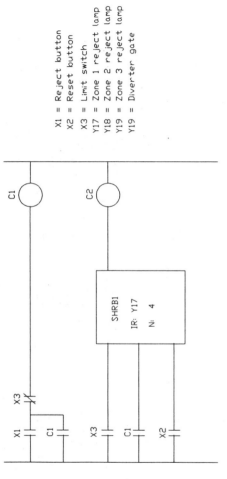

X1 = Reject button
X2 = Reset button
X3 = Limit switch
Y17 = Zone 1 reject lamp
Y18 = Zone 2 reject lamp
Y19 = Zone 3 reject lamp
Y19 = Diverter gate

Figure 12-26 Circuit for Example 12.5.

Solution

Figure 12-26 shows the ladder logic circuit for Example 12-5. In this circuit, pushbutton X1 is the reject button, X2 is the reset, and X3 is a limit switch that initiates the operation of the shift register. Outputs Y17, Y18, and Y19 control the reject lamps, and output Y20 operates the diverter gate.

Figure 12-27 illustrates how the processor shifts a data bit to the right through a group of four words in a file. This register is 64 bits long, and will require 64 input pulses to shift completely through the register. Each successive pulse will cause the first data bits fed into the register to be lost out of the end of the shift register. In this register, the first bit entered is the first bit to be pushed out of the register. This register is occasionally referred to as a First-In, First-Out (FIFO) register.

Figure 12-28 shows an example of an Allen-Bradley bit shift right function block. When input 112 00 is closed, a 1 is loaded into the shift register each time 110 00 changes state. The data bit begins at the most-significant bit and is shifted to the right on each clock pulse. In Figure 12-28, the register is eight bits long. If input 112 00 is high, a 1 will be loaded into address 010 07 on the first clock pulse. Each successive pulse will shift the bit one position to the right until, after eight clock pulses, the bit is shifted to address 010 00. On the ninth clock pulse, output 012 00 becomes energized.

There are two basic types of PLC word shift registers: FIFO and LIFO. A FIFO or First-In, First-Out operation is a file, or queue, where the first data

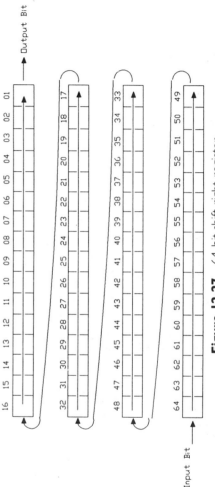

Figure 12-27 64-bit shift right register.

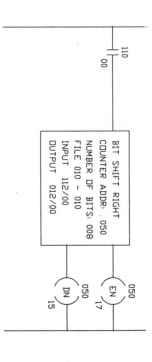

Figure 12-28 Allen-Bradley bit shift right function block.

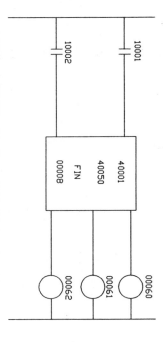

Figure 12-29 Modicon FIFO IN function block.

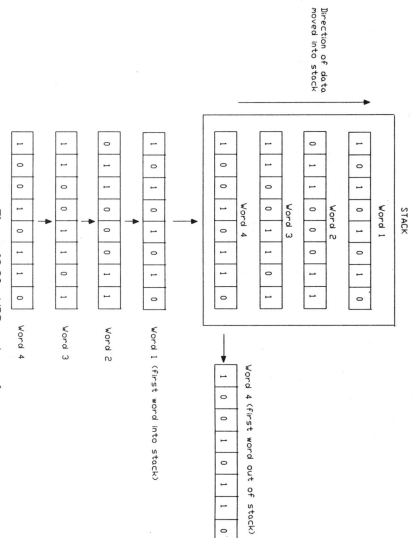

Figure 12-30 LIFO stack transfer.

written into the file are the first data read from the file. PLC systems that have a FIFO instruction generally shift the data one word at a time. The data written into this type of FIFO memory will push, or shift, all subsequent data toward the bottom by one location. For a FIFO instruction with eight locations, this would require that eight data entries be made before the first entry is available to be read at the bottom of the FIFO. The FIFO operation usually consists of two function blocks: FIFO IN and FIFO OUT. FIFO IN loads the queue and FIFO OUT unloads it.

A typical application of a FIFO instruction controls inventory in a manufacturing plant. If 100 different pieces are required to be manufactured, each part would be assigned a different code. As the PLC begins the manufacturing process, each code is automatically pulled out in a sequence determined by the FIFO. Figure 12-29 illustrates a FIFO IN function block used by Modicon PLCs. Register 40050 is the pointer register. Each time input 10001 is closed, the contents of address 40001 are moved to consecutive addresses beginning at 40051. The length of the file is shown as 00008, which means the queue is full after eight input pulses. Output 00060 indicates that the function block is operating. 00061 is energized when the queue is full, and 00062 is ON when the queue is empty. Input 10002 is used to clear the queue and reset the pointer.

A LIFO, or Last-In, First-Out, instruction inverts the order of the data it receives by outputting the last data received first and the first data received last. Essentially, a LIFO is a stack that allows data to be added without disturbing the data already contained in the stack. Figure 12-30 shows the operation of four word locations loaded into and out of a LIFO stack. When the control input logic for the LIFO instruction is activated, Word 1 is loaded into the stack. On the second input pulse, Word 2 is loaded, followed by Word 3, and Word 4. The stack shows the position of the four word locations after four input pulses have been applied. A LIFO OUT instruction will transfer the contents of the stack to an output location in the reverse order that the data were loaded. Consequently, Word 4 is the first location moved from the stack of Figure 12-30.

REVIEW QUESTIONS

12-1. List two types of data transfer.

12-2. What is meant by the term "block transfer?"

12-3. A holding register is
(a) used to transfer more than one register at a time.
(b) used to store data regarding the internal operation of a processor.
(c) the area set aside for the storage of data for discrete I/O.
(d) used for data transfer.

12-4. Input and output registers are
(a) used to store data regarding the internal operation of a processor.
(b) single-bit memory locations set aside for data storage.
(c) 16-bit memory locations.
(d) used for data transfer.

12-5. What are the two number systems PLCs use to store data in registers?

12-6. Describe the purpose of a sign bit.

12-7. The procedure of storing data in a register is called
(a) scanning.
(b) reading.
(c) writing.
(d) shifting.

12-8. When data are transferred from one location to another, are the data erased in the source register? Explain.

12-9. The transfer of data from one word location to another word location is called

    (a) a file-to-file move.

    (b) a file-to-register move.

    (c) a register-to-file move.

    (d) a register-to-register move.

12-10. What are two instructions used by Allen-Bradley for register-to-register moves?

12-11. Pointer registers

    (a) tell the processor the address where data are stored or taken from.

    (b) are used to transfer more than one register at a time.

    (c) are the area set aside for storage of data for discrete I/O.

    (d) are used to store data regarding the internal operation of a processor.

12-12. What is the difference between an input register and a holding register?

12-13. In a table-to-register move, describe the purpose of the pointer register.

12-14. A register-to-table move is the same as

    (a) a file-to-word move.

    (b) a file-to-file move.

    (c) a word-to-file move.

    (d) a word-to-word move.

12-15. File-to-file data transfers are considered to be internally indexed. What does this mean?

12-16. Explain the basic operation of a shift register.

12-17. List two types of shift registers.

12-18. What is a FIFO register?

12-19. Explain the difference between a FIFO register and a LIFO register.

13

Math Functions

Upon completion of this chapter, you will be able to

▶ List three types of data comparison.

▶ Explain the Addition function.

▶ Subtract two numbers using a PLC.

▶ Multiply and divide two numbers.

▶ Define the terms "scaling" and "ramping."

▶ Use the Square Root instruction.

▶ Combine math functions.

13-1 INTRODUCTION

The basic mathematic functions performed by most PLCs are: add, subtract, multiply, and divide. These types of instructions are used by PLCs to gather data from various memory locations, to compare data, and to scale values. Data comparison is an extremely useful programming tool that allows outputs to be energized depending on whether data in one memory location are greater than, less than, or equal to data stored in another memory location. Scaling is also an important application of math functions because it allows numbers which are very small or large to be enlarged or reduced by a fixed constant. The standard format for math functions in a PLC is that the desired math operation is performed on a memory location, and not directly on a number. In other words, if you wish to add two numbers, these numbers must be entered into memory locations, and the contents of the addresses will be added together.

Data comparison is a standard function performed by most PLCs. This instruction can be used to compare the contents of memory locations, to compare a varying count to a fixed value, or to compare varying input values over a certain time period. Most PLCs have the following comparison functions:

Compare Equal:

Generally used to compare the contents of two memory locations for an equal condition. If both locations are equal, the output coil associated with the function will be energized.

Compare Less Than:

If the contents in one register are less than the other, the output coil becomes energized.

Compare Greater Than:

Performed on two memory locations, and will energize an output if the contents of one location are greater than the other.

Figure 13-1 shows an example of an Allen-Bradley Compare Equal instruction. An Equal To comparison is made with the word location designated by the GET instruction. The number 100, which is entered in the Equal To instruction, is the number which is being compared. If the contents of location 070 equal the number 100, output 010 00 will be energized. Output 010 00 will remain OFF for any other value in location 070. If 070 were a counter, output 010 00 would be energized when the accumulative count reaches 100.

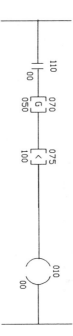

Figure 13-1   Compare Equal instruction.

Figure 13-2 shows an example of an Allen-Bradley Less Than instruction. The value displayed below the Less Than instruction is referred to as the reference value. If the value stored at location 070 is less than the reference value, output 010 00 will be energized. If the GET value is greater than the value at 075, the output coil will be OFF.

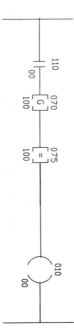

Figure 13-2   Less Than instruction.

An example of an Allen-Bradley Greater Than instruction is shown in Figure 13-3. The Less Than instruction is used for both Less Than and Greater Than instructions. In this circuit, the value retrieved by the GET instruction is the reference value. When the Less Than value is larger than the GET value, output 010 00 becomes energized. For any other value, the output coil remains OFF.

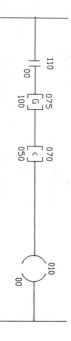

Figure 13-3   Greater Than instruction.

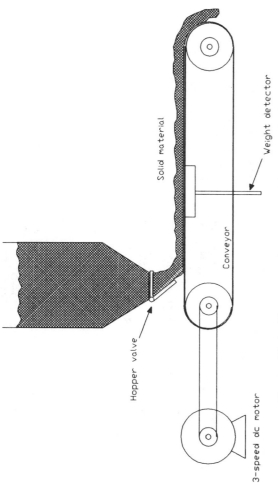

Figure 13-4 Three-speed conveyor with weight detector.

► *EXAMPLE 13-1*

Figure 13-4 is a conveyor system with a weight detector and three-speed motor. The system is designed to move the conveyor belt at a certain speed when a specific value of weight is on the conveyor. If the weight exceeds the preset value, the conveyor speed increases to move the material off the belt at a faster rate. If the weight falls below the preset value, the conveyor speed is reduced. When output 010 00 is energized, the motor runs at normal speed. When 010 01 is ON, resistance is added to the DC motor windings to slow the conveyor down. When 010 02 is energized, resistance is removed from the windings to speed up the motor. Address 200 is the reference location of the weight detector. The preset value is 350. Address 150 stores the data obtained from the weight detector.

Write a ladder logic program using Compare instructions to automatically change the speed of the motor.

Solution

Figure 13-5 shows the ladder logic circuit for Example 13-1. When Start button, 110 01, is pressed, the conveyor begins moving. Address 200 is the reference address and contains the number 350. Address 150 stores the data from the weight detector. If the data in address 150 are equal to the data in address 200, the motor

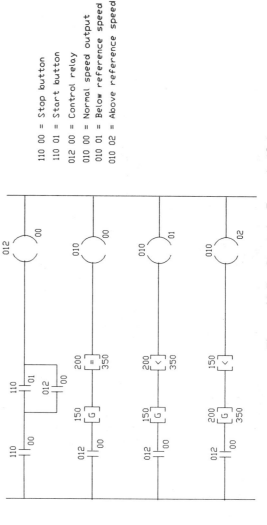

110 00 = Stop button
110 01 = Start button
012 00 = Control relay
010 00 = Normal speed output
010 01 = Below reference speed
010 02 = Above reference speed

Figure 13-5 Circuit for Example 13-1.

Figure 13-6 Modicon Compare function.

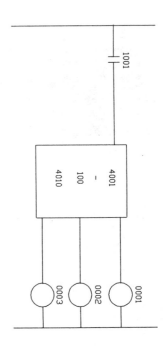

operates at normal speed. If the input data increase above the reference value due to more weight on the conveyor, output 010 02 is energized and the motor speed increases. If the input data fall below the preset of 350, output 010 01 is ON, and the motor speed is reduced.

Modicon PLCs use a subtract function block to perform compare operations. Figure 13-6 shows an example of a Modicon Compare instruction. In this circuit, the number 100 is being compared with the data in memory location 4001. If the data in 4001 are equal to 100, output 0002 will be energized. If the data in 4001 are greater than 100, output 0001 will be energized. If the data in 4001 are less than 100, output 0003 will be ON.

Figure 13-7 illustrates a circuit using a Texas Instruments Compare instruction. When the data stored at memory location V1 are equal to the data stored at location V2, output Y17 will be energized. When the data at V1 are less than the contents of V2, output Y18 is ON. When V2 is less than V1, output Y19 is energized.

Figure 13-7 Texas Instruments Compare function.

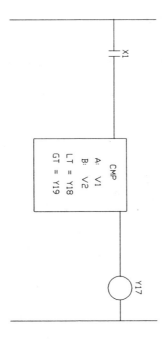

▲
EXAMPLE 13-2

Figure 13-8 shows a paper thickness controlling system that uses a PLC to compare the thickness of the wet fiber to a constant stored in memory. If the data obtained by the measurement transducer are greater than the setpoint, output 0001 is energized and the worm screw motor increases the tension between the movable roller and large fixed motor. If the input data are less than the setpoint, output 0002 is energized and the worm screw motor decreases the tension on the conveyor.

Write a program using a Modicon Compare function to control the system. Use memory location 3001 as the analog input address for the measurement transducer, and assume the number 2500 is the setpoint for data comparison.

Solution

The ladder logic circuit for Example 13-2 is shown in Figure 13-9. When the Start button is pressed, output 0003 is energized and the conveyor begins moving. As the data are loaded into memory location 3001, they are compared to the setpoint value of 2500. If the analog input data are greater than the setpoint, 0001 is energized. If the input data are less than the setpoint, 0002 is energized.

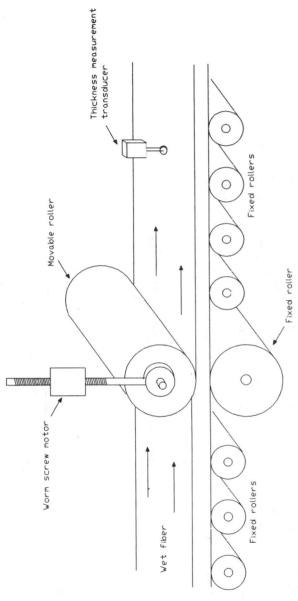

Figure 13-8

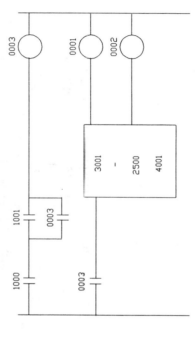

Figure 13-9 Circuit for Example 13-2.

13-3 ADDITION

The Add instruction allows PLCs to add the contents of registers together and store the result in a memory location. Allen-Bradley PLCs use GET instructions to retrieve data from registers. The result of the math instruction is stored at the memory location designated by the function coil. Figure 13-10 shows an example of an Add instruction using an Allen-Bradley PLC. When contact 110 00 is closed, the contents of memory location 070 are added to the contents of location 071, and the result is stored in memory location 072. Therefore, when 110 00 is closed, the number 450 should now be displayed below the Add instruction, because this is the number which is now in location 072.

If the numbers being added together in an Allen-Bradley instruction exceed 999, the overflow bit, bit 14, is energized. In Figure 13-11, when contact 110 00 is closed, the numbers 850 and 900 are added together and the result, 1750, is

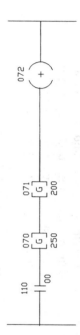

Figure 13-10 Allen-Bradley Add instruction.

stored at 072. Output 010 00 will also be energized because the overflow bit, 072 14, was set.

Once a number has been loaded into a memory location, the only way that number can be erased is by loading the number zero into that address. Figure 13-12 shows a modified version of Figure 13-9 in which a reset instruction has been added for the math function. When contact 110 00 is closed, the number 1750 is loaded into address 072 and output 010 00 becomes energized. The number 750 will appear in the accumulative location below the CTR instruction. Because this location is only three digits long, the last three numbers taken from 072 will be stored at the ACC of the CTR. The fact that only three digits are moved from a math instruction can cause problems if the math destination address is to be used for data transfer or comparison functions. However, the contents of location 072 will be completely erased when 110 01 is closed, even though the true number in 072 was never displayed by the accumulative register of the CTR instruction.

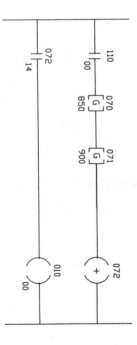

Figure 13-11 Add instruction with overflow bit.

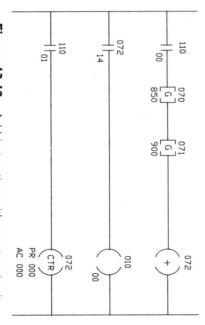

Figure 13-12 Add instruction with counter circuit.

▼
EXAMPLE 13-3

Figure 13-13 shows two conveyors used in a manufacturing process. Each conveyor has a proximity switch to count the workpieces as they pass by. Design a circuit that can obtain a total count from the two individual conveyors.

Solution

The ladder logic circuit for Example 13-3 is shown in Figure 13-14. In this circuit, each time either proximity switch closes, the total count is increased by 1.

Modicon PLCs use function blocks for math operations. The main difference between a Modicon math instruction and an Allen-Bradley PLC-2 math function is that Modicon allows you to directly add numbers together if required. This means that numbers do not have to be placed in memory locations before they are used in a math function. Contents of memory locations can also be used in

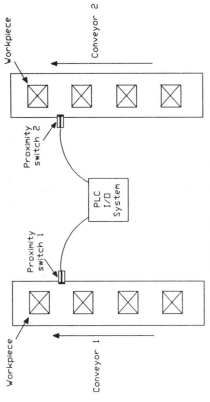

Figure 13-13 Top view of two conveyors.

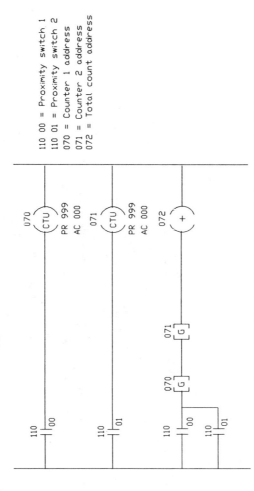

110 00 = Proximity switch 1
110 01 = Proximity switch 2
070 = Counter 1 address
071 = Counter 2 address
072 = Total count address

Figure 13-14 Ladder logic circuit for Example 13-3.

math functions using Modicon PLCs. Some typical addresses for a Modicon PLC are as follows:

3001 to 3032 are input registers
4001 to 4126 are holding registers

Figure 13-15 shows an example of a Modicon Add function where a number is to be added to the contents of a memory location and the result is to be stored in a memory location. In this example, the number 200 is to be added to the contents of register 4001 and the result is to be placed in register 4005. Depending on your Modicon system, the maximum number that can be stored in a register

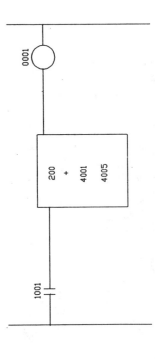

Figure 13-15 Modicon Add function.

is either 999 or 9999. In this circuit, we shall assume 999 is the maximum. Output coil 0001 is an overflow output for the Add instruction. When the numbers being added have a result which is greater than 999, output 0001 is energized. If the number is less than 999, 0001 remains OFF.

With a Modicon Add instruction, it is possible to use the function as a counter. For example, if the number in a memory location is to increase by 1 each time the input is closed, the circuit would appear as shown in Figure 13-16. In this circuit, each time pushbutton 1002 is pressed, the contents of register 4002 increase by 1.

Texas Instruments PLCs also use function blocks to perform math instructions. Inside the function block is A:, B:, and C:. The Add function adds the contents of memory location A to the contents of memory location B, and stores the result in memory location C. The addresses designated by A, B, and C can be either V locations or WY locations. The maximum number that can be stored in a V or WY location is 32,767. Figure 13-17 shows an example of a Texas Instruments Add instruction. In this circuit, the accumulated value of Counter 1 (TCC1) is to be added to the accumulated value of Counter 2 (TCC2), and the result stored in location WY1.

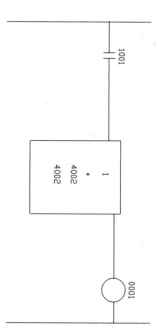

Figure 13-16   Counter circuit using Add instruction.

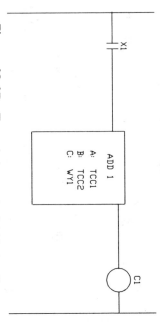

Figure 13-17   Texas Instruments Add instruction.

13-4   SUBTRACTION

The basic operation of subtraction is very similar to that of addition. The subtraction function is more versatile due to its ability to compare quantities and energize one or more outputs based on the value of the quantities. Some PLCs, such as Modicon, use the subtraction function to perform "less than," "greater than," and "equal to" operations.

The Subtraction function for a Modicon PLC allows you to either subtract numbers directly, or subtract the contents of memory locations. Figure 13-18 shows an example of a Modicon Subtraction instruction. The contents of location 4010 are to be subtracted from 4001, and the result is to be entered in address 4020. Contact 1000 is the input instruction, and 0001, 0002, and 0003 are the output

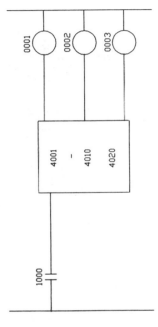

Figure 13-18 Modicon Subtract instruction.

coils. If the contents of location 4001 are greater than 4010, output 0001 will be ON. If 4001 and 4010 are equal, 0002 is ON. If the contents of 4010 are greater than the contents of 4001, output 0003 will be energized.

A typical Allen-Bradley PLC system will use the Subtraction function to subtract the contents of two memory locations and store the result in a third location. When the difference between the two locations is a negative number, the underflow bit, bit 16, is energized. A negative symbol will appear below the Subtraction instruction if the result of the two locations is negative. Figure 13-19 shows an example of a subtraction function using an Allen-Bradley PLC. When contact 110 00 is closed, the contents of memory location 071 are subtracted from 070 and the result is placed in 072. Because 071 contains a larger number than 070, the result is a negative value and the underflow bit is energized. This means that output 010 00 will also become energized when 110 00 is closed.

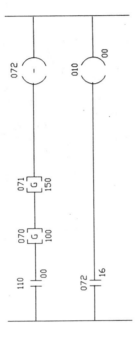

Figure 13-19 Allen-Bradley Subtraction instruction with underflow bit.

▶ *EXAMPLE 13-4*

Figure 13-20 shows a main conveyor with a diverter gate for defective parts to be fed onto a rejection conveyor. If a workpiece fails inspection, the diverter gate is energized and the part is routed onto the reject conveyor. One counter is situated

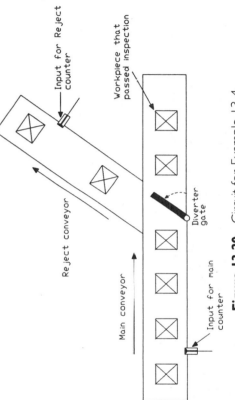

Figure 13-20 Circuit for Example 13-4.

on the main conveyor at the inspection station. The other counter is on the reject conveyor. Write a program using an Allen-Bradley Subtraction function that will determine the number of parts that pass inspection.

Solution

Figure 13-21 shows the ladder logic circuit for Example 13-4. In this circuit, address 070 contains the total number of parts that have been rejected, and address 072 stores the difference between 070 and 071.

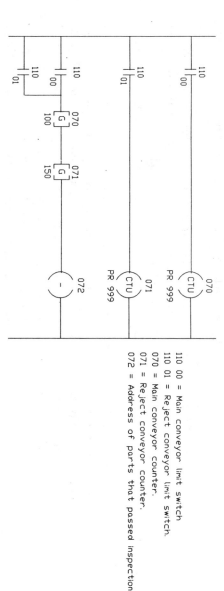

110 00 = Main conveyor limit switch
110 01 = Reject conveyor limit switch.
070 = Main conveyor counter.
071 = Reject conveyor counter.
072 = Address of parts that passed inspection

Figure 13-21 Ladder logic circuit for Example 13-4.

The Subtraction function on a Texas Instruments PLC subtracts the contents in memory location B from the contents in location A and stores the result in memory location C. If the result is a negative number, the value displayed in memory location C will be equal to 65,536 - (B - A). The circuit shown in Figure 13-22 is an example of a Texas Instruments Subtraction function. The number 100 has been entered into location V1, and the number 150 has been entered into location V2. When X1 is closed, V2 is subtracted from V1 and the result is entered in V3. In this example, the result will be negative, so the number which will appear at V3 is equal to 65,536 - (150 - 100), or 65,486.

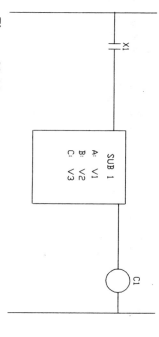

Figure 13-22 Texas Instruments Subtract instruction.

13-5 MULTIPLICATION

Most PLCs require two memory locations as destination addresses for a Multiplication function. This is generally referred to as *double precision*. When a PLC requires two memory locations for a math function, it is recommended that consecutive addresses be used. Allen-Bradley PLC-2 systems use two output coil instructions, as shown in Figure 13-23, to perform this function. The first destination address contains the most-significant digits, and the second word location contains

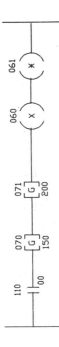

Figure 13-23 Allen-Bradley Multiplication instruction.

the least-significant digits. If the product of the two numbers being multiplied is less than six digits, zeroes will be placed to the left of the result.

The circuit shown in Figure 13-23 will multiply the number stored at location 070 by the number stored at location 071. Because the numbers to be multiplied are 150 and 200, the result, 30,000, will be entered at locations 060 and 061. When contact 110 00 is closed, the values at 060 and 061 will be as follows:

$$060 = 030 \quad 061 = 000$$

The three least-significant digits of the number 30,000 are 000 and the next most-significant digits are 30. Because the register requires three digits, it fills the last digit with 0.

Modicon uses two destination addresses for its Multiplication function. Figure 13-24 shows an example of a Modicon Multiplication instruction. The maximum number that can be entered in any of the memory locations is 999. The result of the Multiplication instruction will be stored at registers 4010 and 4011. If register 4001 contains 150, and 4002 contains 200, the result will be stored in the destination addresses as follows:

$$4010 = 030 \quad 4011 = 000$$

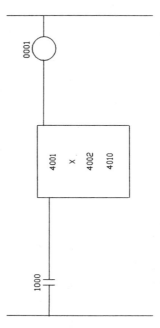

Figure 13-24 Modicon Multiplication function.

These data are stored in the two memory locations of a Modicon system in the same manner as the Allen-Bradley PLC. Consequently, the maximum number that can be stored in the two destination addresses is 999,999.

The Multiplication function is used extensively in control circuits where *scaling* is required. Scaling is the process of multiplying or dividing the contents of a register by a set value. It is often used in motor speed control circuits for *ramping*. Ramp circuits are designed to increase a quantity, such as voltage, at a linear rate. For example, assume an analog output module point has been calibrated to produce 0 - 10 V when the decimal equivalent in its register is between 0 and 32,000. If we want the analog output signal to increase at a rate of 0.1 V/s, it would be necessary to use a scaling function. Figure 13-25 shows a ladder logic circuit that will produce a ramp voltage at address 250. The counter and timer produce a count that increases linearly with time. Every tenth of a second, the data stored at counter 071 increases. The data stored in the accumulated

13-6 DIVISION

count are multiplied by the scaling constant and the result placed in register 250. The scaling constant is determined as follows:

1. The maximum output voltage is 10 V when the number 32,000 is in the analog output register. If the ramp rate is 0.1 V/s, it will take 100 seconds to change from 0 V to 10 V.

2. To reach maximum voltage at a rate of change of 0.1 V/s, 100 increments are required. Therefore, the decimal number in location 250 must change at a rate of

$$32,000/100 = 320$$

The scaling constant is 320 and is stored in register 300, as shown in Figure 13-25. The contents of counter 071 are multiplied by the number 320 every tenth of a second, and the output voltage ramps increase at a linear rate.

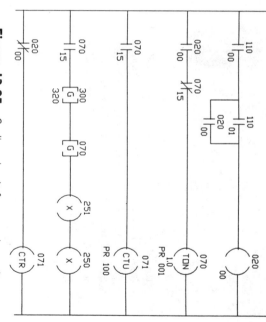

Figure 13-25   Scaling circuit for ramping voltage.

The Division function is often used for scaling operations and for ramping down analog output signals. Allen-Bradley PLCs use the Division function to perform quotient calculation of two numbers. The result of two values stored in GET instructions is placed in two addresses specified by the Division instruction. The first GET is divided by the second GET. The quotient is stored in two DIVIDE instruction words. In Allen-Bradley systems, the quotient is expressed as a decimal, accurate to three decimal places. Fractions are rounded off. The first destination address contains the most-significant digits and the second address contains the least-significant digits. Figure 13-26 shows an example of an Allen-Bradley Division function. When contact 110 00 is closed, the number 35 is divided by 100 and the result appears in the destination addresses as follows:

$$060 = 000 \qquad 061 = .350$$

In Figure 13-26, if address 070 contained the number 100, and 071 contained 35, the destination addresses would contain

$$060 = 002 \qquad 061 = .857$$

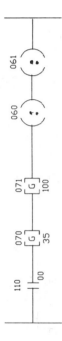

Figure 13-26 Allen-Bradley Division function.

Figure 13-27 shows an example of a Modicon Division instruction. The Modicon Division function requires two consecutive memory locations for the dividend. In Figure 13-27, the dividend is stored in locations 4001 and 4002. The maximum value that can be entered into the quotient, in this case 4010, is 999. The resultant is stored in memory locations 4015 and 4016. The output coil, 0001, will be energized if the resultant is too large for the destination register.

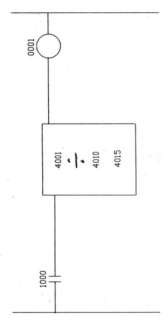

Figure 13-27 Modicon Division function.

13-7 SQUARE ROOT

Some PLCs have a Square Root instruction which is used to calculate the square root of a number and store the value in a memory location. Figure 13-28 shows an example of a Texas Instruments Square Root instruction. This function requires two memory locations for a source address. In Figure 13-28, the source addresses are V1 and V2, and the destination address is V10. When contact X1 is closed, the function calculates the square root of V1 and V2 and places the result in V10. The numbers in locations V1 and V2 must be positive integer values or the function will not be performed.

If the source number is negative, or greater than 32,767, the output coil will not be energized, and a square root error function will occur. In situations, such as scaling functions, when it is critical that a math function take place, it is often necessary to program a warning system into the process to ensure that the operator is aware that a failure has occurred in a math function. Figure 13-29 shows an example of such a warning system. When contact X1 is closed, the Square Root function should be executed. If the function is not completed, output C1 will not energize. This will cause output Y17 to turn ON, which could activate a pilot light or audible alarm to direct attention to the function failure.

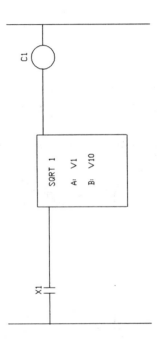

Figure 13-28 Texas Instruments Square Root function.

13-8 COMBINING MATH FUNCTIONS

In many process control systems using math functions, it is often necessary to combine instructions to solve for particular applications. The following examples illustrate some typical applications for combined math functions.

▼ EXAMPLE 13-5

An Allen-Bradley program must convert degrees Fahrenheit to degrees Celsius. The Fahrenheit data are loaded into memory location 200 via a thermocouple and analog input card. The equation for conversion is

$$^\circ C = 5/9 (^\circ F - 32)$$

Solution

The following five registers are used for the above equation:

$$^\circ F = 200$$
$$5 = 275$$
$$9 = 225$$
$$^\circ C = 300$$
$$32 = 350$$

The ladder logic circuit of Figure 13-30 shows how the equation was solved. The contents of register 350 were subtracted from register 200 and stored in register 325. This value was next multiplied by 5 and stored in registers 250 and 251. The result was then divided by 9 and the °C equivalent was stored in address 300.

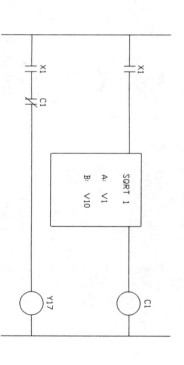

Figure 13-29 Square Root instruction with negative integer indicator.

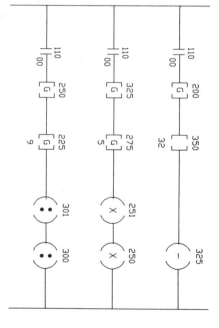

Figure 13-30 Ladder logic circuit for Example 13-5.

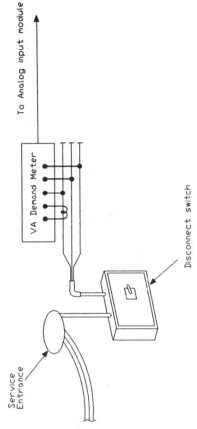

Figure 13-31 Power demand monitoring system.

▶ *EXAMPLE 13-6*

Figure 13-31 shows a power demand monitoring system. In this circuit, an industrial service feed is to be monitored and controlled to maintain a power demand of 500 kVA or less. The 550 V, three-phase power is fed from a 1,000 A disconnect switch. A 0 - 600 kVA demand meter with a linear 0 - 10 V analog output is used to monitor the power feed. Assume an analog input module for the PLC provides full-scale input (10 V) when the integer 4000 is in analog input address 200.

Solution

The ladder logic circuit is shown in Figure 13-32. The setpoint data (500 kVA) are stored in location 300. Multiply and divide instructions scale the analog input. Because 500 kVA is the setpoint and 4000 is the maximum value, the scaling constant per kVA is 500/4000 = 0.125. For a scaling value of this size to be processed by the PLC, it must be multiplied by 1000. Therefore, the number 125 is stored in location 250 and the number 1000 is entered into address 350.

In Figure 13-32, when contact 110 00 is closed, the data from the analog input module are multiplied by the scaling constant 125 and stored in location 400. The data in address 400 are then divided by 1000 and compared to the setpoint data in location 300. If the input data are less than or equal to the reference data, output 010 00 is ON. If the input is greater than the scaling constant, output 010 01 is energized.

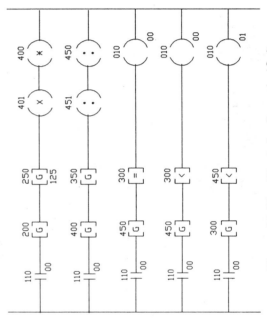

Figure 13-32 Circuit for Example 13-6.

REVIEW QUESTIONS

13-1. List three types of data comparison functions.

13-2. On most PLC systems, the ADD instruction is used to
    (a) add numbers directly.
    (b) add the contents of registers.
    (c) add files.
    (d) none of the above.

13-3. What is the purpose of the overflow bit in an Add instruction?

13-4. In the circuit of Figure 13-33, what is the purpose of output 0001?

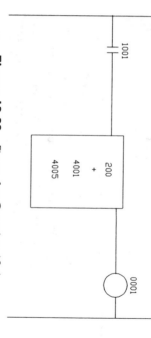

Figure 13-33 Figure for Question 13.4.

13-5. What function does the circuit shown in Figure 13-34 perform?

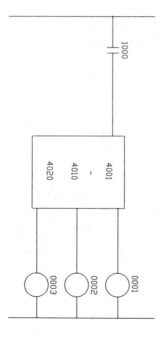

Figure 13-34 Figure for Question 13.5.

13-6. For the circuit shown in Figure 13-35, when does output 010 00 become energized?

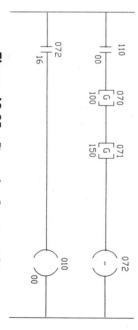

Figure 13-35 Figure for Question 13.6.

13-7. What is meant by the term "double precision"?

13-8. Define "scaling."

13-9. Why would it be necessary to ramp an analog output signal?

13-10. How many memory locations are needed to store the result of a Division function?

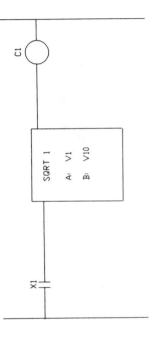

Figure 13-36 Figure for Question 13.11.

13-11. Explain the operation of the circuit shown in Figure 13-36.

Process Control

Upon completion of this chapter, you will be able to

▼ Define process control.

▼ Explain the purpose of block diagrams.

▼ Express the relationship between input and output as a transfer function.

▼ Recognize the symbol for a summing point.

▼ Define the term "transducer."

▼ Differentiate between open-loop and closed-loop control.

▼ Explain transient response.

▼ Understand the purpose of damping.

▼ List the four points required for a successful algorithm.

▼ Draw a flowchart.

▼ Explain proportional, integral, and derivative control.

▼ Understand the application of PID modules.

▼ List three analog input devices.

▼ Name two types of analog output devices.

14-1 INTRODUCTION

In this chapter, we shall examine PLC applications in the field of process control. By definition, *process control* implies the automatic regulation of a control system. The ability of a PLC to perform math functions and utilize analog signals makes it ideally suited for this type of operation. Typical applications of process control systems are in the manufacturing or processing of products in industry. These systems are used extensively in automobile assembly, petrochemical production, oil refineries, nuclear and fossil power plants, food processing, etc. In fact, any operation that requires the manipulation and control of one or more variables is a type of process control system. The most common controlled variables in a process are temperature, flow rate, pressure, and level. Other variables include density, viscosity, color, conductivity, composition, and pH levels.

14-2 BLOCK DIAGRAMS

Block diagrams are often used in control system analysis to represent a process control system as a series of interconnected blocks. Each block represents a component in the system and the lines connecting the blocks represent the signal paths. The advantage of using block diagrams is that it allows the process control system to be analyzed as the interaction of small, simple subsystems.

In mathematical terms, a block diagram is a schematic representation of a system in terms of its component parts where each component is represented by its transfer function. The term *transfer function* describes the relationship between the input and output of any element in the process control system. For example, if a thermocouple produces 0.2 volts for every 1° F change in temperature, the transfer function would be 0.2 volts/°F. In addition to the size relationship between the input and output, transfer functions often indicate the time interval of this relationship.

Figure 14-1(b) shows a basic process control block diagram for a control valve. The position of the valve dial setting in Figure 14-1(a) determines the flow rate through the device. In Figure 14-1(b), the valve setting is shown as the input to the block, and the flow rate of the valve is shown as the output. When two or

Figure 14-1 (a) Needle valve; (b) Block diagram.

more signals intersect in a block diagram, a *summing point* is used to show how the signals are combined. Figure 14-2 shows the block diagram symbol for a summing point and the three signals involved. The setpoint represents the reference value for the system. In process control circuitry, the term *error signal* is considered to be the difference between the measured value and the desired value, or setpoint. In equation form,

$$error = measured\ value - setpoint$$

As mentioned in Chapter 13, the PLC is ideally suited for this type of control because the Compare instruction is able to utilize the measured value and setpoint to produce a corresponding output.

Figure 14-3 shows a typical block diagram for a process control system. This particular system uses a PLC to control the flow rate of a process by actuating a valve positioner. The PLC compares the differential pressure measurement with the setpoint and actuates the valve positioner's voltage-to-pressure transducer. A *transducer* is a device that converts one form of energy to another. The transducer causes the flow rate through the valve to either increase or decrease depending on the signal from the PLC. The process, which in this case is the flow, is then

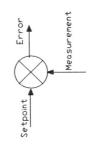

Figure 14-2 Symbol for summing point.

14-3   OPEN-LOOP AND CLOSED-LOOP SYSTEMS

measured and the result sent to the PLC's analog input module via a pressure-to-voltage transducer. This cycle of sampling and correcting can occur as often as thousands of times per second for an infinite time period.

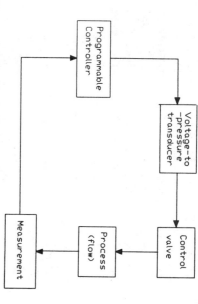

Figure 14-3   Block diagram of a process control system.

The measured signal in Figure 14-3 is referred to as *feedback* because it is taking a portion of the output and returning it to the input. The direction of the feedback is determined by the direction in which the measured value signal travels in the block diagram. The feedback used in process control systems is called *closed-loop*. The term "closed-loop" refers to the loop created by the feedback path. Control systems that do not use feedback are referred to as *open-loop* due to the fact that they have no loop in the block diagram.

Figure 14-4(a) shows an example of an open-loop fluid level control system. In this circuit, a manual valve and sighting tube are used to maintain the fluid level in the tank at a desired level. The valve setting is initially adjusted to establish an inflow, or *manipulated variable*, equal to the outflow rate. This allows the operator to maintain the level, or *controlled variable*, within the prescribed limits

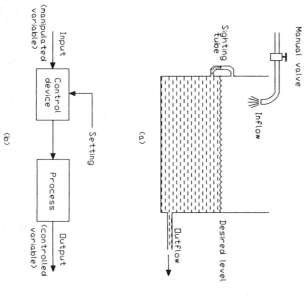

Figure 14-4   (a) Open-loop system; (b) Block diagram.

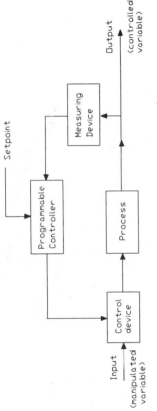

Figure 14-5 Closed-loop fluid-level control system.

of operation. If the outflow rate should vary, the valve setting would have to be manually adjusted to correct the imbalance. Figure 14-4(b) shows the open-loop block diagram for the circuit of Figure 14-4(a).

Essentially, the act of turning a valve to compensate for the change in outflow is a type of feedback. The circuit of Figure 14-4(a) requires a human operator to examine the sighting tube for level, and manually adjust the valve to compensate. If the human is replaced by a PLC, the system would become closed-loop, and would be capable of providing frequent, rapid, and precise corrections for the desired level. Figure 14-5 shows the block diagram for a PLC-controlled closed-loop system. In this system, setpoint data are entered into a memory location in the processor, and the measured variable is compared against the setpoint value. A decision is made by the processor based on these data and the automatic valve positioner is adjusted by the analog output signal from the PLC.

The measuring device shown as a block function in Figure 14-5 is a transmitter, or sensor, that senses the value of the controlled variable and changes it into a usable signal for the PLC. This type of measuring device is usually shown as a single block, although it often consists of both a primary sensing device and signal transducer. The sensing device could be a thermocouple, thermistor, or Resistance Temperature Detector (RTD). The signal transducer converts the primary quantity (resistance, temperature, etc.) into a usable electric signal for the PLC's analog input module. Typical signals produced by these transducers are 0 - 10 V, and 4 - 20 mA.

Four variables associated with closed-loop control are generally taken as the criteria for evaluating the performance of a process control system. These variables are transient response, steady-state error, stability, and sensitivity.

Transient Response. The main function of a process control loop is to maintain a dynamic variable at a prescribed operating point. A *dynamic variable* is any physical parameter that can change either spontaneously, or because of external influences. By using a control loop, external influences that would cause the dynamic variable to fluctuate are minimized. Figure 14-6 shows the output response curves for tank level and valve position used in the system of Figure 14-4. When the valve is open, the tank begins to fill at a fixed rate. If the length of pipe between the valve and tank is quite long, the tank would continue to fill even after the input valve is shut OFF. This is called *overshoot*. Conversely, if the lower limit of the desired level is reached, a certain time delay will occur before liquid from the valve reaches the tank. Because the tank continues to drain during this delay, the liquid may fall below the lower limit required. This is referred to as *undershoot*.

Damping is a method used to reduce overshoot in a process control system. Different types of damping are employed to compensate for external influences on quantities being measured. For example, stepper motors are affected by resonance when controlling high inertia loads. This type of resonance will cause the rotor to fall out of step with the input command. When the natural resonant frequency

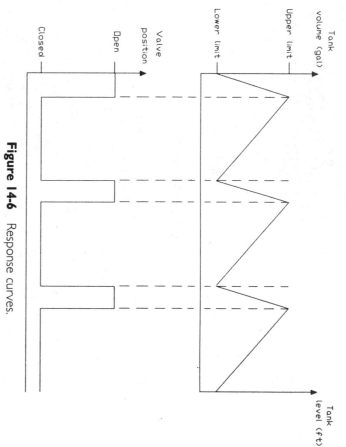

Figure 14-6 Response curves.

of a stepper motor is reached, it will oscillate around a certain point. A typical closed-loop system will have a setpoint for the dynamic variable and an allowable deviation about this setpoint. The *settling time* is the time required for the loop to bring the dynamic variable back to within allowable range after a transient input or change in setpoint has occurred.

Depending on system design, transient response curves will follow any one of the three paths shown in Figure 14-7. Curve 1 represents an underdamped response. The output oscillates, or cycles, before reaching the steady-state condition. In some systems, each successive peak of the oscillation is one-fourth of the preceding peak value. This type of response is called *quarter amplitude decay*. Underdamped response curves are also analyzed mathematically using the *minimum Integral of Absolute Error (ITAE)*. This criterion uses calculus to minimize the total shaded area on the curve. Curve 2 shows a critically damped response. This type of damping is used when overshoot above the setpoint is undesirable. The overdamped response curve shown in Figure 14-7 also prevents overshoot, but takes longer to reach steady-state.

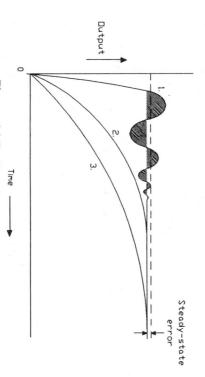

Figure 14-7 Transient response curves.

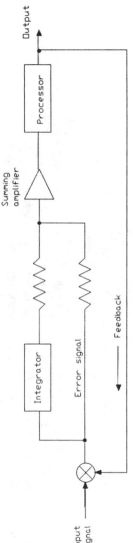

Figure 14-8 Integral damping circuit.

Steady-state Error. The difference between the final steady-state output reached and the value called for by the input is called the steady-state error, or *offset*. By increasing the gain of a system, it is possible to reduce the steady-state error. However, increasing the gain of a system to offset the output variable's fluctuations may make the system unstable. Unstable means that the system causes large variations in the value of the controlled variable as it rapidly "hunts" for the proper controller output. This hunting action occurs from the system overreacting to an error, thereby causing an even larger error in the opposite direction. The system then tries to correct the opposite error and overreacts again, causing a fluctuation in the other direction.

On its own, gain will not eliminate steady-state error. Consequently, integral action is often employed. An *integrator* is a ramping circuit that will automatically dampen oscillations. Figure 14-8 shows an example of integral damping to reduce steady-state error. When the input signal is first applied, the integrator output is zero, and the system operates as if the integrator were not present in the circuit. Initially, the change in input signal causes an immediate and relatively large error. The summing amplifier output drives the analog input signal to the PLC in a direction that eliminates the error. As time elapses, the error signal decreases and the integrator output increases. If the integrator were not used, a small residual error signal would be present when the PLC output signal stopped. However, by using the integrator, the error signal will eventually be removed because the integrator continues to ramp as long as any residual error voltage is present at its input.

Stability. This variable refers to the ability of a control system to dampen out any oscillations that result from disturbances. An unstable system will cause the output to oscillate above and below the desired value, as shown in the under-damped response curve of Figure 14-7.

Sensitivity. The sensitivity of a control system specifies the level of input required to obtain a desired output. This variable identifies the effectiveness of the system in correcting for small input changes. For example, thermocouple sensitivity is measured in volts output per degree Celsius.

14-4 ALGORITHMS AND FLOWCHARTS

To quickly and accurately reduce fluctuations in a control system, it is often necessary to solve for conditions by using mathematical equations. These equations are referred to as **algorithms.** An algorithm is any fixed set of instructions that is guaranteed to solve a particular type of problem in a finite number of steps. In a PLC-based system, the CPU implements these instructions in the process of calculating signals to be sent to process actuators. Although algorithms are generally thought of as complex mathematical equations, any sequence of processing steps that must occur within a program to produce output control is an algorithm.

For an algorithm to operate properly in a PLC-controlled process system, the following four points must be taken into consideration:

1. *Process model:* The basic parameters of how the system is expected to function; i.e., how should the system respond to setpoint changes and disturbances.

2. *Model uncertainty:* Most processes are nonlinear, or have different operating conditions at different points in time.

3. *Type of input:* Setpoint changes will often have the shape of steps, or ramps. Disturbances to the system can be modelled as steps, entering a lag.

4. *Performance objectives:* Ideally, the system model should closely approximate "real world" conditions for maximum reliability and performance.

Most algorithms can be expressed symbolically by the use of a block diagram or flowchart. A **flowchart** is a pictorial description of an algorithm, showing the points of decision, relevant operations, and the sequence in which they should take place to solve the problem correctly. Flowcharts typically use four basic symbols: the oval, parallelogram, diamond, and rectangle. These symbols are linked in a sequential manner using arrows to indicate direction. The oval symbol shown in Figure 14-9 indicates either the beginning or end of an algorithm.

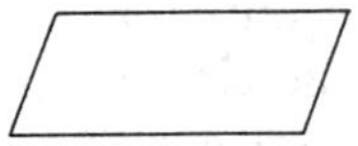

The parallelogram symbol of Figure 14-10 indicates either the need for information by the algorithm (input) or the availability of information in the form of a partial or complete answer (output).

The diamond symbol shown in Figure 14-11 indicates a point of decision in the algorithm. Decisions compare the algebraic magnitudes of two numbers, variables, or combinations of quantities, with connectors indicating either a "yes" or "no" concerning the comparison. For example, if quantity A in Figure 14-11(b) was greater than quantity B, the answer to A=B? would be NO, and the algorithm would proceed to the next step indicated at the tip of the NO arrow.

Figure 14-9 Flow-chart Start and Stop symbols.

Figure 14-10 Input/Output symbol.

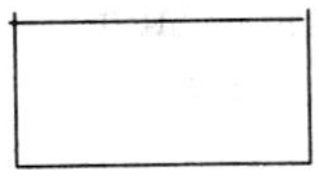

Figure 14-12 Operation symbol.

Figure 14-12 shows the fourth symbol used in flowcharts. The rectangle indicates that some type of computational processing or operation is to take place at this point in the algorithm.

Table 14-1 is a table of flowchart symbols, definitions, and number of arrows flowing into or out of each symbol.

The defining and symbolizing of a process control problem into an algorithm requires a substantial amount of thinking and planning. The symbolic algorithm is the thought pattern that the PLC is going to follow once the algorithm has been translated into a set of instructions. The finished flowchart precisely specifies the solution of the problem and must therefore take into account all aspects inherent in the problem. Figure 14-13 shows a flowchart describing the steps to be taken when making a phone call. Although this flowchart is fairly concise, it still leaves out many details. For example: Where do we look up the number?, How long do we wait for someone to answer?, etc.

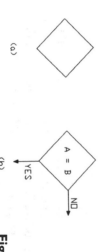

(a)

(b)

Figure 14-11 Decision symbol.

Symbol	Meaning	Possible number of IN arrows	Possible number of OUT arrows
START	Indicates the beginning of the flowchart.	None	One only
(parallelogram)	Input/Output takes place	A minimum of one	One only
(diamond)	Decision point usually of magnitudes of numbers	A minimum of one	Two (Yes and No)
(rectangle)	Computation or other type of operation	A minimum of one	One only
STOP	Indicates the end of the flowchart	A minimum of one	None

TABLE 14-1 Flow Chart Symbols and Arrow Properties

Figure 14-14 shows an example of a process control flowchart for measuring temperature using an analog input. If the temperature is greater than 300°F, the PLC jumps to a subroutine. If the temperature is less than 300°F, a heater coil is energized. The first step in the chart after START is to input the preset values for the decision-making process. A Pushbutton (PB) is pressed each time a temperature reading is required. When thc PB is pressed, the temperature is sampled by the analog input device and the data are stored in a memory location.

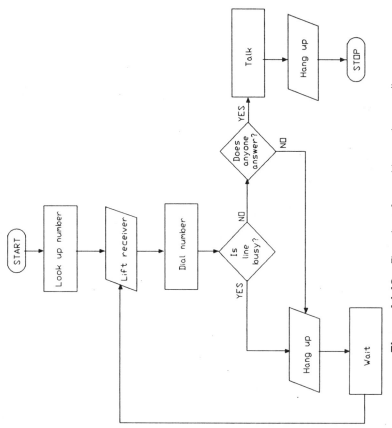

Figure 14-13 Flowchart for making a phone call.

14-5 PROPORTIONAL-INTEGRAL-DERIVATIVE (PID) CONTROL

Proportional-Integral-Derivative, or PID, control is used for virtually any process condition to provide feedback to a PLC. As mentioned earlier in this chapter, feedback is defined as taking a portion of an output signal and feeding it back into the input to cause a change. There are four main types of feedback used in PLC-controlled systems. They are

1. ON-OFF feedback: Used to send a full-ON or full-OFF signal to the controller to indicate whether a discrete output has been energized. Controlling activity is achieved by the period of ON-OFF cycling action.

2. Proportional feedback: Sends a signal which is proportional to the output back to the input.

3. Derivative feedback: Used when sudden changes in signal occur which can drastically affect system operation. This type of feedback is used when a fast response is required to reduce the possibility of overshoot.

4. Integral feedback: Used when offset signals must be taken into account. An offset signal can be an error voltage which is in the system and is adversely affecting process control.

Proportional Control. Proportional control operates on the principle that it creates a permanent residual error in the operating point of the controlled variable when a change in load occurs. This error is referred to as the offset. The main disadvantage of proportional feedback is that if a long-term or steady-state distur-

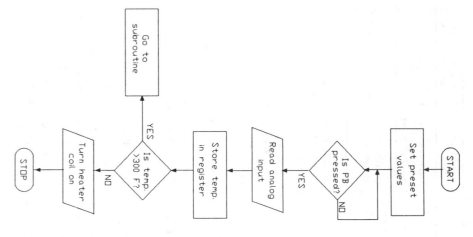

Figure 14-14 Flowchart for monitoring temperature.

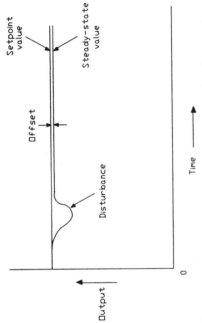

Figure 14-15 Transient response for proportional control system.

bance occurs, the manipulated variable cannot make the controlled variable return to the setpoint value. Because proportional-mode feedback systems require an error signal to control the manipulated variable, the magnitude of the error signal decreases as the controlled variable's signal approaches the setpoint value. At some point, the strength of the error signal is not sufficient to control the manipulated variable and a point of equilibrium is reached, as shown in Figure 14-15. The net result of this action is an offset signal that is slightly lower than the setpoint value. Depending on the PLC application, this offset may or may not be acceptable.

Figure 14-16 shows an example of a proportional control system. A capacitance probe is an electronic device that makes a direct height measurement of the contents of a tank containing liquid. The flow of liquid into the tank is controlled to maintain the liquid level within designated limits. Assume that the outflow causes the level to fluctuate over a wide range above and below a preset value. In a properly designed system, the maximum inflow will equal the maximum outflow. A pneumatic valve controller operates between 0% and 100% to maintain level control, and is set for normal operation at 50%. At this setting, no error signal exists and the valve opening is automatically maintained at 50%. Although often not practical, the 50% setpoint value is ideal because it allows an equal maximum amount of correction of the controlled variable above and below the setpoint.

Integral Control. The integral control mode changes the output of a PLC by an amount proportional to the integral of the error signal. The main purpose for introducing an integral term into a process control system is to remove any steady position errors. An everyday example of integrator action is the distance travelled

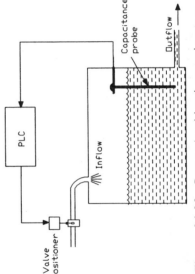

Figure 14-16 Proportional level control system.

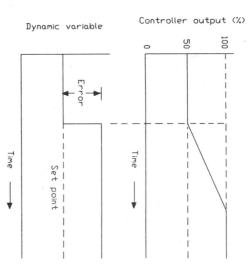

Figure 14-17 Integral control response curves.

by an automobile. Distance travelled is the integral of speed and time. The greater the speed and longer the time, the greater the distance travelled. At a fixed speed, distance travelled depends on running time. When the speed drops to zero, the distance from the start position remains fixed. In process control systems, the integral mode is also known as *floating control*.

The response curve for an integral controller is shown in Figure 14-17. The percent output changes until it reaches 100% of scale, or until the measurement is returned to the setpoint. This graph is again using the 50% reference, which means the output signal will also change until it reaches 0%. Integral control provides a continuous change in output that is dependent on the error. This mode is often referred to as *reset action*. The reset action is inversely related to the time constant of the control loop. Consequently, when the reset rate is high, the integral response will be quickly affected in the loop. The disadvantage of pure integral control is that damping in the feedback loop is reduced, thus causing a decrease in the relative stability of the system.

Proportional plus Integral Control. In many industrial applications, the offset caused by proportional control is not acceptable. To overcome this problem, another mode of control is added. By using integral control, or reset action, it is possible to integrate any difference between the measurement and the setpoint. A PLC's output will change until the difference between the measurement and setpoint is zero. The integral part of the control continually repositions the final correcting device until the setpoint is attained, regardless of the load change or process reaction delay. This allows the proportional band of control to be widened, and consequently the PLC can begin reducing the correcting device sooner and more forcefully as the controlled variable recovers to the setpoint. As a result, overshoot and cycling are dramatically reduced.

When PLCs operate valve positioners using proportional plus integral control, the position of the control valve is determined by the following two factors:

1. *Magnitude of error signal:* This value represents the proportional part of a control system.

2. *Time integral of error signal:* This mathematical quantity represents the magnitude of the error multiplied by the time it has persisted.

The integral control action essentially performs the task of a human operator by manually adjusting the bias in a proportional control system. This is done by

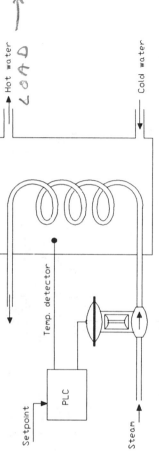

Figure 14-18 Proportional plus integral control for a steam-heated water system.

shifting the proportional band in a direction opposite to that of the measurement change. Consequently, an increasing measurement signal results in a decreasing output. The integral action effectively provides a reset of the zero error output after a load change occurs.

Figure 14-18 shows an example of a system utilizing proportional plus integral control. In this system, the water in a tank is to be heated by steam. If we assume the water temperature is low (below setpoint), the proportional mode output calls for an increase in steam flow. This causes the steam valve to open and the steam flow increases, bringing the water temperature toward the setpoint. If the water temperature remains low, the integral mode gradually adds to the output and the steam valve opens further. As long as there is a control error present, the integral mode continues adding to the output, the valve continues opening, and the temperature rises until it finally reaches the setpoint. When the control error is reduced to zero, the output and valve position will remain constant until the temperature is disturbed again. When the temperature changes again, the control system responds to the deviation from the setpoint. The additive action of the integral mode reinforces the action of the proportional mode in either direction, up or down.

Derivative Control. Derivative action, or *rate control*, is used by PLC systems to speed up the transient response of the control system. This type of control cannot be used alone because when the error is zero, or constant, the controller has no output. Consequently, derivative action is always accompanied by proportional control; integral control is used only when necessary. The advantage of rate control is that it reduces the initial overshoot and dampens the oscillatory nature of the process control system. Derivative feedback is based on the principle that the control system is "looking" at the rate of change of the variable, and will anticipate the level of the variable in the future. The ability of the control system to anticipate the future level of the variable substantially reduces the delay or lag that is present and causing oscillation.

PID Control. Essentially, a PID control system has a feedback loop that is proportional plus derivative plus integral. In this type of system, the zero error term of the proportional mode is not necessary due to the integral mode automatically accommodating for offset and nominal setting. The derivative action is used to increase the speed of response, while the integral action prevents steady-state errors from taking place in the process flow rate or actuator position. The integral action of a PID control system is generally used when the system is trying to maintain the process variable at its nominal operating value and where changes in the process variable will only take place as a result of changes in the load.

If PID control were applied to the steam-heated water system of Figure 14-18, the derivative mode would help to speed up the response speed to temperature

14-6 PID MODULES

PID modules are used by PLCs to process data obtained by feedback circuitry. PID operations are generally complex, mathematically-based algorithms. Because PID programs can be quite long and complex, most PID modules are equipped with microprocessors which solve the algorithm without burdening the CPU with these mathematical equations. The PID's microprocessor will receive analog signals from transducers and compare these data to pre-programmed values, or setpoints, and will determine appropriate output signals based on these data.

Figure 14-19 shows a standard block diagram of a PID module and its relationship to various components in the control process. The setpoint is an analog value that is in the PLC's program. The transducer generates an output signal from the process being controlled, and feeds it into the PID module. The module determines the difference between the setpoint and measured value and generates an error signal. The error signal is fed into a correcting device, such as a valve positioner, motor control circuit, voltage amplifier, etc.

In a PID module, the proportional mode produces an output signal which is proportional to the difference between the measurement being taken and the setpoint entered in the PLC. The integral control function produces an output which is proportional to the amount and length of time that the error signal is present. The derivative section produces an output signal which is proportional to the rate of change of the error signal. PID modules are used in situations where the PLC must be able to respond to very rapid analog signal changes, and in cases where there is a long lag time between applying corrective action, the appearance of the results of the corrective action, and the appearance of a noticeable change as a result of the corrective action.

The corrective action taken by a PID-controlled system will overcome the magnitude of the error signal, as well as the time integral of the error signal. The PID module also takes into account the rate of change of the error signal, because a rapidly changing error causes a greater corrective action than an error signal that changes slowly.

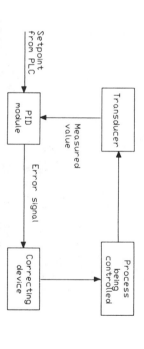

Figure 14-19   Block diagram of process control system with PID module.

change. The derivative mode changes the control signal according to how fast the control error changes. If the error is not changing, the derivative mode does nothing. A slow-changing error signal produces an output signal that changes slowly. If the controlled variable is changing quickly, the control signal is quickly increased to compensate. PID control is generally used on processes that exhibit rapid and large disturbances in error signals.

In many process control situations, it is necessary for the PID module to predict, or estimate, what a condition will be. For example, if liquid flowing into a tank is to be heated by a steam coil and then discharged, the PID module must be able to process the following variables:

Liquid flow rate
Liquid temperature
Specific heat of the liquid
Heat of vaporization of water at the pressure inside the steam coil

The PID module must be able to calculate the steam flow in the heating coil, the amount of heat required, and must also compensate for: (a) variations in the flow-in liquid into the tank, and (b) the temperature of the liquid entering the tank. Either of these variations could cause drastic changes in the heating load, and the corresponding flow of steam heat. For the PID module to compensate for such variations, *feedforward control* is often used. Feedforward control, or *output bias*, is a method of calculating the amount of heat required versus the cold-liquid requirement at every instant. It then provides the exact value of steam heat needed. To make this calculation, an algorithm is developed which uses a mathematical model to simulate the performance of the liquid-heating process.

Manufacturers such as Allen-Bradley use algorithms called PID equations to program process control instructions. The output of the PID equation goes to a control device. In some situations, an additional value called the *bias term* is added to the PID equation to decrease the offset. The purpose of the PID equation is to drive the quantity that is being controlled toward the set-point. The PID equation is derived as follows:

$$\text{PID equation} = \text{Proportional term} + \text{Integral term} + \text{Derivative term} + \text{Bias term}$$

There are two general types of PID equations:

Dependent Gains Equation: In this PID equation, a variation in the proportional term will have an effect on the integral and derivative terms.

Independent Gains Equation: This equation allows the proportional, integral, and derivative terms to be adjusted independently.

The Dependent Gains equation is an algorithm which is based on calculus equations. The following variables and symbols are available in a Dependent Gains equation:

K_C = Controller Gain
CO = Control Output
T_D = Derivative Time Constant, in minutes
T_i = Integral Time Constant, in minutes
dt = Sampling Rate, in minutes
PV = Process Variable
$Bias$ = Output Bias
E = Error (This value equals the process variable or setpoint.)
$E(n-1)$ = Error from Last Sample
$PV(n-1)$ = Process Variable from Last Sample

14-7 PID TUNING PARAMETERS

The *tuning* of a PID control system refers to the adjustment of its modes. This is done on-line, while the process is actually running. The initial settings of the control system are estimated and the three modes are fine-tuned to eventually reach the optimum control settings. There are three basic methods of tuning a PID system: the open-loop transient response method, the Ziegler-Nichols method, and the frequency response method.

The open-loop method of determining control parameters is accomplished when a system is in the manual mode of operation. Although this method does not include the PLC's influence on the process loop, it is a relatively easy tuning method that can be quite effective. The basic idea of open-loop tuning is that the process control loop is opened so that no feedback occurs. This is typically done by disconnecting the controller output from the final control element. A chart recorder with adjustable speed, adjustable sensitivity, and adjustable zero is used to continually record the controlled variable. The tuning begins by operating the process on manual control until the measured variable remains constant. A step change in the manipulating device is then introduced and the response of the controlled variable is recorded. The controlled variable is allowed to respond to the manipulated variable change, and the parameters used in the tuning equations are determined. The parameters that are obtained from chart recording include the process lag and process rate.

The Ziegler-Nichols closed-loop tuning method is also known as the *ultimate cycle method*. This method is based on adjusting a loop until steady oscillations occur. The two measurements obtained from this method are the minimum controller gain and the period of the oscillation. The minimum controller gain, or ultimate gain, is the amount of gain required to cause the control system to oscillate. The period of oscillation is also known as the ultimate period. The following steps are taken to determine the ultimate gain and ultimate period:

1. Reduce the integral and derivative modes to their least-effective settings.
2. Gradually increase the gain setting until the controlled variable begins oscillating. The final gain setting that produces oscillation is the ultimate gain.
3. The period of these oscillations, measured in minutes, is the ultimate period.

The frequency response method of PID tuning involves the use of Bode plots for the process and control loops. Bode plots, named after Hendrik W. Bode, represent straight-line approximations of the magnitude and phase angle response to frequency. Bode plots of frequency response are obtained by opening the loop and providing a variable frequency disturbance of the controlling variable.

14-8 ANALOG INPUT DEVICES

Analog signals are defined as signals that vary in both time and magnitude. Unlike digital signals, analog values are continuous and change smoothly over a given range. Figure 14-20(a) shows a sine wave, which is a typical analog signal. The horizontal axis represents time, and the vertical axis represents magnitude. As the sine wave passes through 360°, the magnitude of the signal increases and decreases in strength. At 180°, the signal crosses the zero axis and the polarity of the sine wave is considered to be negative.

The peak voltage of a sine wave is taken from the zero axis to the maximum positive or negative value. In Figure 14-20(a), the peak voltage is measured between the zero reference line and the 90° point, or the zero and 270° point in the sine wave. The peak-to-peak voltage of an analog signal is the potential difference

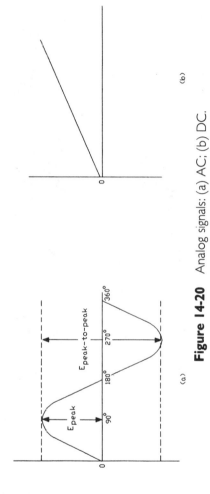

Figure 14-20 Analog signals: (a) AC; (b) DC.

between the maximum positive and negative voltages. This signal is classified as *alternating current* because it crosses the zero axis. The waveshape shown in Figure 14-20(b) is considered to be *direct current* because it does not cross the zero axis. However, this particular waveform would be classified as an analog signal because the signal strength varies with time.

The RMS, or Root-Mean-Square, voltage is the voltage which an AC voltmeter reads when connected across two points in a circuit. The RMS value is calculated as 0.707 of the peak voltage. RMS voltages are the standard reference for AC values. For example, when an electrical appliance is rated at 10 amperes and 120 V, both values are assumed to be RMS quantities.

In addition to voltage and current signals, analog values also include pneumatic, hydraulic, temperature, humidity, etc. A PLC analog input module only responds to changes in voltage and current. For a PLC to monitor signals which are not electrical in nature, a transducer must be used. Because a transducer is a device which converts one form of energy into another form, a thermocouple would be considered to be a transducer because it converts temperature into voltage. The following transducers are typical components which are interfaced with PLCs: thermocouples, Resistance Temperature Detectors (RTDs), pressure transducers, humidity transducers, and photovoltaic transducers.

Thermocouples. A thermocouple is a device which converts temperature to voltage. Thermocouples operate on the principle that when a temperature differential is maintained across a metal, the vibration of atoms and motion of electrons will cause a potential difference to exist across the metal. As the temperature of the metal varies, so does the voltage produced by the metal. Thermocouples typically use two types of metals to produce voltage outputs. Table 14-2 shows the main types of thermocouples used in industry and their normal temperature operating ranges.

The output voltage produced by a thermocouple is very small. Figure 14-21 shows some typical voltage versus temperature curves for type E, J, K, and R thermocouples. The maximum output voltage produced by these thermocouples is under 100 mV. Type R thermocouples produce 0.006 mV for each degree Celsius

TABLE 14-2

Type	Materials	Normal Range
J	Iron-constantan	−180°C to 750°C
T	Copper-constantan	−200°C to 370°C
K	Chromel-alumel	−190°C to 1260°C
E	Chromel-constantan	−100°C to 1260°C
S	90% Platinum + 10% rhodium	0°C to 1482°C
R	87% Platinum + 13% rhodium	0°C to 1482°C

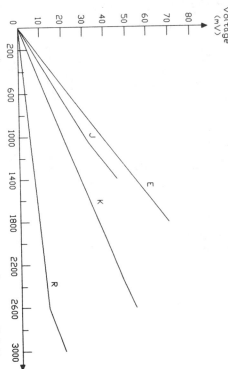

Figure 14-21 Voltage versus temperature curves for types E, J, K, and R thermocouples.

change in temperature. For this reason, to interface a thermocouple with an analog input card of a PLC, it is necessary to use a voltage amplifier to increase the strength of the signal to a value that the PLC will recognize. Typically, analog input modules respond to 0 to 10 V values, and 4 to 20 mA signals. A thermocouple used with an amplifier is often called a *temperature-measuring transmitter*.

Figure 14-22 shows a typical curve for a temperature-measuring transmitter. This particular device produces an output signal between 4 and 20 mA, depending on the temperature being measured. At minimum temperature, the output signal is 4 mA. This signal is often referred to as the *zero setting*. At maximum temperature, the output current is 20 mA. The difference between the maximum temperature and minimum temperature is called the *span setting*. The curve shown in Figure 14-22 is basically a straight line that varies evenly. This type of curve is *linear* because the signal changes proportionately between two quantities, i.e., voltage/temperature, current/time, etc.

Thermocouples are extremely susceptible to electrical noise. Extreme caution should be taken when interfacing thermocouples to PLC systems. If possible, twist the lead wires from the thermocouple, and use foil shielding wrapped around the lead wires. If possible, use an instrumentation amplifier with a high common mode rejection ratio. These types of amplifiers are operational amplifiers, or **op-amps**, which are used as differential amplifiers. A differential amplifier has the ability to reject electrical noise and only amplify the signal from a thermocouple. Some PLC manufacturers have actual thermocouple modules for installation in the I/O rack. These modules eliminate the need for signal amplification and special filtering considerations. By using a thermocouple module, the thermocouple is connected directly to the module itself.

Resistance Temperature Detectors (RTDs). A Resistance Temperature Detector, or RTD, is used to detect the change in resistance of a metal over a range in temperature. Because pure metals have positive temperature coefficients, temper-

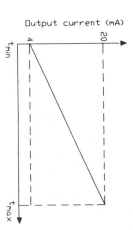

Figure 14-22 Input temperature versus output current for a temperature-measuring transmitter.

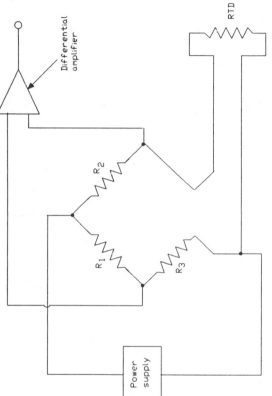

Figure 14-23 Bridge circuit using RTD and differential amp.

ature and resistance are directly proportional; as the temperature of a metal increases, the resistance also increases.

There are many different RTDs used in industrial applications. Because the RTD is a transducer which converts temperature to resistance, to monitor the signal with an analog input module, the signal must be converted from resistance to voltage. The circuit shown in Figure 14-23 consists of an RTD in a bridge circuit. A differential output amplifier is connected to the output of the bridge. When the resistance of the RTD is at, for example, ambient temperature, the potential difference at the bridge output is 0 V, and the differential output is 0 V. If the temperature of the RTD changes, the resistance changes, and the bridge is no longer balanced. This causes a potential difference to exist across the bridge, and the output of the differential amplifier produces an output voltage which could be fed into the analog input module of the PLC.

As was the case with thermocouples, some PLC manufacturers have actual RTD modules which are connected directly to pure metal conductors such as platinum or nickel. When the temperature of the metal changes, the resistance change is detected by the RTD module, and the PLC processes the information provided by the RTD module.

Pressure Transducers. Pressure transducers are used by PLCs to measure and control fluids such as liquid and gas. There are a great number of pressure transducers on the market, although the principle of operation is essentially the same for all of them. *Pressure* is defined as the force per unit area that a fluid exerts on its surroundings. Static pressure refers to fluid that is not in motion, i.e., being pumped though a pipe. Dynamic pressure refers to fluid in motion. The standard unit of measurement of pressure is the pascal, which is measured in newtons per square meter.

Pressure transducers often incorporate differential transformers to measure pressure. The *Linear Variable Differential Transformer*, or *LVDT*, measures force in terms of the displacement of the ferromagnetic core of the transformer. Figure 14-24 shows an LVDT with two secondary coils, a primary coil, and a movable core. The output voltage, which is connected to the analog input of the PLC, will vary between 0 and 10 V, depending on the positioning of the core. In its normal resting place, the core is centered between the two secondary coils. In this position, the induced emfs in the secondary winding are equal and opposite to each other. Consequently, the output voltage is zero. If the core moves to the left, coil 1 has a larger value of induced emf than coil 2. The polarity of the voltage is affected by the direction that the core was moved, and the magnitude of the voltage is determined by the distance that the core was moved.

Pressure transducers also use resistance, inductance, and capacitance to measure displacement, and employ devices such as diaphragms or bellows. A bellows converts a pressure differential into a physical displacement. The circuit shown in Figure 14-25 is a pressure transducer. In this type of system, the inductance value of the coil is determined by the position of the core in the windings. If the pressure increases or decreases, the bellows will either expand or contract. The coil is arranged in a center-tap configuration so that as the inductance of one coil increases, the inductance of the other coil decreases. The signal converter changes the varying inductance into a proportional voltage or current signal.

Flow Transducers. The main applications for flow transducers are in the measurement of solid flow and liquid flow. Solid flow measurement includes the measurement of solid particles, such as crushed or powdered material. Solid flow measurement usually incorporates a conveyor and load cell, as shown in Figure 14-26. In this system, material is taken from an input hopper, transported across a weighing platform, and deposited in an output hopper.

A load cell uses the same principle as the LVDT. The greater the force on the load cell, the greater the displacement of the movable core. In a system like the one shown in Figure 14-26, the flow rate is directly proportional to the speed of the conveyor. As the conveyor speed increases, so does the flow rate.

The standard method of measuring liquid flow involves using Bernoulli's principle. This principle states that as the velocity of a fluid increases, its pressure decreases. Therefore, when a fluid flows through a restriction, its velocity will increase and the pressure will decrease.

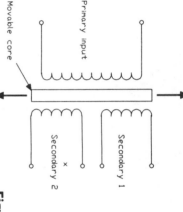

Figure 14-24 LVDT with dual voltage output.

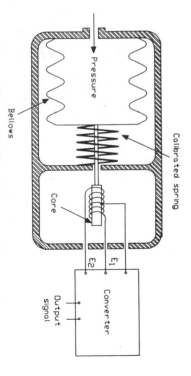

Figure 14-25 Pressure transducer.

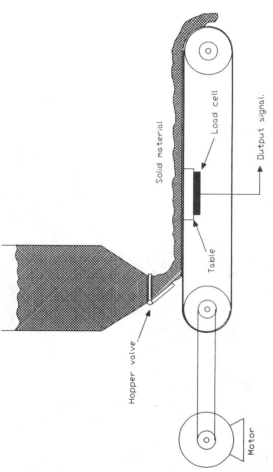

Figure 14-26 Weight detection system using load cell.

Figure 14-27 shows a differential pressure flowmeter with a venturi. The venturi is the section of pipe where the passageway is reduced. By restricting the channel, the fluid's velocity is increased through the venturi. In Figure 14-27, point P_1 is before the venturi and P_2 is in the venturi. When there is flow in the pipe, according to Bernoulli's principle, the pressure at P_1 will be greater than at P_2. This will cause the bellows at P_1 to extend and force the core of the LVDT to the right. When there is no flow, Bernoulli's principle has no effect, and the core of the LVDT is centered. Once again, the LVDT is connected to the analog input module of the PLC, and any change in output voltage from the LVDT can be monitored.

Humidity Transducers. PLCs are frequently used to control environmental conditions with variables such as temperature, light, and humidity. When a PLC is required to supervise the moisture content of air, or a material such as soil, it must be able to differentiate between the amount of moisture required, and the amount of moisture present. The measurement of relative humidity involves interfacing the analog input module of the PLC with a humidity transducer. Humidity is defined as the moisture content of air. Relative humidity is the ratio of moisture to the maximum amount of water vapor that air can possibly hold.

The two most common humidity transducers in use in industrial applications are *hygrometers* and *psychrometers*. Hygrometers operate on the principle that hygroscopic materials, such as human hair, change in length as humidity increases. By placing a hygroscopic material under tension, an LVDT is used to transmit an electrical signal as the length of the material varies with humidity. A resistive

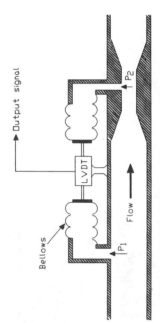

Figure 14-27 Differential pressure flowmeter.

hygrometer is shown in Figure 14-28. It consists of metal electrodes encased in a plastic form and coated with lithium chloride. As the relative humidity of the air surrounding the hygrometer increases, the lithium chloride film absorbs more water, causing the resistance of the electrodes to decrease. At 100% humidity, the hygrometer has a resistance of approximately 75,000 Ω. At 10% relative humidity, the hygrometer has a terminal resistance of about 350 MΩ.

A psychrometer, as shown in Figure 14-29, consists of two temperature transducers and two bulbs. One transducer is in the ambient air and is connected to a dry bulb, the other is submerged in wet fibre and is connected to a wet bulb. A wick and reservoir are used to maintain the wet condition of the second transducer. The wet bulb is colder than the dry bulb due to the evaporation of liquid contained in the fibrous material. If the relative humidity is low, the water evaporates more quickly, and the wet bulb has a lower temperature. If the relative humidity is high, the liquid will evaporate at a slower rate, and the temperature of the wet bulb is higher. The two transducers produce varying voltage outputs for changes in temperature. The change in output signal from the psychrometer can be used by the PLC's analog input to respond to changes in humidity levels.

Photovoltaic Transducers. A photovoltaic transducer is a device that will generate a voltage which is proportional to light intensity. As the light which is shining on the device increases, the voltage generated increases. As the light decreases, the voltage which is generated by the transducer decreases. Figure 14-30 shows the structure of a typical photovoltaic cell. The cell operates on the same principle that applies to any semiconductor device. That is, when electron-hole pairs are formed, minority carriers are created which will move across the pn junction.

The photocell is constructed of a p-type substrate and an n-type substrate. The connection point of these two substrates is called the *depletion layer*. As light falls on the photovoltaic cell, electron-hole pairs are created, the depletion layer decreases, and minority carriers travel across the pn junction. If a load is connected between the p-type substrate and the n-type substrate, current will flow. The amount of current which flows is directly proportional to the amount of carriers formed by the light intensity.

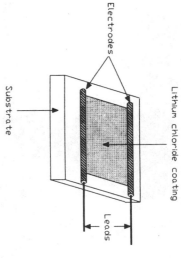

Figure 14-28 Resistance hygrometer.

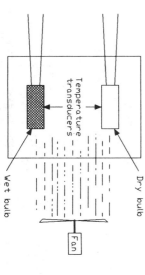

Figure 14-29 Psychrometer humidity sensor.

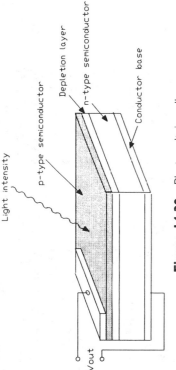

Figure 14-30 Photovoltaic cell.

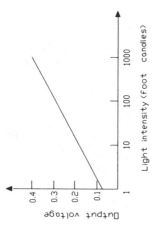

Figure 14-31 Open circuit voltage curve of photocell.

Figure 14-31 shows the open circuit voltage generated by a typical photovoltaic cell. Light intensity, shown on the horizontal axis, is measured in foot candles and is logarithmic in nature. From the graph, it can be seen that the cell is more sensitive to lower levels of light. A change from 10 foot candles to 100 foot candles almost doubles the output voltage.

Because the output voltage generated by a photovoltaic cell is too small to be utilized by the analog input module of a PLC, it is necessary to use a voltage amplifier to increase the magnitude of the signal. Figure 14-32 shows the op-amp connected in series between a photovoltaic cell and the analog input module of a PLC.

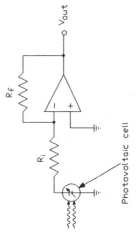

Figure 14-32 Op-amp combined with photovoltaic cell.

14-9 ANALOG OUTPUT DEVICES

The devices discussed in this chapter have dealt with analog signals which are being sent into a PLC. PLCs are also used in applications, such as motor speed control, where a varying analog output signal is required. To vary the speed of AC or DC motors, a PLC must be able to control the actual speed of the motor. Because the output voltage and current of an analog output module are very small, the PLC will not be directly connected to the motor. Instead, the analog output module is connected to an AC or DC drive system.

Speed control of DC motors is accomplished by reducing the voltage applied to the armature circuit. Generally, the voltage is changed in the armature circuit by either inserting or removing resistance. As resistance in the armature circuit increases, the speed of the motor decreases. The speed of a DC shunt motor can also be varied by changing the amount of voltage which is applied to the field winding. As field voltage is increased, motor speed decreases.

The disadvantage of field control is that it consumes more energy. Although either method can be used in DC drive systems, for this discussion of DC speed control, we will assume that voltage across the armature is being varied.

Figure 14-33 shows the basic circuit operation of a DC drive system using a *DC chopper*. A chopper is essentially an ON-OFF switch that connects and disconnects the load to a DC voltage source. This type of control is also referred to as *Pulse Width Modulation (PWM)*. Because the SCR cannot switch itself OFF once in the conducting state, a commutating circuit is required to apply a negative voltage on the SCR for a brief instant. The diode shown in parallel with the DC motor is called a *freewheeling diode*. These diodes are popular in motor control circuits to suppress high induced voltage when equipment is de-energized. In Figure 14-33, the armature current, I_a, initially increases after the SCR is switched ON, and the speed of the motor picks up. When the SCR is commutated, the armature current decreases through the freewheeling diode. When the SCR is triggered again, the cycle repeats. Consequently, motor speed is controlled by varying the ON-OFF times of the SCR. The longer the SCR is ON, the greater the voltage across the motor.

A typical DC drive has a potentiometer mounted on the front of the chassis. As the potentiometer is varied, the voltage in the armature circuit of the DC motor is altered. The potentiometer is in the control circuit of the DC drive. By turning the potentiometer, the voltage in the control circuit is varied between 0 and +10 V DC. If the potentiometer is turned so that there is no voltage in the control circuit, the voltage in the power circuit of the DC drive is interrupted and the motor does not turn. As the voltage is increased in the control circuit, the voltage across the armature of the DC motor increases, and the shaft of the motor begins to rotate. Therefore, the voltage in the control circuit of the DC drive is directly proportional to the speed of the DC motor.

Analog output modules are ideally suited for controlling the speed of a DC motor because the module produces a voltage level which is quite suitable for control circuit values in the drive system. By simply disconnecting the potentiometer on the front of the drive, and connecting the output voltage from the analog output module, it is possible to control the speed of a DC motor by varying the output voltage of the PLC's analog module.

To change the speed of an AC motor, the frequency of the motor must be altered. It is not possible to change the speed of an AC motor simply by reducing the armature voltage. The speed of an AC motor will be reduced when armature voltage decreases, but the speed regulation of the motor also decreases substantially. This means that the AC motor is unable to maintain a constant speed output

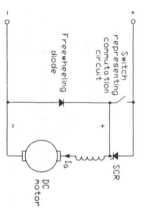

Figure 14-33 DC motor driven by a chopper.

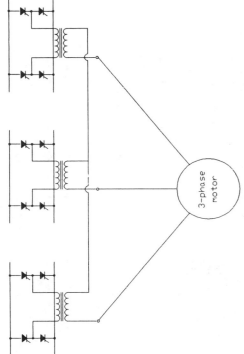

Figure 14-34 Six-step inverter for motor speed control.

as the torque on the motor shaft is varied. Changing motor frequency is usually accomplished by **inverters**, or *cycloconverters*, which are electronic control systems that change the speed of an AC motor without having an effect on the torque or speed regulation of the motor. An inverter converts a DC source into AC by triggering a group of SCRs in a specific sequence. A cycloconverter converts an AC source into a lower frequency AC source by controlling the firing angles of the SCRs.

Figure 14-34 shows a basic three-phase six-step inverter driving a wye-connected motor. By switching the SCRs ON and OFF in the proper sequence, the DC supply voltage is switched across the stator windings in such a way that a rotating magnetic field is created that duplicates the action of a three-phase AC source. The inverter output voltage can be smoothly adjusted from a maximum value to zero by retarding the control signals for one pair of SCRs with respect to each other.

Figure 14-35 shows the basic cycloconverter components required for the speed control of a three-phase induction motor. Three dual converters are used for the power electronics, one for each motor phase. A waveform generator is also required in the drive system to supply the AC reference to each dual converter. The waveform generator must control the phase sequence to set the motor rotation, as well as the amplitude, to control the motor torque and frequency to control the motor speed. The output frequency is determined by the number of gate pulses per half-cycle of the output waveform.

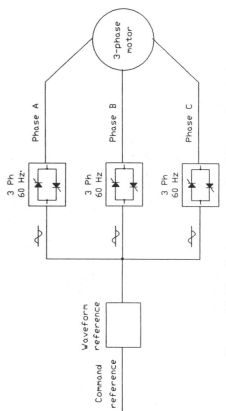

Figure 14-35 Cycloconverter for AC speed control.

Although the control circuitry for an AC variable speed drive is more complex than for a DC drive, the actual control circuit still operates on a varying 0 to +10 V DC signal. Once again, a typical AC drive will have a potentiometer mounted on the front of the drive system. When the potentiometer is varied, the frequency of the motor will be altered and the motor will change speed. The control circuits for both AC and DC drive systems use this 0 to 10 V value. Thus, an analog output module can be used to control either AC or DC motors. By disconnecting the potentiometer in the control circuit of a variable frequency drive and connecting the output voltage leads from an analog output module, it is possible to control the speed of an AC motor with a PLC.

Motor speed control is a very important PLC function. Many industrial applications require the speed of a motor to be varied. Standard industrial equipment requiring speed control includes assembly line conveyors, mining machines, cranes, elevators, food processing equipment, lathes, fans, etc. By interfacing an analog output module to a variable-speed drive, it is possible to obtain exact speed control of motors for almost any application.

REVIEW QUESTIONS

14-1. Define the term "process control."

14-2. What is the purpose of a block diagram?

14-3. "Transfer function" is

    (a) the automatic regulation of a control system.

    (b) a process control system represented by a series of interconnected blocks.

    (c) the relationship between the input and output of any element in a process control system.

    (d) a symbol used to show how two or more signals are combined.

14-4. When is a summing point used in a block diagram?

14-5. Define the term "error signal."

14-6. What is a transducer?

14-7. Why is feedback used in process control systems?

14-8. What is the difference between open-loop and closed-loop control?

14-9. Define the following terms:

    (a) Manipulated variable

    (b) Controlled variable

14-10. List the four variables associated with closed-loop control.

14-11. A dynamic variable is

    (a) the outflow rate in a control system.

    (b) any physical parameter that can change either spontaneously or due to external influence.

    (c) a method used to reduce overshoot.

    (d) the difference between the measured value and setpoint.

14-12. Define the following terms:

    (a) Overshoot

    (b) Undershoot

14-13. Describe one example of damping in a control system.

14-14. What is meant by the term "settling time"?

14-15. The term "offset" refers to
(a) transient response.
(b) damping.
(c) steady-state error.
(d) sensitivity.

14-16. The "stability" of a process control system specifies
(a) the level of input required to obtain a desired output.
(b) the basic parameters of how a system is expected to function.
(c) the difference between the final steady-state output reached and the value called for by the input.
(d) the ability of a control system to dampen out any oscillations that result from a disturbance.

14-17. What is an algorithm?

14-18. List the four requirements necessary for an algorithm to operate in a PLC-controlled system.

14-19. What is the advantage of using a flowchart?

14-20. Describe the four main types of feedback used in process control systems.

14-21. Proportional control
(a) is used to send a full-ON or full-OFF signal to the controller.
(b) creates a permanent residual error in the operating point of a controlled variable.
(c) is used when sudden changes in signal occur that can drastically affect system operation.
(d) is used when offset signals must be taken into account.

14-22. Another name for floating control is
(a) proportional control.
(b) integral control.
(c) derivative control.
(d) proportional plus derivative control.

14-23. When PLCs operate valve positioners using proportional plus integral control, what two factors determine the position of the control valve?

14-24. Another name for rate control is
(a) proportional control.
(b) integral control.
(c) derivative control.
(d) proportional plus integral control.

14-25. Describe the basic operation of a PID control loop.

14-26. What principle do PID modules employ to anticipate changes in control variables?

14-27. List the two general types of PID equations.

14-28. Name four types of analog input devices.

14-29. Explain the basic operating principle of a Linear Variable Differential Transformer (LVDT).

14-30. What are the two main applications for flow transducers in process control?

14-31. Name the two most common types of humidity transducers.

14-32. How is speed control of a DC motor accomplished?

14-33. List two types of variable frequency control.

Data Highways

15-1 INTRODUCTION

Upon completion of this chapter, you will be able to

▼ Define the term "data highway."

▼ Understand the term "protocol" as it applies to PLC systems.

▼ Explain the principle of token passing.

▼ Name two types of topology.

▼ List four factors affecting transmission media.

▼ Describe the two types of bandwidth used in data highway systems.

▼ Define response time.

▼ Explain proprietary networks.

▼ Understand the term "manufacturing automation protocol (MAP)."

▼ Name the seven MAP layers.

Data highway is a term associated with PLC systems that refers to Local Area Networks, or LANs. A LAN is a system which interconnects data communications components in an area with a radius of no more than a few miles. Essentially, a LAN is a private, on-site communications system that allows communication between computers, PLCs, robots, etc. In computer systems, LANs are used to communicate between microcomputers and peripheral devices. The communication speed between LAN components is limited by the access speed of shared storage media and by the way the software used by the microcomputer interacts with the LAN. The rate at which characters can be transmitted along a communications line is dependent on the number of bits of binary information that can be sent at a given time. This transfer of information is measured in bits per second, or **baud.**

Communications conductors used by LANs are twisted pair, coaxial cable, and fiber optics. Any device connected in a LAN is referred to as a workstation, or **node.** The maximum distance between nodes in a LAN is typically one mile. The transmission speed between nodes ranges from 40 kilobaud to 10 megabaud.

15-2 PROTOCOL

In the traditional sense of the word, protocol is defined as being a set of rules which are mutually agreed upon. The term is popular in military and diplomatic procedure, and it is also a common term used in communications systems. Protocol is the method used by a LAN to establish criteria for receiving and transmitting data through communications channels. It is, in effect, the way a LAN directs traffic on its data highway.

There are two main protocols used by LANs: token passing and Carrier Sense Multiple Access/Collision Detection, or CSMA/CD, which is also referred to as collision detection. In collision detection, each node that has a message to transmit waits until there is no traffic on the data highway and then it transmits. Carrier sense refers to how a node "listens" to the data highway to determine if there are any data being transmitted by another node. Nodes will not transmit when they sense, or "hear," traffic on the highway. When a node is transmitting data, the collision detection circuitry is checking for the presence of another transmitting node. If two nodes are transmitting simultaneously, a collision occurs, and the node must wait a predetermined amount of time before re-transmitting. The limitation of this type of system is the time lost while a node retries transmitting data when a collision occurs.

15-3 TOKEN PASSING

Token passing is a method of transmitting and receiving data by assigning each node in a LAN a logical position in an ordered sequence. Using this method, the nodes form a ring where the last node follows the first. A token is a binary combination which circulates between nodes when there is no traffic on the highway. At any time, a node may access the token. Once a node has the token, it is given exclusive, but temporary, use of the data highway. The node only has use of the token for the duration of its transmission. Once the node is finished transmitting, the token is automatically recirculated among the nodes in the LAN. The time required to circulate the token entirely around the LAN is determined by multiplying the token holding time by the number of nodes in the network. Token passing eliminates the delays caused by collisions in a CSMA/CD system.

15-4 TOPOLOGY

Topology is a term used to describe the pattern of connection for nodes in a LAN. The standard topologies used in PLC-based LANs are: star, ring, and common bus. In the star topology, each node is connected via a point-to-point link to a central, or control, node. Figure 15-1 shows a typical star topology with a control node and eight PLCs. The control node can be either a computer or another PLC. In this configuration, all traffic routing is performed by the control node. This type of system works best when information is primarily being transmitted between the main controller and remote PLCs. However, if most communication is to occur between PLCs, the operation speed, or throughput, is affected. Also, the star system can use substantial amounts of communication conductors to connect all remote PLCs back to one central location.

In the ring topology, nodes are connected in series with each other to form a loop. Transmitted messages travel from node to node in the loop. This type of system is popular for token passing protocol. The token, or bit pattern, is used by a node to gain control of the communications channel. The main disadvantage of this type of topology is that because it is basically a loop, if any node fails, the system crashes. However, advances have been made in this topology to greatly reduce downtime in the event of a node failing. An example of ring topology is shown in Figure 15-2.

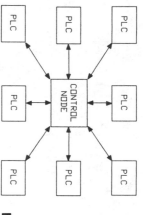

Figure 15-1 Star topology.

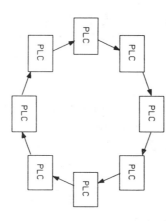

Figure 15-2 Ring topology.

Common bus topology, unlike star topology, does not require switching. Communication can take place between any two nodes without information having to be routed through a central node. This is a sort of parallel communications system where the bus is simply the communications cable which connects the PLCs. An inherent problem in this type of topology is the danger of data collision. Any data which are transmitted by a node can be received simultaneously by more than one node by using this system. It is also quite inexpensive to add additional nodes onto a LAN using common bus topology. Figure 15-3 shows an example of common bus topology.

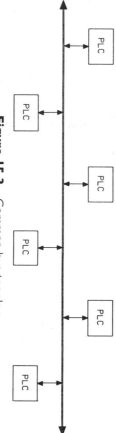

Figure 15-3 Common bus topology.

Some systems which use common bus topology have a network consisting of a central controller, which acts as a master, and several remote PLCs, which are referred to as slaves. In this configuration, the master sends data to the slaves. If data are required from a slave, the master will query the slave and wait for a response. There is no communication on the bus unless it is initiated by the master.

Master/slave topology uses two pairs of conductors. One pair of wires is used for the master to transmit data and the slave to receive them. On the other pair, the slaves transmit and the master receives.

15-5 TRANSMISSION MEDIA

The term transmission media refers to the types of conductors used to interconnect PLC systems on a data highway. When selecting the proper transmission media for a data highway, the following points must be considered:

1. *Range:* Each type of media has limitations in terms of transmission distances. For example, twisted pair conductors are limited to ranges of less than 100 m, while fiber optic cables can transmit data up to 10 km.

2. *Bandwidth:* The bandwidth of a transmission medium will have an effect on a network's ability to move data and how this capacity is used.

3. *Noise immunity:* Media such as flat multi-conductors and telephone lines are highly susceptible to electromagnetic interference.

4. *Relative cost:* The importance of the three previous points has a significant impact on the cost of the transmission media. Fiber optic cable has the best characteristics for use in PLC data highways, but it is also three times the cost of coaxial cable.

Twisted pair conductors are very popular in industry and are capable of handling a transmission speed in excess of 250 kilobaud over distances up to 4000 feet. One limitation of twisted pair in LANs is that the performance of the conductor decreases as the number of nodes connected increases. Typically, when using twisted pair with PLC data highways, data transmission should not exceed 20 kilobaud to ensure error-free transmission.

There are two types of bandwidth used in data highway systems: **broadband** and **baseband.** Broadband systems use one cable to carry several frequencies that are assigned to specific devices connected to the cable. Baseband systems allow several devices to use one cable by using a time-sharing principle. Each device is assigned a specific time slot for data transmission. Baseband transmissions require less expensive cabling than broadband systems, although broadband systems allow for much higher transmission speeds.

Coaxial cable is available as either a baseband or broadband transmission medium. Baseband coax is typically 3/8 in. in diameter and can be used to transmit at speeds up to 10 Megabits Per Second (MPS) over distances exceeding 15,000 feet. Baseband transmission uses the entire frequency bandwidth for one channel. Digital signals are transmitted directly without modulation. Broadband systems use multiple frequencies which act as a multilane highway. All broadband systems use centralized control transmission, which is essentially a token bus configuration.

Broadband coax is usually between 1/2 in. and 1 in. in diameter and can carry signals up to 100 megabaud at distances exceeding 25 miles. Broadband transmission divides frequency into a number of independent channels. These channels are allocated bandwidths which can also be used to carry audio and video messages in addition to data. The main difference between broadband and baseband transmission is that baseband signals can only travel in one direction, unlike broadband signals which are bidirectional.

Although broadband signals are capable of transmitting in both directions, broadband cable is inherently one direction. This problem is alleviated by splitting transactions into transmission and reception. This splitting may be accomplished by using two cables, or by splitting the cable bandwidth into three parts: one range for data transmission, the second for reception, and the third for a dead band between the first two. The conversion of frequencies between data transmission and reception is accomplished by a device called a *headend*. This technique, called midsplit, reduces the installation cost because only a single cable is used.

Another method of physically connecting PLCs on a data highway is by fiber optics. This transmission medium is relatively new in PLC-based applications, although it is extremely impressive in terms of transmission speed and distance. Typically, a fiber optic cable can carry a 1,000-megabaud signal over 35,000 feet. Compared with twisted pairs of wire, or coaxial cables, fiber optic cables have advantages such as their small size, no electromagnetic interference, and long transmission ranges. The initial installation costs for fiber optic cable are very high compared to coax cable, but this medium is extremely reliable and the cost is expected to drop in the future. These types of cables have very large bandwidths so they are well-suited to high-speed transmission in noisy environments. Fiber optic cables use either Light-Emitting Diodes (LEDs) or injection lasers for the transmission of data. The data are received at the other end of a fiber optic cable by devices such as PIN diodes and avalanche detectors.

Table 15-1 is a comparison of transmission media commonly used for PLC data highways. From this table it is apparent that although shielded twisted pair is the least expensive medium, it can only carry signals a short distance. Because we are assuming the PLC network considered in this book to be a relatively small LAN, we have excluded microwave communications from Table 15-1.

As previously mentioned, the protocol of a LAN refers to the rules governing the operation of the data communications system. The protocol for PLC data highways includes everything from data transmission speed to voltage levels of communication conductors. Most PLCs adhere to the protocols established by the International Standards Organization, or ISO. The ISO has divided the various functions required by PLC systems into seven hierarchical layers known as the *Reference Model of Open Systems Interconnection*, or ISO-OSI. The OSI model takes into account the hardware, software, protocols, and network architecture that are needed for any two machines to communicate. The actual connections between machines are physical, while the connections between layers in the model are logical.

To interconnect Data Termination Equipment, DTE, such as PLCs, computers, and peripherals, an interface standard is necessary. The Electronic Industries Association, EIA, produced the RS-232-C, which is generally acknowledged as the industry standard for PLC data highway systems. However, the RS-422 is also quite popular in both PLC and computer communication devices. The RS-232-C will transmit at a speed of 19.2 kilobaud for up to 50 feet, while the RS-422 will transmit at speeds in excess of 10 megabaud over distances of more than 4000 feet. PLC networking is usually achieved through a separate interface that will either use a programming port, or will have access to a fast parallel bus within the PLC. The software aspects of data transmission between PLC systems becomes complex only if extensive data preparation is required before transmission.

TABLE 15-1 Properties of Communications Media

Medium	Range	Bandwidth	High Freq. Loss	Noise Immunity	Relative Cost
Twisted Pair	<100 m	<10 MHz	High	Very good	Low
Shielded	<1200 m	<100 kHz	High	Poor	High
Flat Multi.	<100 m	<10 MHz	High	Fair	High
Coaxial	<2 km	<400 MHz	6.5 dB/km	Poor	High
Fiber Optics	2–10 km	500 MHz/km	8 dB/km	Excellent	High
Telephone	—	60 kHz	60 dB/km	Poor	Low

Distance and speed of data highways are determined primarily by the number of devices on the bus and the transmission medium used. The total cable length required for interconnection is generally divided into the main cable length and the drop cable required from the main cable to the PLC. The cable lengths allowed are dependent on the type of medium and data highway used. Because each cable drop has an impact on the highway, the number of taps and the drop length must be taken into consideration when installing or modifying a data highway.

The transmission speed of a data highway is also determined by response time. **Response time** is defined as the time required between an input transition at one node and the corresponding output transition at another node. This response time, or communication time, is determined by the following equation:

$$R_T = I_T + 2 \times ST_1 + PT_1 + A_T + T_T + PT_2 + 2 \times ST_2 + O_T$$

where

I_T = Input delay time, or the time required to detect external contact for input transition.

ST_1 = Scan time for sending node (PLC1).

ST_2 = Scan time for receiving node (PLC2).

PT_1 = Processing time to prepare data transmission.

PT_2 = Processing time to receive data and have data ready to be operated on by the program logic.

A_T = Access time, or the time involved in network access for transmitting and receiving data.

T_I — Transmission time at current baud rate.

O_T = Output delay time, or the time required to produce an external closure, or output transition.

15-6 DATA HIGHWAY TYPES

Each PLC manufacturer has a different name for its data highway. AEG Modicon refers to its system as Modbus, and the communication instructions as Modbus Protocol. Texas Instruments uses the TIWAY system, and Allen-Bradley's is simply called Data Highway. Table 15-2 lists the differences between the three data highway systems.

Depending on the manufacturer, a PLC system will either require a host controller for communication, or will be able to communicate directly. The Allen-Bradley Data Highway allows PLCs to communicate directly with each other without the need for a computer to oversee system operation. Data Highway functions as a floating master system where each station on the highway takes control before passing supervision to the next station.

Texas Instruments' TIWAY II modules allow 500 series processors to communicate directly with each other, as well as providing an interface to other PLC products on the data highway. Figure 15-4 shows a TIWAY network using broadband transmission to allow video and voice communications to be simultaneously transmitted with data.

TABLE 15-2 Data Highway Comparison

Manufacturer	Max. Nodes	Max. Baud Rate	Access Method
Allen-Bradley	64	56k	Token
Modicon (Modbus)	247	19.2k	Master-slave
Texas Instruments (TIWAY II)	2^{32}	5M	Token

Systems such as those mentioned in Table 15-2 are referred to as *proprietary networks*. These networks are based on whether the equipment to be interconnected is supplied by the same manufacturer. If this is the case, it makes sense to use the vendor's proprietary network to reduce installation costs and minimize integration problems. The disadvantage of proprietary networks is that when equipment is supplied from only one vendor, the user becomes locked into that vendor and technology. This means the user is unable to take advantage of technological advances made by other manufacturers. In most practical situations, it is unlikely that all the equipment used in a control system is made by one vendor. Consequently, the difficulties of interfacing equipment of different manufacturers has led to the development of an industry standard known as Manufacturing Automation Protocol, or *MAP*.

Figure 15-4 TIWAY system.

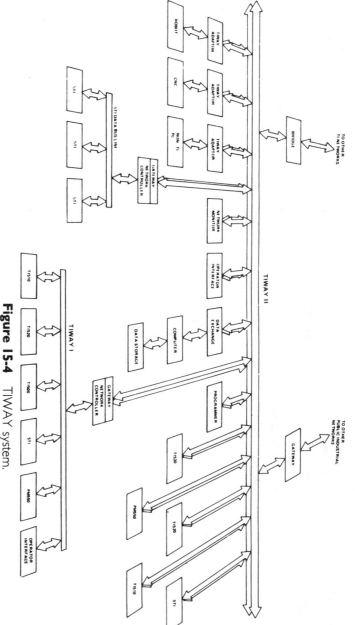

15-7 MANUFACTURING AUTOMATION PROTOCOL (MAP)

Manufacturing Automation Protocol (MAP) is a token passing bus LAN patterned after the seven-layer ISO/OSI model. MAP is a set of rules governing how machines made by any manufacturer should communicate.

For two machines of different makes to communicate, seven different functions, or layers, must be standardized. For example, if an Allen-Bradley PLC is required to communicate with a Modicon PLC, a seven-layer MAP system would be used. Figure 15-5 shows the seven layers used in a conventional MAP system.

The seven MAP layers are

1. *Physical:* This layer provides the physical connection between communicating devices. It is at this layer that voltage levels, baud rates, connector standards, and all other aspects of physical interfacing are taken into account.

2. *Data link:* The data link breaks the data being transmitted into groups, or frames. The counting and numbering of frames are controlled by the data link, as are error detection and re-transmittal of data when required.

Layer	Definition
7	Application
6	Presentation
5	Session
4	Transport
3	Network
2	Data link
1	Physical

Figure 15-5 The seven layers of a MAP system.

3. *Network:* The network provides traffic control and routing of data frames. It performs message routing for data transfer between non-adjacent nodes.

4. *Transport:* Provides error-free transmittal of data from source to destination. This layer allows transparent, reliable data transfer from end node to end node.

5. *Session:* This layer provides name/address translation, access security, and synchronization and management of data. This is the interface point between the user and network. Typically, the session allows the user to log in to the system by typing a password.

6. *Presentation:* Restructures data to and from standardized formats used within the network. Allows incompatible devices to communicate.

7. *Application:* Provides all services directly comprehensible to application programs.

Figure 15-6 illustrates the seven basic tasks required for communication between two systems. Data are transferred from a sender through each of the seven layers and onto the network. At the receiving end, the data travel back up through the layers. As the data are sent, each communication layer manages or alters the message in some way and adds information for its counterpart in the form of a message header. When this header is added to the original message, it forms part of the data unit. Before data are transmitted on the message frame, data bits such as error detection and address codes are added. These bits complete the message frame that is transmitted over the physical layer of the network to PLC System B. As the data unit passes through System B, each layer removes and reads the header intended for it, executes the data instructions, and passes the data unit on to the next layer above.

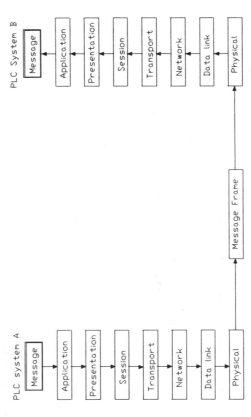

Figure 15-6 MAP interconnection layers and message frame.

REVIEW QUESTIONS

15-1. What is a data highway?

15-2. Define the term "Local Area Network."

15-3. The rate at which characters can be transmitted along a communications line is called
  (a) LAN.
  (b) node.

(c) baud.

(d) protocol.

15-4. What is the definition of protocol as it applies to a LAN system?

15-5. The two main protocols used by LANs are

(a) broadband and baseband.

(b) token passing and CSMA/CD.

(c) MAP and broadband.

(d) ring and star.

15-6. Token passing is

(a) the method used by LANs to establish criteria for receiving and transmitting data.

(b) a term that is used to describe the pattern of connection for nodes in
a LAN.

(c) the time required between an input transition at one node and a corresponding output transition at another node.

(d) a method of transmitting and receiving data by assigning each node a
logical position in an ordered sequence.

15-7. Define "topology."

15-8. What is the difference between ring topology and star topology?

15-9. What is the main disadvantage of using common bus topology?

15-10. List the four points that must be taken into account when selecting a
transmission medium.

15-11. Name one limitation of using twisted pair conductors in a LAN system.

15-12. What are the two types of bandwidth used in data highway systems?

15-13. A "headend" is a device used to

(a) convert frequencies using a midsplit technique.

(b) transmit data at speeds greater than 10 megabits per second.

(c) transmit data through fiber optic cables.

(d) ensure that data travel in only one direction.

15-14. A typical fiber optic cable can carry data

(a) under 100 m.

(b) under 2 km.

(c) up to 10 km.

(d) up to 100 km.

15-15. Response time is

(a) the timing method used by LANs to communicate with nodes.

(b) the pattern of connection for nodes in a LAN.

(c) a method of transmitting and receiving data.

(d) the time required between an input transition at one node and a corresponding output transition at another node.

15-16. What is a proprietary network?

15-17. Name the seven MAP layers.

15-18. What is the advantage of using a MAP system?

16

Number Systems and Codes

Upon completion of this chapter, you will be able to

▶ Define the term "radix."
▶ Understand the binary number system.
▶ Express a negative number in binary form.
▶ Differentiate between the least-significant bit and the most-significant bit.
▶ Add binary numbers.
▶ Add and subtract using 2's complement.
▶ Multiply and divide binary numbers.
▶ Convert binary numbers to decimal, and decimal numbers to binary.
▶ Understand the octal number system.
▶ Convert octal numbers to binary, and binary numbers to octal.
▶ Explain the hexadecimal number system.
▶ Convert hexadecimal numbers to binary, and binary numbers to hexadecimal.
▶ Differentiate between natural binary and Binary Coded Decimal (BCD).
▶ Understand the parity bit, Gray code, and ASCII code.

16-1 INTRODUCTION

A number system is, essentially, a code consisting of symbols which are assigned for each individual quantity. Once a code is memorized, it is possible to count using this code. The decimal number system uses ten basic symbols, or digits: 0

16-2 DECIMAL NUMBER SYSTEM

The decimal number system uses combinations of ten individual digits to represent any number imaginable. Because there are ten digits in this system, the decimal number system is referred to as a base 10 system. As the digits move to the left of the decimal place, they increase by a power of 10. As the digits move to the right, they decrease by a power of 10. For example, in the decimal number 5053.72, the digit to the immediate left of the decimal point has a value of 3×10^0, or 3; the next digit to the left of the decimal point has a value of 5×10^1, or 50; and the digit to the immediate right of the decimal place has a value of 7×10^{-1}, or 0.7.

The total value of the decimal number 5053.72 is determined as follows:

$$
\begin{aligned}
2 \times 10^{-2} &= 0.02 \\
7 \times 10^{-1} &= 0.7 \\
3 \times 10^{0} &= 3 \\
5 \times 10^{1} &= 50 \\
0 \times 10^{2} &= 0 \\
5 \times 10^{3} &= \underline{5,000} \\
&\ 5,053.72
\end{aligned}
$$

From the above example, it is apparent that each position in a decimal number has a value that is 10 times the value of the next position to the right. Therefore, each position value is a multiple of 10 and can be expressed as 10 raised to some exponent.

▼ **EXAMPLE 16-1**

Express the decimal number 123 in exponential form.

Solution

$$
\begin{aligned}
123 &= 1 \times 100 + 2 \times 10 + 3 \times 1 \\
&= 1 \times 10^2 + 2 \times 10^1 + 3 \times 10^0
\end{aligned}
$$

16-3 BINARY NUMBER SYSTEM

The binary number system is based on two digits: 1 and 0. Any number imaginable can be expressed in binary form as a combination of 1s and 0s. To process numbers in electronic circuitry, such as in a PLC, it is necessary to represent numerical quantities by electrical signals. If digital equipment processed decimal numbers, each of the ten digits would have to be assigned a specific voltage level, and combinations of these ten different voltages would represent a decimal number. This would mean that a six-digit decimal number would require voltage levels on

through 9. Each digit represents a specific quantity. When the digits are grouped together, larger quantities can be expressed.

The **radix**, or *base*, of a number system is the total number of individual symbols in that system. The largest-valued symbol always has a magnitude of one less than the radix. For example, the decimal number system has a radix of 10, so the largest single digit is 10 - 1, or 9.

All number systems use position weighting to represent the significance of an individual digit in a group of numbers. As digits move to the left of a decimal point, the value of the digit increases by its base power. If a digit is to the right of the decimal place, it decreases by its base power.

six different conductors. Having ten different voltage levels would considerably complicate the circuitry required to process data.

The binary number system is ideally suited for processing data because only two voltage levels are required to represent all the different digits in the binary system. Typically 5 volts is used to represent binary 1, and 0 volts is used to represent binary 0. As mentioned in previous chapters, a single binary digit is referred to as a **bit**, and a combination of bits is called a word. An eight-bit binary word would be represented inside a PLC as a combination of voltage levels. For example, the binary word 10110111 would appear as the following voltage levels:

$$5 \text{ V}, 0 \text{ V}, 5 \text{ V}, 5 \text{ V}, 0 \text{ V}, 5 \text{ V}, 5 \text{ V}, 5 \text{ V}$$

When the processor "sees" these voltage levels, it considers the binary number 10110111 to be present.

Because only two symbols, or digits, are used in the binary number system, the base, or radix, is two. Therefore, the position weighting that is assigned to a binary symbol will double each position a digit is moved to the left of the decimal point, and it will decrease by 1/2 each position a digit is moved to the right of the decimal point. The digit of a binary number that has the lowest weight is called the *Least-Significant Bit*, or LSB, and the digit with the highest value is called the *Most-Significant Bit*, or MSB.

▶ *EXAMPLE 16-2* Express the binary number 1011 in exponential form.

Solution

$$1 \times 2^0 + 1 \times 2^1 + 1 \times 2^2 + 0 \times 2^3 + 1 \times 2^4$$

16-4 NEGATIVE NUMBERS

In the decimal number system, a negative number is represented by a subtraction symbol in front of the number. For example, the number negative 5 is represented as −5. This implies that each number has both a magnitude and a sign. If a decimal number is positive, it has a plus sign; if a number is negative, it has a minus sign. This method of representing numbers is referred to as *sign-magnitude* representation.

In digital equipment, such as a PLC, it is not possible to use positive and negative symbols to represent the polarity of a number. The simplest method of representing a binary number as either a positive or negative value, is to use an extra digit, or *sign bit*, at the MSB side of the number. In the sign bit position, a 0 usually indicates that the number is positive, and a 1 indicates a negative number. Figure 16-1 shows a four-bit binary number expressed in sign-magnitude form.

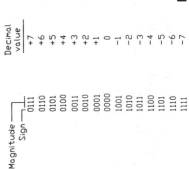

Magnitude		Decimal value
Sign		
0	111	+7
0	110	+6
0	101	+5
0	100	+4
0	011	+3
0	010	+2
0	001	+1
0	000	0
1	001	−1
1	010	−2
1	011	−3
1	100	−4
1	101	−5
1	110	−6
1	111	−7

Figure 16-1 Signed binary numbers.

Another method of expressing a negative number in a digital system is by using the complement of a binary number. If a binary number has the value 1, the complement would be 0. Conversely, if the binary number is 0, the complement would be 1. This is known as the 1's complement form of a binary number. In other words, the 1's complement of 1001 is 0110. When negative numbers are represented in 1's complement, each negative number magnitude is the 1's complement of the corresponding positive number magnitude. Figure 16-2 shows the sequence of four-digit binary numbers, using the 1's complement form.

The 2's complement of a number is similar to the 1's complement in the sense that one extra digit is used to represent the sign. Digital equipment, such as PLCs, use the 2's complement method for performing subtraction. By using the 2's complement, binary numbers are actually added together to produce a subtraction operation. This is an advantage in a PLC because it means that the same digital circuitry can perform both addition and subtraction. The 2's complement is the binary number that results when 1 is added to the 1's complement:

2's complement = 1 + 1's complement

Figure 16-3 is a summary of common representations of signed binary numbers.

Magnitude		Decimal value
Sign ┐		
0	111	+7
0	110	+6
0	101	+5
0	100	+4
0	011	+3
0	010	+2
0	001	+1
0	000	0
1	110	-1
1	101	-2
1	100	-3
1	011	-4
1	010	-5
1	001	-6
1	000	-7

Figure 16-2 1's complements.

Signed decimal	Signed binary	Sign-magnitude	One's complement	Two's complement
+7	+111	0111	0111	0111
+6	+110	0110	0110	0110
+5	+101	0101	0101	0101
+4	+100	0100	0100	0100
+3	+11	0011	0011	0011
+2	+10	0010	0010	0010
+1	+1	0001	0001	0001
0	0	0000	0000	0000
-1	-1	1001	1110	1111
-2	-10	1010	1101	1110
-3	-11	1011	1100	1101
-4	-100	1100	1011	1100
-5	-101	1101	1010	1011
-6	-110	1110	1001	1010
-7	-111	1111	1000	1001

Figure 16-3 Common representations of signed binary numbers.

16-5 ADDING BINARY NUMBERS

The rules for adding binary numbers are basically the same as for adding decimal numbers. That is, when two digits are added, these two digits produce a sum and possibly a carry. If the largest digit in the number system is exceeded, the carry is transferred to the next most-significant digit. Because there are only two digits

Chapter 16 / Number Systems and Codes

in the binary number system, when a result is greater than 1, it must be carried. The following five cases show the different combinations of adding binary numbers:

$$0 + 0 = 0$$
$$0 + 1 = 1$$
$$1 + 0 = 1$$
$$1 + 1 = 10$$
$$1 + 1 + 1 = 11$$

The last case occurs when two bits in a certain position are 1 and there is a carry from the previous position. In the last two cases, the result can create some confusion if it is related to the decimal numbers 10 and 11. Binary 10 represents a quantity of two units, not ten units, and binary 11 represents three units, not eleven. To avoid confusion between the two number systems, subscripts are used to represent the base of the number system. Binary numbers use the subscript 2, and decimal numbers use the subscript 10.

10_2 = binary form 10_{10} = decimal form

▶ *EXAMPLE 16-3*   Add the following binary numbers:

(a) 101 and 110
(b) 011 and 110
(c) 1010 and 1101
(d) 10.110 and 11.011

Solution

(a)
```
   101
 + 110
 -----
  1011
```

(b)
```
   011
 + 110
 -----
  1001
```

(c)
```
   1010
 + 1101
 ------
  10111
```

(d)
```
   10.110
 + 11.011
 --------
  110.001
```

(a)
1st column: $1 + 0 = 1$
2nd column: $0 + 1 = 1$
3rd column: $1 + 1 = 10$ (0, carry 1)

(b)
1st column: $1 + 0 = 1$
2nd column: $1 + 1 = 10$ (0, carry 1)
3rd column: $1 + 1 = 10$ (0, carry 1)

(c)
1st column: $0 + 1 = 1$
2nd column: $1 + 0 = 1$
3rd column: $0 + 1 = 1$
4th column: $1 + 1 = 10$ (0, carry 1)

(d)
1st column: $0 + 1 = 1$
2nd column: $1 + 1 = 10$ (0, carry 1)
3rd column: $1 + 1 = 10$ (0, carry 1)
4th column: $1 + 0 + 1 = 10$ (0, c. 1)
5th column: $1 + 1 + 1 = 11$ (1, c. 1)

16-6 ADDITION AND SUBTRACTION USING 2'S COMPLEMENT

In arithmetic functions, the initial numerical quantities that are to be combined by subtraction are the **minuend** and **subtrahend.** The result of the subtraction process is called the *difference*, represented as:

```
   A   (minuend)
 − B   (subtrahend)
 ---
   C   (difference)
```

The procedure for subtracting numbers using the 2's complement is

1. Determine the 2's complement of the subtrahend. Include the sign bit. If the subtrahend is negative, the 2's complement will result in a positive number.
2. After the 2's complement of the subtrahend is obtained, it is *added* to the minuend. The result of the addition is the difference. If the sign bit of the difference is 1, the number is negative, if the sign bit is 0, the number is positive.

The advantage of using the 2's complement system when adding or subtracting binary numbers is that it allows positive and negative numbers to be represented. Also, numbers can be added together to produce a result which is the same as if the same numbers were subtracted. The following example shows the method used to add a positive and negative number.

Add the binary number 110 to the negative binary number −101.

1. Convert −101 to a 2's complement value.
   −101 = 010 + 1 = 011
2. Add the two numbers together.

$$\begin{array}{r} 110 \\ +\ 011 \\ \hline 1001 \end{array}$$

3. When a carry is generated in the last stage of addition, it is always disregarded. Therefore, the result of adding 110 and −101 is 001. Because the sign bit is 0, the result is a positive binary number.

▶ **EXAMPLE 16-4**

Solve the equation $1011_2 - 110_2$.

Solution

Determine the 2's complement of 110_2, including the sign bit, and add the two numbers together.

Original #	1's complement	2's complement
0110	1001	1010

$$\begin{array}{r} 1011 \\ +\ 1010 \\ \hline 1\ 0101 \end{array}$$

The overflow bit, 1, is ignored. The answer is 0101. The 0 in the MSB column indicates a positive number. Therefore, the difference between 1011 − 110 is 101.

▶ **EXAMPLE 16-5**

Solve the equation $10011_2 - 10001_2$.

Solution

Determine the 2's complement of the subtrahend.

010001 = 101110 + 1 = 101111

$$\begin{array}{r} 010011 \\ +\ 101111 \\ \hline 1\ 000010 \end{array}$$

The overflow bit, 1, is ignored. The answer is 000010. The 0 in the MSB column indicates a positive number. The difference between 10011 and 10001 is 10_2.

16-7 BINARY MULTIPLICATION AND DIVISION

Binary numbers are multiplied in the same manner as decimal numbers. Binary multiplication is actually easier than decimal because there are only four possible combinations.

$$0 \times 0 = 0$$
$$0 \times 1 = 0$$
$$1 \times 0 = 0$$
$$1 \times 1 = 1$$

To multiply numbers with more than one digit, form partial products and add them together. The following example illustrates the multiplication of two unsigned binary numbers:

$$
\begin{array}{r}
101 \\
\times\ 110 \\
\hline
000 \\
101 \\
101 \\
\hline
11110
\end{array}
$$

▶ **EXAMPLE 16-6**

Multiply the following unsigned binary numbers: 101.1 and 10.10.

Solution

$$
\begin{array}{r}
101.1 \\
\times\ 10.10 \\
\hline
000\ 00 \\
101\ 1 \\
0000 \\
1011 \\
\hline
1101.110
\end{array}
$$

PLC's that use the 2's complement system require both numbers to be in true binary form. If both numbers are positive, they are already in true binary form. If both numbers are negative, each must be 2's complemented to be converted to true binary form. If one number is positive and one number is negative, the product will be negative, meaning that the negative number being multiplied and the product must both be 2's complemented.

▶ **EXAMPLE 16-7**

Multiply the following signed binary numbers: 0110 and 1110.

Solution

1110 is a negative number. It must be 2's complemented.

$$1110 = 0001 + 1 = 0010$$

$$
\begin{array}{r}
0110 \\
\times\ 0010 \\
\hline
0000 \\
0110 \\
0000 \\
0000 \\
\hline
0001100
\end{array}
$$

The product is a negative number, so it is also 2's complemented.

$$0001100 = 1110011 + 1 = 1110100$$

The sign bit is 1, indicating the product is negative.

The process for dividing one binary number by another is the same for both binary and decimal numbers. In most PLC systems, the subtraction operation, which is part of the division process, is carried out using the 2's complement method.

▶ EXAMPLE 16-8

Divide the following unsigned binary numbers: 1110 and 10.

Solution

$$
\begin{array}{r}
111 \\
10\overline{)1110} \\
\underline{10} \\
11 \\
\underline{10} \\
10 \\
\underline{10} \\
00
\end{array}
$$

The division of signed binary numbers is carried out in the same way as the multiplication of signed binary numbers. Negative numbers are 2's complemented, and then divided. If the dividend and divisor both have the same sign, the quotient is assigned a positive value and given a sign bit of 1.

16-8 BINARY-TO-DECIMAL CONVERSION

Although digital equipment processes data in binary form, the data must be converted to decimal values to be utilized in visual applications. For example, a calculator may perform math instructions in binary form, but to be relevant to the user, the data must be displayed in decimal form. The conversion of binary digits to decimal is referred to as *decoding*. In a digital machine, such as a calculator, there is an integrated circuit chip called a decoder which performs this function. When a number is manually converted from binary to decimal, the position weight of each binary digit is added together. The result is the equivalent decimal number. The following example illustrates the conversion of a binary number to decimal form:

1001_2 to decimal

$$
\begin{array}{cccc}
1 & 1 & 0 & 0 & 1 \\
\end{array}
$$

- $1 \times 2^0 = 1$
- $0 \times 2^1 = 0$
- $0 \times 2^2 = 0$
- $1 \times 2^3 = 8$
- $1 \times 2^4 = \underline{16}$
- 25

The sum of $1 + 8 + 16 = 25$. Therefore, the decimal equivalent of binary number 11001 is 25.

▶ EXAMPLE 16-9

Convert binary number 101101 to decimal form.

Solution

$$1 \times 2^0 = 1$$
$$0 \times 2^1 = 0$$
$$1 \times 2^2 = 4$$
$$1 \times 2^3 = 8$$
$$0 \times 2^4 = 0$$
$$1 \times 2^5 = \underline{32}$$
$$45$$

1 0 1 1 0 1

Decimal number 45 is the equivalent of binary number 101101.

▶ **EXAMPLE 16-10** Convert binary number 110110.010 to decimal form.

Solution

1 1 0 1 1 0 . 0 1 0

$$0 \times 2^{-3} = 0$$
$$1 \times 2^{-2} = 0.25$$
$$0 \times 2^{-1} = 0$$
$$0 \times 2^0 = 0$$
$$1 \times 2^1 = 2$$
$$1 \times 2^2 = 4$$
$$0 \times 2^3 = 0$$
$$1 \times 2^4 = 16$$
$$1 \times 2^5 = \underline{32}$$
$$54.25$$

Decimal number 54.25 is the equivalent of binary number 110110.010.

16-9 DECIMAL-TO-BINARY CONVERSION

Decimal values entered into a digital machine must be converted, or **encoded**, into decimal form. This is accomplished by using an encoder chip. To convert a decimal number into binary form, divide the decimal number by 2 and record the remainders as shown below:

25_{10} to binary

$$\frac{25}{2} = 12 + \text{remainder of } 1$$

$$\frac{12}{2} = 6 + \text{remainder of } 0$$

$$\frac{6}{2} = 3 + \text{remainder of } 0$$

$$\frac{3}{2} = 1 + \text{remainder of } 1$$

$$\frac{1}{2} = 0 + \text{remainder of } 1$$

$$\text{MSB} \, 1 \quad 1 \quad 0 \quad 0 \quad 1 \, _{\text{LSB}}$$

The equivalent binary number of decimal number 25 is 11001.

The number determined in decimal-to-binary conversion can be proven by converting the binary number back to decimal form.

Solution

Convert 175_{10} to binary and prove that it is correct.

$175 \div 2 = 87$ with a remainder of 1 (LSB)
$87 \div 2 = 43$ with a remainder of 1
$43 \div 2 = 21$ with a remainder of 1
$21 \div 2 = 10$ with a remainder of 1
$10 \div 2 = 5$ with a remainder of 0
$5 \div 2 = 2$ with a remainder of 1
$2 \div 2 = 1$ with a remainder of 0
$1 \div 2 = 0$ with a remainder of 1 (MSB)

$$175_{10} = 10101111_2$$
$$10101111_2 = 175_{10}$$

$1 \times 2^0 = 1$
$1 \times 2^1 = 2$
$1 \times 2^2 = 4$
$1 \times 2^3 = 8$
$0 \times 2^4 = 0$
$1 \times 2^5 = 32$
$0 \times 2^6 = 0$
$1 \times 2^7 = 128$

$$\underline{\qquad}$$
$$175$$

16-10 OCTAL NUMBER SYSTEM

The octal number system is used by some PLC manufacturers, such as Allen-Bradley, for I/O addressing. The octal number system has a base of eight, which means that it has eight possible digits: 0, 1, 2, 3, 4, 5, 6, and 7. Position weighting is applied to the octal system in the same way it is applied to the decimal and binary systems. That is, as digits move to the left of the decimal place, they increase by the power of their base. Because octal uses the base 8 number system, the numbers increase by the power of 8 as they move to the left, and decrease by the power of 8 as they move to the right of the decimal place.

The weights of the digit positions in an octal number are as follows:

$$8^n.....8^4 \quad 8^3 \quad 8^2 \quad 8^1 \quad 8^0 \quad . \quad 8^{-1} \quad 8^{-2} \quad 8^{-3} \quad 8^{-4}...8^{-n}$$

To convert an octal number to a decimal number, multiply each octal digit by its weight and add the resulting products. For example, octal number 17 is converted to decimal in the following manner:

$$1(8^1) + 7(8^0) = 8 + 7 = 15 \quad \text{decimal}$$

Solution

Convert 362_8 to decimal.

$$3(8^2) + 6(8^1) + 2(8^0) = 192 + 48 + 2 = 242_{10}$$

Decimal numbers can be converted to octal numbers by dividing the decimal number by 8. The remainders form the decimal number, with the first remainder being the least-significant digit and the last remainder being the most-significant digit. An example of converting 214_{10} to octal is

$$\frac{214}{8} = 26 \text{ with a remainder of 6}$$

$$\frac{26}{8} = 3 \text{ with a remainder of 2}$$

$$\frac{3}{8} = 0 \text{ with a remainder of } \frac{3}{326}$$

When converting a decimal fraction to octal, the decimal number is multiplied instead of divided. Also, the first number divided is now the most-significant digit, and the last number is the least-significant digit. For instance, to change 0.35_{10} to octal, proceed as follows:

$$0.35 \times 8 = 2.8 = 0.8 \text{ with a carry of 2}$$
$$0.8 \times 8 = 6.4 = 0.4 \text{ with a carry of 6}$$
$$0.4 \times 8 = 3.2 = 0.2 \text{ with a carry of } \frac{3}{0.263}$$
$$\text{etc.}$$

▶ **EXAMPLE 16-13**

Convert the following decimal numbers to octal: (a) 624 (b) 0.472 (c) 25.5.

Solution

(a) 624/8 = 78 with a remainder of 0
78/8 = 9 with a remainder of 6
9/8 = 1 with a remainder of 1
1/8 = 0 with a remainder of $\frac{1}{1,160}$

(b) 0.472 × 8 = 3.776 = 0.776 with a carry of 3
0.776 × 8 = 6.208 = 0.208 with a carry of 6
0.208 × 8 = 1.664 = 0.664 with a carry of $\frac{1}{0.361}$
etc.

(c) 25/8 = 3 with a remainder of 1
3/8 = 0 with a remainder of $\frac{3}{31}$

0.5 × 8 = 4.0 = 0 with a carry of 4
$25.5_{10} = 31.48$

16-11 OCTAL-TO-BINARY CONVERSION

An octal number is converted to its binary equivalent by changing each octal digit to its three-bit binary equivalent. The eight possible digits are converted as shown in Table 16-1.

TABLE 16-1

Octal Number	Binary Equivalent
0	000
1	001
2	010
3	011
4	100
5	101
6	110
7	111

The following example illustrates how to convert an octal number to its binary equivalent:

▲ *EXAMPLE 16-14*

Convert each of the following octal numbers to binary: (a) 25 (b) 177 (c) 13.65.

Solution

(a) 2   5
     ↓   ↓
    010   101

The binary equivalent of 25_8 is 010 101, or 10 101.

(b) 1   7   7
     ↓   ↓   ↓
    001   111   111

The binary equivalent of 177_8 is 001 111 111, or 1 111 111.

(c) 1   3   6   5
     ↓   ↓   ↓   ↓
    001 011   110   101

$13.65_8 = 001\ 011\ .\ 110\ 101$
$= 1\ 011\ .\ 110\ 101$

16-12 BINARY-TO-OCTAL CONVERSION

The conversion from binary to octal is very simple, and requires only that a given binary number be divided into three-bit sections, beginning at the least-significant digit side of the number. Each three-bit portion of the binary number is then converted into an octal number, using the same 4-2-1 weighting that was applied in the octal-to-binary conversion process.

In situations where the binary number does not divide evenly into groups of three, add 0s to the most-significant digit side of the binary number. The following example illustrates binary-to-octal conversion.

▲ *EXAMPLE 16-15*

Convert the following binary numbers to equivalent octal numbers: (a) 1011101011 (b) 11011011011011 (c) 100011.1011.

Solution

(a) 010 | 111 | 011 | 011
      ↓   ↓   ↓   ↓
      2   7   3   3

$1011101011_2 = 2733_8$

(b) $001 \mid 101 \mid 101 \mid 110 \mid 111 \mid 011$

$\quad\ \downarrow\quad\ \downarrow\quad\ \downarrow\quad\ \downarrow\quad\ \downarrow\quad\ \downarrow$

$\quad\ 1\qquad 5\qquad 5\qquad 6\qquad 7\qquad 3$

$110110111011011_2 = 155673_8$

(c) $100 \mid 011 \mid . \mid 101 \mid 100$

$\quad\ \downarrow\quad\ \downarrow\quad\ .\quad\ \downarrow\quad\ \downarrow$

$\quad\ 4\qquad 3\qquad .\qquad 5\qquad 4$

$100011.1011_2 = 43.54_8$

16-13 HEXADECIMAL NUMBER SYSTEM

The hexadecimal system uses base 16. This means it has 16 possible digit symbols. The hexadecimal number system uses the ten digits in the decimal system, 0 through 9, as well as the first six letters of the alphabet, A, B, C, D, E, and F. It is important to remember that the six alphabetic letters used are equivalent to decimal numbers 10, 11, 12, 13, 14, and 15. Table 16-2 shows a comparison between decimal, binary, and hexadecimal digits.

The use of letters to represent numbers may seem strange initially, although any number system is actually a set of symbols. As was the case with octal numbers, the hex code is simple to interpret in terms of binary digits and is easy to read. This makes the hexadecimal system well-suited for representing binary numbers and digital codes.

Any hexadecimal number can be converted to its decimal equivalent in a manner similar to an octal number being converted to decimal. The hexadecimal system uses base 16, which means position weighting moves to the left of the decimal place by the power of 16.

$$16^4 \quad 16^3 \quad 16^2 \quad 16^1 \quad 16^0 \quad . \quad 16^{-1} \quad 16^{-2} \quad 16^{-3} \quad 16^{-4}$$

The following example illustrates a hexadecimal-to-decimal conversion:

$$539_{16} = 5 \times 16^2 + 3 \times 16^1 + 9 \times 16^0$$
$$= 1{,}280 + 48 + 9$$
$$= 1{,}337_{10}$$

TABLE 16-2

Decimal	Binary	Hexadecimal
0	0000	0
1	0001	1
2	0010	2
3	0011	3
4	0100	4
5	0101	5
6	0110	6
7	0111	7
8	1000	8
9	1001	9
10	1010	A
11	1011	B
12	1100	C
13	1101	D
14	1110	E
15	1111	F

EXAMPLE 16-16

Convert the following hexadecimal numbers to their decimal equivalents: (a) 3AF (b) B2E7 (c) FACE.

Solution

(a) $3AF_{16} = 3 \times 16^2 + 10 \times 16^1 + 15 \times 16^0$
$= 768 + 160 + 15$
$= 943_{10}$

(b) $B2E7_{16} = 11 \times 163 + 2 \times 16^2 + 14 \times 16^1 + 7 \times 16^0$
$= 45,056 + 512 + 224 + 7$
$= 45,799_{10}$

(c) $FACE_{16} = 15 \times 16^3 + 10 \times 16^2 + 12 \times 16^1 + 14 \times 16^0$
$= 61,440 + 2,560 + 192 + 14$
$= 64,206_{10}$

To convert from a decimal number to a hexadecimal number, divide the decimal number by 16 and keep track of the remainders. The remainders will form the hexadecimal equivalent number. For example, to convert the decimal number 283 to hex,

$283/16 = 17$ with a remainder of 11 (B)
$17/16 = 1$ with a remainder of 1

The hexadecimal equivalent of the decimal number 283_{10} is $1B_{16}$.

▼ EXAMPLE 16-17

Convert the following decimal numbers to their hexadecimal equivalents: (a) 2377 (b) 62 (c) 35599.

Solution

(a) $2377/16 = 148$ with a remainder of 9
$148/16 = 9$ with a remainder of 4
$9/16 = 0$ with a remainder of 9

$2377_{10} = 949_{16}$

(b) $62/16 = 3$ with a remainder of 14 (E)
$3/16 = 0$ with a remainder of 3

$62_{10} = 3E_{16}$

(c) $35599/16 = 2224$ with a remainder of 15 (F)
$2224/16 = 139$ with a remainder of 0
$139/16 = 8$ with a remainder of 11 (B)
$8/16 = 0$ with a remainder of 8

$35599_{10} = 8B0F_{16}$

16-14 HEXADECIMAL-TO-BINARY CONVERSION

Hexadecimal numbers are converted to binary form by determining the four-bit equivalent binary digit for each hexadecimal digit. This method is also known as the 8-4-2-1 system. The following example illustrates hex-to-binary conversion:

3A16₁₆ to binary

8421	8421	8421	8421
3	A	1	6
↓	↓	↓	↓
0011	1010	0001	0110

$$3A516_{16} = 0011\ 1010\ 0001\ 0110, \text{ or } 11\ 1010\ 0001\ 0110$$

▶ **EXAMPLE 16-18** Convert the following hexadecimal numbers to their binary equivalents: (a) E277 (b) 92F6 (c) FFA3B.

Solution

(a)
E	2	7	7
↓	↓	↓	↓
1110	0010	0111	0111

(b)
9	2	F	6
↓	↓	↓	↓
1001	0010	1111	0110

(c)
F	F	A	3	B
↓	↓	↓	↓	↓
1111	1111	1010	0011	1011

16-15 BINARY-TO-HEXADECIMAL CONVERSION

This conversion is the reverse process of that discussed in the previous section. A binary word is divided into groups of four bits, and the equivalent hexadecimal number is determined. 0s are added to the most-significant digit side of the binary number to form groups of four.

▶ **EXAMPLE 16-19** Convert the following binary numbers into hexadecimal numbers: (a) 11101110101011101 (b) 101011101010100110101 (c) 1100110010101100111.

Solution

(a)
0001	1101	1101	0101	1101
↓	↓	↓	↓	↓
1	D	D	5	D

$$11101110101011101_2 = 1DD5D_{16}$$

(b)
0101	0111	0101	0011	0101
↓	↓	↓	↓	↓
5	7	5	3	5

$$101011101010100110101_2 = 57535_{16}$$

(c)
0110	0110	0101	0110	0111
↓	↓	↓	↓	↓
6	6	5	6	7

$$1100110010101100111_2 = 66567_{16}$$

16-16 BINARY CODED DECIMAL (BCD)

Binary Coded Decimal (BCD) is a modification of the decimal number system where the decimal digits are independently coded as four-bit binary numbers. There are many types of BCD codes, with the 8-4-2-1 code being the most popular.

TABLE 16-3 BCD Code with Binary and Decimal Equivalents

Decimal	BCD	Binary
0	0000	0
1	0001	1
2	0010	10
3	0011	11
4	0100	100
5	0101	101
6	0110	110
7	0111	111
8	1000	1000
9	1001	1001
10	0001 0000	1010
11	0001 0001	1011
12	0001 0010	1100
13	0001 0011	1101
14	0001 0100	1110
15	0001 0101	1111

In this discussion of BCD codes, we will consider the 8-4-2-1 system to be the only BCD system under consideration. The designation 8-4-2-1 indicates the binary weights of the four bits (2^3, 2^2, 2^1, 2^0). The BCD system was developed to make the conversion from decimal numbers to binary easier. Using four bits, it is possible to count from 1 to 15. However, in the BCD system, the six numbers over 9 are not valid. For example, 1011 is not a legitimate BCD number because 1011 does not convert to a single decimal digit. Any number over 9 must be represented by two BCD numbers, or eight bits. Table 16-3 illustrates the relationship between the BCD system, the natural binary system previously discussed, and the decimal number system.

To express any decimal number in BCD, simply replace each decimal digit by the appropriate four-bit code. To illustrate the BCD code, consider the number 375. Each digit is changed to its binary equivalent as follows:

```
  3      7      5    (decimal)
  ↓      ↓      ↓
0011   1110   0101
```

In the above example, 0011 1110 0101 is the BCD equivalent of the decimal number 375. Because the 0s on the most-significant digit side can be ignored, 11 1110 0101 is also the correct expression for the decimal number 375.

▲
EXAMPLE 16-20

Convert the following decimal numbers into BCD: (a) 27 (b) 458 (c) 72.6.

Solution

(a)
```
  2      7
  ↓      ↓
0010   0111
```

(b)
```
  4      5      8
  ↓      ↓      ↓
0100   0101   1000
```

(c)
```
  7      2     .6
  ↓      ↓      ↓
0111   0010 . 0110
```

It is also quite simple to determine a decimal number from a BCD number. Start at the least-significant bit and break the code into groups of four bits. The decimal digit represented by each four-bit group is then written.

▶ EXAMPLE 16-21

Convert the following BCD numbers into decimal numbers: (a) 1001 0110 0101 (b) 1000 0001 (c) 1000 0111 . 1001.

Solution

(a) 1001   0110   0101
    ↓   ↓   ↓
    9   6   5

(b) 1000   0001
    ↓   ↓
    8   1

(c) 1000   0111 . 1001
    ↓   ↓   ↓
    8   7 . 9

16-17 THE PARITY BIT

PLC data highways and communication systems use a binary digit to check the accuracy of data transmission. For example, when data are being transferred between PLCs or from a PLC to a peripheral device, one of the binary digits may be accidently changed from a 1 to a 0. This can happen due to a transient, noise, or by a failure in some portion of the transmission network. A parity bit is used to detect errors that may occur while a word is being moved.

Even parity is a method of adding a binary digit to a word to make the total number of 1s in the word even. For example, consider the binary word 010101. There are three 1s in this word. To make the word conform to even parity, a 1 is added to the word, which results in 0101011.

Odd parity is used to make the number of 1s odd. Table 16-4 shows the 8-4-2-1 code with even and odd parities.

TABLE 16-4

8-4-2-1 Code	Even Parity Bit	Odd Parity Bit
0000	0	1
0001	1	0
0010	1	0
0011	0	1
0100	1	0
0101	0	1
0110	0	1
0111	1	0
1000	1	0
1001	0	1

▶ EXAMPLE 16-22

Encode the following numbers into 8-4-2-1 code and attach an even parity bit to the end of each word: (a) 277 (b) 3276 (c) 93544.

Solution

(a) 277 = 0010 0111 0111
    There are seven 1s, so a 1 is added to the end.
    0010 0111 0111 1

(b) 3276 = 0011 0010 0111 0110

There are eight 1s, so 0 is added.

0011 0010 0111 0110 0

(c) 93544 = 1001 0011 0101 0100 0100

There are eight 1s, so 0 is added.

1001 0011 0101 0100 0100

16-18 GRAY CODE

The Gray code is a special type of binary code that does not use position weighting. In other words, each position does not have a definite weight. The Gray code is set up so that as we progress from one number to the next, only one bit changes. For this reason, the Gray code can be quite confusing for manual counting, but it is ideal for systems such as computers and PLCs. The Gray code is considered to be an error-minimizing code because it greatly reduces the possibility of ambiguity in the electronic circuitry when changing from one state to the next. Because only one bit changes at a time, the speed of transition for the Gray code is considerably faster than codes such as BCD.

A standard application for the Gray code in a PLC system is in encoder circuits. An **absolute encoder** is a position transducer which uses the Gray code to determine angular position. Table 16-5 shows the Gray code and binary equivalents for comparison.

TABLE 16-5

Gray Code	Binary
0000	0000
0001	0001
0011	0010
0010	0011
0110	0100
0111	0101
0101	0110
0100	0111
1100	1000
1101	1001
1111	1010
1110	1011
1010	1100
1011	1101
1001	1110
1000	1111

16-19 ASCII CODE

ASCII stands for American Standard Code for Information Interchange. It is an alphanumeric code, which includes letters as well as numbers. The characters accessed by the ASCII code include 10 numeric digits, 26 lower-case and 26 upper-case letters of the alphabet, and about 25 special characters, including those found on a standard typewriter, i.e., @, #, $, %, *, etc.

ASCII code is a seven-bit code in which decimal digits are represented by the 8-4-2-1 BCD code preceded by 011. Upper-case letters are preceded by 100 or 101. Lower-case letters are preceded by 110 or 111. Character symbols are preceded by 010, 011, 101, and 111. This seven-bit code provides all possible combinations of characters used when communicating with peripherals or interfaces in a PLC system.

TABLE 16-6 Partial Listing of ASCII Code

Character	7-bit ASCII
A	100 0001
B	100 0010
C	100 0011
D	100 0100
E	100 0101
F	100 0110
G	100 0111
H	100 1000
I	100 1001
J	100 1010
K	100 1011
L	100 1100
M	100 1101
N	100 1110
O	100 1111
P	101 0000
Q	101 0001
R	101 0010
S	101 0011
T	101 0100
U	101 0101
V	101 0110
W	101 0111
X	101 1000
Y	101 1001
Z	101 1010
0	011 0000
1	011 0001
2	011 0010
3	011 0011
4	011 0100
5	011 0101
6	011 0110
7	011 0111
8	011 1000
9	011 1001
blank	010 0000
.	010 1110
;	010 1100
+	010 1011
–	010 1101
#	010 0011
(	010 1000
%	010 0101
=	011 1101

Table 16-6 is a partial listing of the ASCII code. In some cases, an eighth bit is added to the standard seven-bit code for error checking. The eighth bit is the parity bit. If the parity is supposed to be even, the letter B would be represented by 0100 0010, which has an even number of 1s in the word. If odd parity is used, the letter B would have an ASCII code of 1100 0010.

REVIEW QUESTIONS

16-1. What is a number system?

16-2. Define the term "radix."

16-3. Express the decimal number 285 in exponential form.

16-4. What is sign-magnitude representation?

16-5. Express the binary number 11011 in exponential form.

16-6. Define the term "sign bit."

16-7. What are the two most common methods of expressing a negative number in a digital system?

16-8. What is the difference between the 2's complement of a number and the 1's complement?

16-9. Add the following binary numbers:

(a) 110 and 111

(b) 101 and 011

(c) 1100 and 1011

16-10. What is the advantage of using the 2's complement system when adding or subtracting binary numbers?

16-11. Subtract the following binary numbers:

(a) 1101 − 101

(b) 1001 − 110

(c) 10111 − 10010

16-12. Multiply the following unsigned binary numbers:

(a) 110 × 110

(b) 010 × 101

(c) 101.11 × 11.10

16-13. Multiply the following signed binary numbers:

(a) 0101 × 1101

(b) 101 × 1011

(c) 1111 × 0101

16-14. Divide the following unsigned binary numbers:

(a) 1011 by 10

(b) 1100 by 11

(c) 110110 by 101

16-15. What is meant by the term "decoding"?

16-16. Convert the following binary numbers to decimal form:

(a) 1010101

(b) 1101101

(c) 10101.011

16-17. Define the term "encoding."

16-18. Convert the following decimal numbers to binary form:

(a) 185

(b) 577

(c) 2396

16-19. Change the following octal numbers to decimal form:

(a) 176

(b) 235

(c) 7263

16-20. Convert the following decimal numbers to octal:

(a) 839

(b) 0.568

(c) 29.3

16-21. Change each of the following octal numbers to binary:

(a) 37

(b) 271

(c) 14.77

16-22. Convert the following binary numbers to equivalent octal numbers:
   (a) 11011010101
   (b) 110111110101
   (c) 1010101011011

16-23. List the 16 digits used in the hexadecimal number system.

16-24. Convert the following hexadecimal numbers to their decimal equivalents:
   (a) 1B7
   (b) DE6C
   (c) F2E9

16-25. Change the following decimal numbers to their hexadecimal equivalents:
   (a) 2492
   (b) 83996
   (c) 492648

16-26. Convert the following hexadecimal numbers into binary form:
   (a) 2E3
   (b) 9FF6
   (c) A73FE

16-27. Change the following binary numbers into hexadecimal numbers:
   (a) 1010110101
   (b) 111011101101101
   (c) 101010111110101

16-28. What is the difference between Binary Coded Decimal (BCD) and binary?

16-29. Convert the following decimal numbers to BCD:
   (a) 35
   (b) 971
   (c) 87.5

16-30. Why are parity bits used?

16-31. What is the difference between even parity and odd parity?

16-32. Encode the following decimal numbers into 8-4-2-1 code and attach an even parity bit to the end of each word:
   (a) 296
   (b) 4879
   (c) 92965

16-33. What is Gray code and how is it unique?

16-34. Name one standard application for Gray code in PLC-controlled systems.

16-35. What is ASCII code?

Digital Logic

17

Upon completion of this chapter, you will be able to

▼ Apply truth tables to troubleshooting digital circuits.

▼ List five logic gates.

▼ Describe the basic operation of an inverter.

▼ Explain the purpose of Boolean algebra.

▼ Understand logic gate combinations.

▼ Convert digital logic to ladder logic.

▼ Name eight Boolean theorems.

▼ Apply DeMorgan's theorem to ladder logic circuits.

17-1 INTRODUCTION

All digital equipment, regardless of its complexity, is constructed from combinations of logic gates. A logic gate is a decision-making element. The gate produces an output that is high or low, depending on its input conditions. In this chapter, we shall examine the principles of logic gates and how they apply to PLCs. We will see how logic gates can be combined to form logic circuits. Truth tables will also be discussed in this chapter as both a troubleshooting tool as well as a method of understanding the operation of logic gates. A **truth table** is basically a graphical illustration of the relationship between input and output logic levels of a gate circuit.

The concept of Boolean algebra will also be introduced in this chapter. Boolean algebra is an essential mathematical language in the study of PLCs. Many PLCs use this language to write complex programs containing many variables. In our discussion of process control systems, it was noted that as the number of variables to be controlled increases, the usefulness of ladder logic decreases. In these situations, languages such as Boolean are ideally suited for solving complex control problems.

The five logic gates that we shall discuss in this chapter are the AND, OR, NOT, NAND, and NOR gates. In a logic gate circuit, input and output signals can only assume one of two possible logic levels, or states. These logic levels are indicated by the binary numbers 0 and 1. In addition to logic gates and Boolean algebra, we shall also examine the parallels between digital logic circuits and ladder logic.

17-2 AND GATES

Electric circuits are composed of combinations of series and parallel connected elements. The same is true for digital circuits. Figure 17-1 shows two switches connected in series. For lamp Z to be energized, both switches must be closed. It can therefore be stated that for output Z to be energized, switch A "AND" switch B must both be closed.

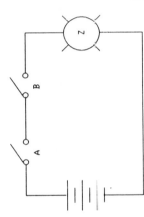

Figure 17-1 Electrical series circuit.

A truth table shows how a circuit's output responds to various combinations of input signals. The truth table for the circuit of Figure 17-1 would be as shown in Figure 17-2.

Switch A	Switch B	Output Z
Open	Open	OFF
Open	Closed	OFF
Closed	Open	OFF
Closed	Closed	ON

Figure 17-2 Truth table for circuit of Figure 17-1.

If we assume binary 1 is a closed switch and binary 0 is an open switch, the truth table for Figure 17-1 would be as shown in Figure 17-3. Boolean algebra is often used to express the mathematical function of a logic gate. Boolean algebra was developed by George Boole in 1847. However, it wasn't until 1938 that an engineer by the name of Claude Shannon showed how Boolean algebra could be used to analyze the two-state switching of relay logic circuits.

Switch A	Switch B	Output Z
0	0	0
0	1	0
1	0	0
1	1	1

Figure 17-3 Another truth table scenario for the circuit of Figure 17-1.

The · symbol is used to express the AND operation in Boolean terms. The Boolean equation for a two-input AND gate would be as follows:

$$A \cdot B = Z$$

The · symbol is optional for the AND function. If two letters are together with no symbol, the AND operation is implied. For example, the above equation could also be expressed as

$$AB = Z$$

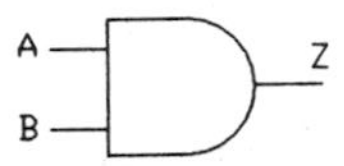

The equivalent logic gate for the circuit of Figure 17-1 would be the two-input AND gate shown in Figure 17-4. For any AND gate, regardless of the number of inputs, the output is high only when all the inputs are high. The total number of possible combinations of binary inputs is determined by the following equation:

$$N = 2^n$$

where N = the total possible combinations
n = the number of input variables

▼
EXAMPLE 17-1

Determine the total possible combinations of input states for a four-input AND gate.

Solution

$$
\begin{aligned}
N &= 2^n \\
&= 2^4 \\
&= 16
\end{aligned}
$$

▼
EXAMPLE 17-2

Derive a truth table for a three-input AND gate.

Solution

The truth table for a three-input AND gate is shown in Figure 17-5.

A	B	C	Z
0	0	0	0
0	0	1	0
0	1	0	0
0	1	1	0
1	0	0	0
1	0	1	0
1	1	0	0
1	1	1	1

Figure 17-5 Truth table for three-input AND gate.

17-3 OR GATES

Figure 17-6 shows two switches connected in parallel. For output Z to be energized, either or both switches must be closed. Therefore, Switch A "OR" Switch B must be closed to energized output Z.

The equivalent logic gate for the circuit shown in Figure 17-6 is the OR gate. The OR gate is essentially a parallel circuit that produces an output voltage when

Figure 17-4 Two-input AND gate.

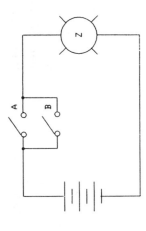

Figure 17-6 Parallel circuit.

a voltage appears at any input. The schematic symbol for a two-input OR gate is shown in Figure 17-7.

Figure 17-7 Two-input OR gate.

The truth table for a two-input OR gate is shown in Figure 17-8.

The + symbol is used to express the OR function in Boolean algebra. The Boolean equation for a two-input OR gate would be as follows:

$$A + B = Z$$

A	B	Z
0	0	0
0	1	1
1	0	1
1	1	1

Figure 17-8 Truth table for two-input OR gate.

17-4 THE INVERTER

An inverter is a digital circuit which takes a digital input and produces an output which is the opposite state of the input. For example, if the input to an inverter were binary 0, the output would be binary 1. Conversely, a binary 1 input results in a binary 0 output.

The electrical circuit shown in Figure 17-9 is the basic equivalent of a digital inverter. If switch A is "NOT" closed, the output will be ON. Closing switch A turns OFF the output.

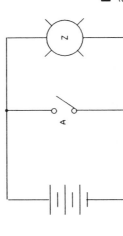

Figure 17-9 Equivalent electrical circuit for an inverter.

Figure 17-10 shows the two basic symbols that are used to represent an inverter. The inversion is indicated by the small circle on either the input or output side of the triangle. The triangle symbol itself is used to represent a buffer amplifier. A buffer amplifier is essentially a current source which does not amplify voltage.

Figure 17-10 Schematic symbols for an inverter.

The Boolean equation for an inverter with A designated as the input and Z as the output is as follows:

$$A = \overline{Z}$$

A	Z
0	1
1	0

Figure 17-11 Truth table for an inverter.

The line above the output implies an inversion. The truth table for the inverter is shown in Figure 17-11.

17-5 THE NAND GATE

The NAND gate is simply an AND gate with an inverter connected to the output, as shown in Figure 17-12(a). The schematic symbol for a NAND gate is shown in Figure 17-12(b). The circle on the output of the AND gate shown in Figure 17-12(b) denotes the inversion operation.

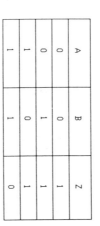

(a)   (b)

Figure 17-12 (a) AND gate with inverter; (b) NAND gate.

The output of the NAND gate is exactly the opposite of the AND gate for the same combinations of inputs. Therefore, the output of the NAND will only be low when *all* inputs are high. When *any* of the inputs are low, the output will be high. The truth table for a two-input AND gate is shown in Figure 17-13.

A	B	Z
0	0	1
0	1	1
1	0	1
1	1	0

Figure 17-13 Truth table for two-input NAND gate.

The Boolean equation for a two-input NAND gate with inputs labelled A, B, and the output labelled Z, would be as follows:

$$A \cdot B = \overline{Z}$$

or,

$$\overline{A \cdot B} = Z$$

Both of the above equations would adequately represent a two-input NAND gate. Inverting either the entire input or entire output would produce a similar mathematical result.

17-6 THE NOR GATE

The NOR gate is an OR gate with an inverter connected to the output, as shown in Figure 17-14(a). The schematic symbol for the NOR gate is shown in Figure 17-14(b).

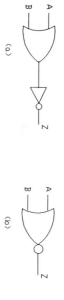

(a)   (b)

Figure 17-14 (a) OR gate with inverter; (b) NOR gate.

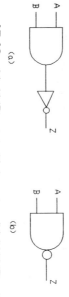

The output of the NOR gate is exactly the opposite of the OR gate for the same combinations of inputs. The output of the NOR gate is low when *any* of the inputs are high. The output is high only when *all* the inputs are low. The truth table for a two-input NOR gate is shown in Figure 17-15.

A	B	Z
0	0	1
0	1	0
1	0	0
1	1	0

Figure 17-15 Truth table for two-input NOR gate.

The Boolean equation for a two-input NOR gate with inputs A, B, and output labelled Z would be as follows:

$$A + B = \overline{Z}$$

or,

$$\overline{A + B} = Z$$

17-7 LOGIC GATE COMBINATIONS

As logic circuits become more complex, the need to express these circuits in Boolean form becomes greater. A simple logic gate is quite straightforward in its operation. However, by grouping these gates into combinations, it becomes more difficult to determine which combinations of inputs will produce an output. Consider the circuit of Figure 17-16. Two OR gates and one AND gate form a logic gate combination that will cause output Z to become energized when a specific input combination is applied at A, B, C, and D.

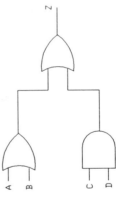

Figure 17-16 A logic gate combination.

The Boolean equation for the circuit of Figure 17-16 would be as follows:

$$(A + B) + (CD) = Z$$

The above Boolean equation tells us that if inputs A or B are high, the output will be high. Also, if inputs C and D are high, the output will be high. Output values for the truth table are derived from the Boolean equation, as shown in Figure 17-17.

▶ **EXAMPLE 17-3** For the circuit of Figure 17-18, determine the Boolean equation and truth table.

Solution

The output of gate 1 is AB, the output of gate 2 is BC, and the output of gate 3 is BCD. Because gate 4 is the output of gates 1 and 3, the Boolean equation is

$$AB + BCD = Z$$

The truth table is shown in Figure 17-19.

A	B	C	D	Z
0	0	0	0	0
0	0	0	1	0
0	0	1	0	0
0	0	1	1	1
0	1	0	0	0
0	1	0	1	1
0	1	1	0	1
0	1	1	1	1
1	0	0	0	0
1	0	0	1	1
1	0	1	0	1
1	0	1	1	1
1	1	0	0	1
1	1	0	1	1
1	1	1	0	1
1	1	1	1	1

Figure 17-17 Truth table for logic gate combination of Figure 17-16.

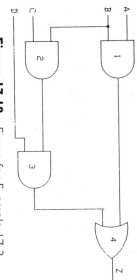

Figure 17-18 Figure for Example 17-3.

A	B	C	D	Z
0	0	0	0	0
0	0	0	1	0
0	0	1	0	0
0	0	1	1	0
0	1	0	0	0
0	1	0	1	0
0	1	1	0	1
0	1	1	1	0
1	0	0	0	0
1	0	0	1	0
1	0	1	0	0
1	0	1	1	0
1	1	0	0	0
1	1	0	1	1
1	1	1	0	0
1	1	1	1	1

Figure 17-19 Truth table solution for Example 17-3.

▶ **EXAMPLE 17-4**   Draw the logic circuit for the following Boolean equation:

$$AB + \overline{B}C = Z$$

Solution

The circuit in Figure 17-20 illustrates a logic gate combination that meets the requirements of the above Boolean equation. The inversion over B in the second portion of the equation is solved by connecting an inverter at the input of AND gate 2.

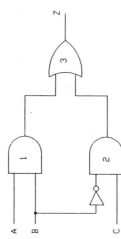

Figure 17-20   Circuit solution to Example 17-4.

▶ **EXAMPLE 17-5**   For the circuit of Figure 17-21, determine the Boolean equation and truth table.

Solution

The output of gate 1 is AC, the output of gate 2 is $B+\overline{C}$, and the output of gate 3 is $A\overline{B}$. Because the output of gate 4 depends on gates 1, 2, and 3, the Boolean equation is as follows:

$$AC + B + \overline{C} + A\overline{B} = Z$$

Figure 17-22 shows the truth table for the circuit of Figure 17-21.

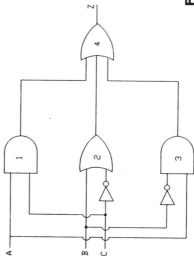

Figure 17-21   Circuit for Example 17-5.

A	B	C	Z
0	0	0	1
0	0	1	0
0	1	0	1
0	1	1	1
1	0	0	1
1	0	1	1
1	1	0	1
1	1	1	1

Figure 17-22   Truth table solution for Example 17-5.

17-8 CONVERTING DIGITAL LOGIC TO LADDER LOGIC

A digital logic circuit can be implemented on a PLC by either converting each individual gate to an equivalent ladder logic network, or by determining an equivalent ladder logic program based on the Boolean equation for the digital circuit.

Because the AND gate is essentially two series connected contacts, the equivalent ladder logic circuit for the two-input AND gate of Figure 17-23(a) is shown in Figure 17-23(b).

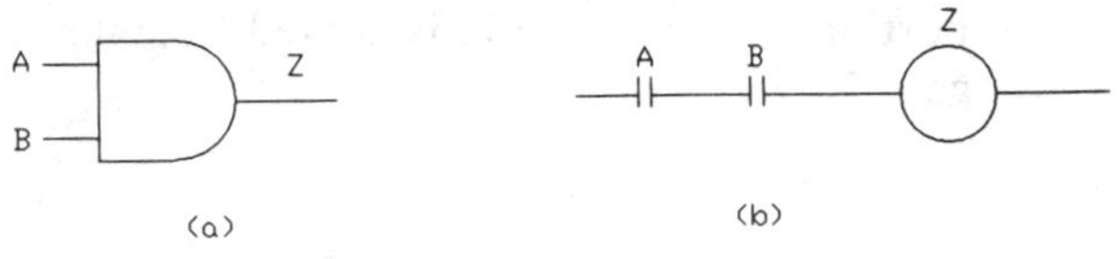

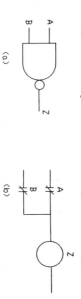

Figure 17-23 (a) AND gate; (b) Equivalent circuit.

The equivalent ladder logic of the two-input OR gate shown in Figure 17-24(a) is the ladder logic network of Figure 17-24(b).

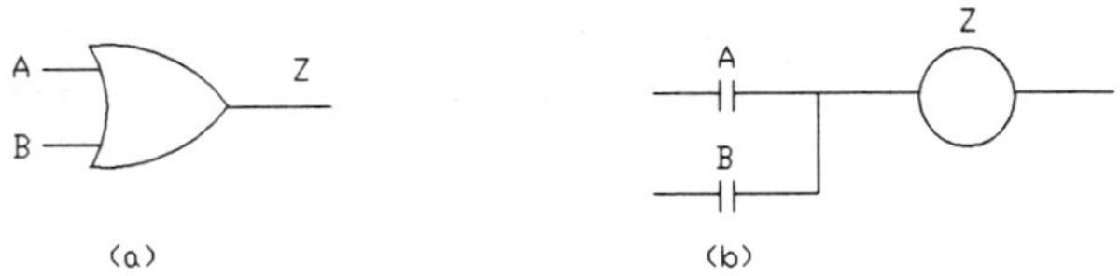

Figure 17-24 (a) OR gate; (b) Equivalent circuit.

The equivalent ladder logic circuit for the inverter of Figure 17-25(a) is shown in Figure 17-25(b). For this type of equivalent circuit, we are assuming that binary 0 represents a contact in its normal state, and binary 1 represents a contact in its changed state. In other words, when A is not changed, Z is ON. When A is changed from closed to open, Z turns OFF.

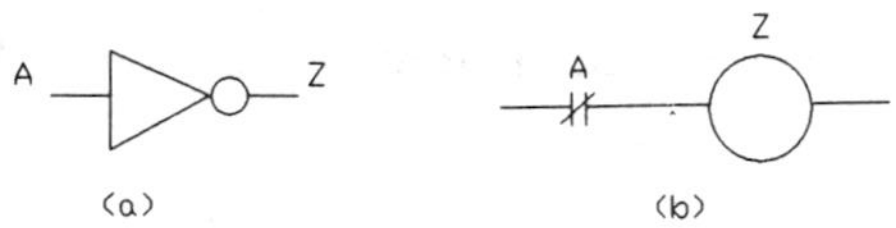

Figure 17-25 (a) Inverter; (b) Equivalent circuit.

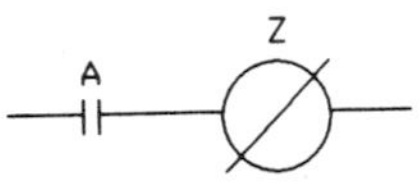

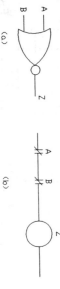

Figure 17-26 Inverse circuit from that illustrated in Figure 17-25.

Some PLCs, such as those made by Texas Instruments, have coils which perform the inverse function. That is, when no power reaches the coil it is ON, and when power reaches the coil it turns OFF. An equivalent inverter circuit for this type of coil is shown in Figure 17-26.

If we assume binary 0 is a contact in its normal resting state, and binary 1 is a contact in its changed state, the NAND gate of Figure 17-27(a) is represented in ladder logic form by the circuit of Figure 17-27(b). Because both input contacts are normally closed, if both inputs are at binary 0 the output is ON.

Figure 17-27 (a) NAND gate; (b) Equivalent circuit.

The equivalent ladder logic circuit for the NOR gate shown in Figure 17-28(a) is shown in Figure 17-28(b). Once again, we are assuming that binary 0 is a contact in its normal resting state, and binary 1 is a contact in its changed state.

Figure 17-28 (a) NOR gate; (b) Equivalent circuit.

► **EXAMPLE 17-6**

Convert the digital circuit shown in Figure 17-29 into an equivalent ladder logic circuit.

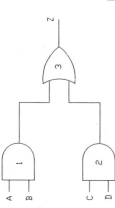

Figure 17-29   Figure for Example 17-6.

Solution

Because the digital circuit of Figure 17-29 has four inputs, the equivalent ladder logic circuit requires four contacts and one output coil. Logic gates 1 and 2 are AND gates, which means contacts A and B, as well as C and D must be in series. Gate 3 is an OR gate, so the two scts of contacts will be in parallel with each other. The equivalent ladder logic circuit is shown in Figure 17-30.

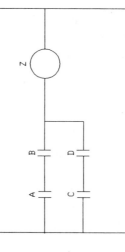

Figure 17-30   Ladder logic circuit solution for Example 17-6.

► **EXAMPLE 17-7**

Write the Boolean equation for the ladder logic circuit shown in Figure 17-31.

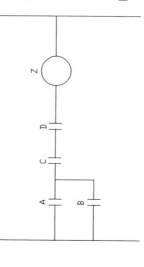

Figure 17-31   Circuit for Example 17-7.

Solution

The circuit of Figure 17-31 has two contacts in series and two in parallel. Therefore, the Boolean equation would be

$$(A + B) \cdot CD = Z$$

► **EXAMPLE 17-8**

Determine the equivalent digital logic circuit for the ladder logic circuit of Figure 17-31.

Solution

Contacts A and B would be represented by an OR gate. Contacts C and D would be an AND gate. Because A and B are in series with C and D, the output stage of the circuit would also be an AND gate. The circuit of Figure 17-32 is an equivalent digital circuit for the ladder logic circuit of Figure 17-31.

▼
EXAMPLE 17-9

Convert the digital circuit shown in Figure 17-33 into an equivalent ladder logic circuit.

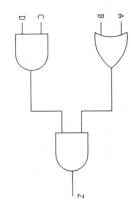

Figure 17-32 Digital circuit solution to Example 17-8.

Solution

It is easier to analyze the circuit of Figure 17-33 when shown as a Boolean equation. The output of gate 1 is AB, the output of gate 2 is $A\overline{B}$, the output of gate 3 is $\overline{B}C$, and the output of gate 4 is $A\overline{B} + \overline{B}C$. Because gates 1 and 4 are the inputs to gate 5, the Boolean equation is as follows:

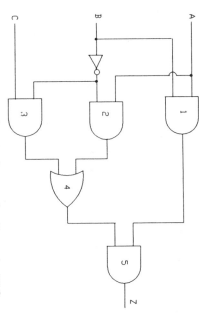

Figure 17-33 Circuit diagram for Example 17-9.

$$(A\overline{B} + \overline{B}C)AB = Z$$

From this equation, it can be seen that an NC contact will be required in the circuit. The equivalent ladder logic circuit is shown in Figure 17-34.

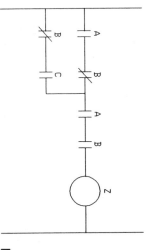

Figure 17-34 Solution to Example 17-9.

17-9 BOOLEAN THEOREMS

To program PLCs which use Boolean as a programming language, it is necessary to understand the basic concepts of Boolean algebra. In the previous chapter, Boolean equations for basic logic gates were derived. As Boolean equations increase in size and complexity, it becomes necessary to simplify these statements to their most basic form. Boolean theorems are used to reduce the size and complexity of Boolean equations. There are eight single variable theorems and seven multivariable theorems. The single variable theorems with equivalent ladder logic functions are shown in Table 17-1.

The seven multivariable theorems involve more than one variable. They are

9. x + y = y + x
10. xy = yx

(Theorems 9 and 10 are referred to as the *commutative laws*. They indicate that the order in which variables are added or multiplied is unimportant.)

11. x + (y + z) = (x + y) + z = x + y + z
12. x(yz) = (xy)z = xyz

(Theorems 11 and 12 are the *associative laws*, which state that it is possible to group the terms of a sum or product in any order that is desired.)

13. x(y + z) = xy + xz

(Theorem 13 is the *distributive law*, which states that an expression can be expanded by multiplying term by term, as in ordinary algebra.)

14. x + xy = x
15. x + $\overline{xy}$ = x + y

TABLE 17-1 Single Variable Theorems

Theorem	Ladder logic form	Reduced form	Boolean form
1.	A A	A	A·A = A
2.	A open circuit	open circuit	A·0 = 0
3.	A short circuit	short circuit	A+1 = 1
4.	A $\overline{A}$	short circuit	A+$\overline{A}$ = 1
5.	A A	A	A+A = A
6.	A $\overline{A}$	open circuit	A·$\overline{A}$ = 0
7.	A short circuit	A	A·1 = A
8.	A open circuit	A	A+0 = A

EXAMPLE 17-10 Simplify the ladder logic circuit shown in Figure 17-35.

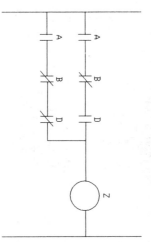

Figure 17-35 Circuit diagram for Example 17-10.

Solution

First, write the Boolean equation for the circuit.

$$A\overline{B}D + AB\overline{D} = Z$$

Factor out the common variables AB using Theorem 13.

$$AB(\overline{D} + D) = Z$$

According to Theorem 8, the term in brackets is equal to 1. Therefore,

$$Z = AB \cdot 1$$
$$= AB \text{ (according to Theorem 2)}$$

The simplified ladder logic program is shown in Figure 17-36. From Example 17-10, it is apparent that Boolean algebra can also be used in ladder logic applications to simplify existing ladder logic circuits.

Figure 17-36

EXAMPLE 17-11 Simplify $(\overline{A} + B)(A + \overline{B}) = Z$.

Solution

Multiply out the following terms:

$$\overline{A}A + \overline{A}\overline{B} + BA + B\overline{B} = Z$$

$\overline{A}A$ and $B\overline{B}$ are equal to zero (Theorem 4). Therefore,

$$Z = 0 + \overline{A}\overline{B} + BA + 0$$
$$= \overline{A}\overline{B} + BA$$

EXAMPLE 17-12 Simplify $ACD + \overline{A}BCD = Z$.

Solution

Factor out common variables CD by

$$CD(A + \overline{A}B) = Z$$

Use Theorem 15 to replace $A + \overline{A}B$ with $A + B$

$$Z = CD(A + B)$$

$$= ACD + BCD$$

17-10 APPLYING DEMORGAN'S THEOREMS TO LADDER LOGIC CIRCUITS

DeMorgan was a logician and mathematician who proposed two theorems that are an important part of Boolean algebra. DeMorgan's theorems are stated as follows:

1. The complement of a sum equals the product of the complements.
2. The complement of a product equals the sum of the complements.

In equation form,

$$\overline{A \cdot B} = \overline{A} + \overline{B}$$

$$\overline{A + B} = \overline{A} \cdot \overline{B}$$

DeMorgan's theorems are used mainly for simplifying logic circuits. The following examples illustrate how DeMorgan's theorems can be used to reduce digital and ladder logic circuits.

▶ **EXAMPLE 17-13**   Reduce the digital circuit in Figure 17-37 using DeMorgan's theorems.

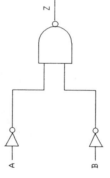

Figure 17-37   Circuit diagram for Example 17-13.

Solution
First, write the Boolean equation.

$$\overline{A} \cdot \overline{B} = \overline{Z}$$

Mathematically, whatever you do to one side of an equation, you can do to the other side. Therefore, if the entire output is inverted, the entire input could also be inverted.

$$\overline{\overline{A} \cdot \overline{B}} = \overline{Z}$$

Apply DeMorgan's theorem to the above equation.

$$\overline{\overline{A}} + \overline{\overline{B}} = Z$$

If an input is inverted twice, the double inversion cancels out.

$$A + B = Z$$

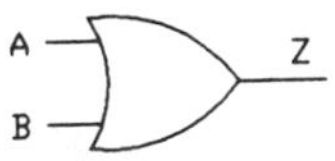

According to DeMorgan's theorems, the logic circuit of Figure 17-37 reduces to the OR gate shown in Figure 17-38.

Figure 17-38   OR gate solution to Example 17-13.

▲
EXAMPLE 17-14

Convert the digital logic circuit shown in Figure 17-39 to an equivalent ladder logic circuit using DeMorgan's theorems.

Solution

First, write the Boolean equation for the circuit.

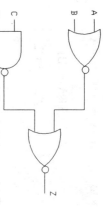

Figure 17-39 Circuit diagram for Example 17-14.

$$\overline{(A + B) + \overline{(C \cdot D)}} = \overline{Z}$$

$$\overline{(A + B)} + \overline{\overline{(C \cdot D)}} = Z$$

Apply DeMorgan's theorems.

$$\overline{(A + B)} \cdot \overline{(\overline{C \cdot D})} = Z$$

Remember, the double inversions cancel out.

$$(A + B) \cdot (C \cdot D) = Z$$

The equivalent ladder logic circuit is shown in Figure 17-40.

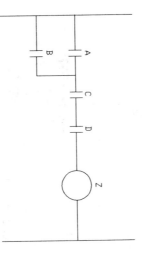

Figure 17-40 Solution circuit for Example 17-14.

▲
EXAMPLE 17-15

Convert the digital logic circuit shown in Figure 17-41 to ladder logic using DeMorgan's theorems.

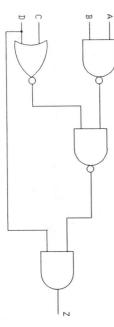

Figure 17-41 Circuit diagram for Example 17-15.

Solution

First, write the Boolean equation.

$$\overline{(A + B) \cdot (C \cdot D)} = Z$$

Apply DeMorgan's theorem.

$$\overline{\overline{(A \cdot B)} + \overline{(C + D)}} \cdot D = Z$$

The double inversions cancel out.

$$[(A \cdot B) + (C + D)] \cdot D = Z$$

$$ABD + CD + DD = Z$$

$$D(AB + C + 1) = Z$$

The equivalent ladder logic network is shown in Figure 17-42.

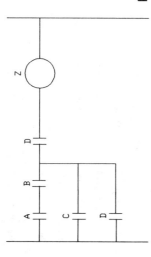

Figure 17-42

From Figure 17-42, it is apparent that if contact D is closed, output Z will be energized. Therefore, the circuit could be reduced further, as shown in Figure 17-43.

Figure 17-43

REVIEW QUESTIONS

17-1. What is a truth table?

17-2. Name the five types of logic gates.

17-3. What is meant by a "logic level"?

17-4. An AND gate operates on the same principle as
   (a) a series circuit.
   (b) a parallel circuit.
   (c) a series-parallel circuit.
   (d) none of the above.

17-5. Why use Boolean algebra in digital circuits?

17-6. Write the Boolean equation for a three-input AND gate.

17-7. Determine the total possible combinations of input states for a five-input AND gate.

17-8. Derive the truth table for a four-input AND gate.

17-9. An OR gate operates on the same principle as
   (a) a series circuit.
   (b) a parallel circuit.
   (c) a series-parallel circuit.
   (d) none of the above.

17-10. Write the Boolean equation for a two-input OR gate.

17-11. Derive the Boolean equation and truth table for the circuit shown in Figure 17-44.

17-12. Draw the schematic symbol for an inverter.

Figure 17-44 Figure for Question 17.11.

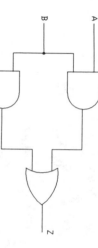

17-13. Write the Boolean equation for a two-input NAND gate.

17-14. Derive the truth table for a three-input NAND gate.

17-15. A NOR gate is
    (a) an AND gate with an inverter connected to the output.
    (b) an OR gate with an inverter connected to the output.
    (c) equivalent to a series circuit.
    (d) equivalent to a parallel circuit.

17-16. Write the Boolean equation for a four-input NOR gate.

17-17. Derive the truth table for a three-input NOR gate.

17-18. For the circuit of Figure 17-45, determine the Boolean equation and truth table.

17-19. Draw the logic circuit for the following Boolean equation:

$$(A+\overline{B}) \cdot (\overline{BC}) = Z$$

Figure 17-45 Figure for Question 17.18.

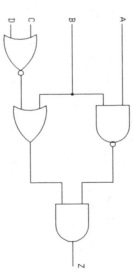

17-20. For the circuit of Figure 17-46, determine the Boolean equation and truth table.

17-21. What is the equivalent ladder logic circuit for a three-input AND gate?

17-22. Draw the equivalent ladder logic circuit for a two-input NOR gate.

17-23. Convert the digital circuit shown in Figure 17-47 into an equivalent ladder logic circuit.

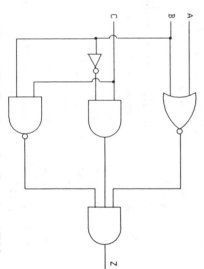

Figure 17-46 Figure for Question 17.20.

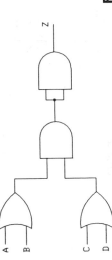

Figure 17-47 Figure for Question 17.23.

17-24. Write the Boolean equation for the ladder logic circuit shown in Figure 17-48.

17-25. Determine the equivalent digital logic circuit for the ladder logic circuit of Figure 17-48.

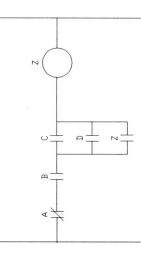

Figure 17-48 Figure for Question 17.24.

17-26. What are the two types of Boolean theorems?

17-27. Name the three laws associated with Boolean theorems.

17-28. Use Boolean theorems to simplify the ladder logic circuit shown in Figure 17-49.

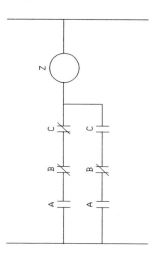

Figure 17-49 Figure for Question 17.28.

17-29. Simplify the following Boolean equation:

$$(A + \overline{B})\,(\overline{A} + B) = Z$$

17-30. Reduce the digital circuit in Figure 17-50 using DeMorgan's theorems.

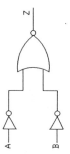

Figure 17-50 Figure for Question 17.30.

Review Questions

275

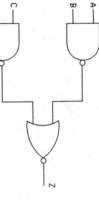

Figure 17-51 Figure for Question 17-31.

17-31. Convert the digital logic circuit shown in Figure 17-51 to an equivalent ladder logic circuit using DeMorgan's theorems.

Glossary of Terms

Abort: Terminates a process command.

Absolute encoder: A rotating device that transmits coded information back to a PLC indicating its various positions.

AC input module: Converts AC input signals into logic levels used by a PLC.

AC output module: Converts PLC logic signals into AC output voltages.

Across-the-line: Method of starting a motor by directly connecting the motor to the supply line when started.

Address: A reference number, label, or name assigned to an individual memory location. Each memory location in a processor has an address.

Algorithm: Mathematical procedure for problem-solving.

Alphanumeric: Character set used to represent any combination of numbers, letters, and symbols.

Alternating Current (AC): Current which changes in both magnitude and direction.

Ambient temperature: The temperature surrounding a device.

Ampacity: The maximum current rating of a conductor.

Ampere: Unit of electrical current.

Analog input module: A module which converts an analog signal into a digital signal.

Analog output module: A module which converts a digital signal into an analog signal.

Analog signal: A signal that depends entirely on magnitude to express a quantity.

AND gate: A combinational logic element that causes an output signal to appear only when there is an input signal present at all input points.

ANSI: American National Standards Institute.

Application memory: A section of system memory that is designated for the storage of application programs and related information.

Argument: An independent variable. For example, a number which identifies the memory location of a desired value.

Arithmetic Logic Unit (ALU): A processor subsystem that can perform arithmetic and logic gate functions.

Array: A combination of panels, such as LEDs, coordinated in structure and function.

ASA: American Standards Association.

ASCII: American Standard Code for Information Interchange. A seven-bit character code for representing letters, numbers, and symbols.

Assembly language: A symbolic language which is capable of being directly converted into machine language instructions.

Base number: The radix of a number system. Ten (10) is the radix of the decimal system. 8 is the radix of the octal system, and 2 is the radix of the binary system.

Baseband: Transmission of modulated or unmodulated signals in single form.

Baud: A unit of signalling speed equal to the number of discrete conditions or signal events per second. Often defined as the number of binary digits transmitted per second.

BCD: Binary Coded Decimal. A number system used to represent decimal data in binary code. Each decimal digit is represented by a four-digit binary combination.

Binary: A system of counting using only 1s and 0s.

Binary word: A binary code of stated length given a specific meaning. Typically, 8 or 16 binary digits form a binary word.

Bit: A single binary digit, having a value of 0 or 1.

Bit pick: Used by PLCs to determine the status of an input or output device. A 1 implies an energized state, and a 0 means the input or output is OFF.

Bit rate: The speed at which binary digits pass a given point in a communications circuit.

Boolean algebra: A shorthand notation that expresses logic functions based on algebra formulated by George Boole (1815-1864).

Boolean equation: Expression of relations between logic functions written in Boolean algebra.

Boolean operators: Logic gates such as AND, OR, and NOT, which are used individually or in combination to form logical statements.

Branch: A parallel logic path within a user program rung.

Broadband: Transmission of two or more channels in a simultaneous mode by use of frequency division multiplexing.

Buffer: A temporary storage area used by digital equipment to compensate for a difference in the rate of flow of data when transmitting from one device to another.

Bug: A system defect or error that causes a malfunction. Can be caused by either software or hardware.

Burn-in: The operation of PLC components at increased temperatures prior to final installation. Intended to stabilize characteristics and identify early failures.

Bus: One or more electrical conductors used to transmit and receive signals.

Busway: A system of enclosed power transmission that is operated by current and voltage.

Byte: A sequence of binary digits operated upon as a unit. Although a byte is usually considered to be eight bits, the exact number depends on the system.

Carry bit: A binary digit that is 1 if the last operation generated a carry from the most-significant bit.

Cascading: A programming technique used to extend the maximum accumulated values of timers and counters.

Cassette recorder: A peripheral device used by PLCs to transfer data between magnetic tape and the memory of the PLC. In record mode, the recorder makes a permanent record of a program existing in the processor's memory. In playback mode, the recorder enters previously recorded data from the tape into the memory of the processor.

Cathode-Ray Tube: Commonly referred to as a CRT. An electron-beam tube in which the beam is focused to a small cross-section on a luminescent screen. The beam is varied in position and intensity to produce a visible pattern.

Central Processing Unit: Also referred to as a CPU or processor. The central control unit of a PLC that includes the circuits controlling the interpretation and execution of instructions.

Channel: 1. A group of I/O modules that are separately connected to the CPU. Typically, a channel can contain 128 inputs and 128 output connection points. 2. A combination of transmission media and equipment capable of receiving signals at one point and delivering related signals at another point.

Channel capacity: The maximum information that can be transmitted per second on a given communications channel.

Character: One symbol of a set of elementary symbols, such as a letter of the alphabet or decimal number.

Checksum: A technique used for error detection where a logical sum of data is equal to the character placed at the end of the block of data.

Chip: Another name for an integrated circuit. A small piece of semiconductor material (usually silicon), on which electronic components are formed.

Clear: A command to remove data from one or more memory locations. Returns the contents of a memory location to a non-programmed state, typically zero.

Clock: A circuit that generates periodic signals used for the synchronization of digital equipment.

Clock rate: The speed at which a microprocessor operates. Determined by the speed that binary digits are transferred through internal logic sequences.

CMOS: Abbreviation for Complementary Metal Oxide Semiconductor. An integrated circuit device with the characteristics of high-noise immunity and low-power consumption.

Coaxial cable: An electric conductor consisting of outgoing and returning cable paths having a common axis, of which one of the paths completely surrounds the other throughout its length.

Code: 1. A system of symbols or bits for representing data or characters. 2. The characters or expressions of a source programming language, each correlated with an equivalent expression in a target language.

Coil: A symbol designated as the output instruction of a PLC. When energized, a coil will change the status of all associated contacts.

Command: One of a set of several signals, or groups of signals, that occurs as a result of interpreting an instruction. A command will initiate the individual steps that form the process of executing the instruction's operation.

Commissioning tests: Tests applied to a PLC after installation to verify that the system has been installed in a correct manner and is able to function satisfactorily.

Common carrier: A public utility company that provides communication services to the public.

Compare function: A program instruction that compares one number against another number to see if a "less than," "greater than," or "equal to" condition exists.

Complement: A logical operation that inverts a signal or binary digit. The complement of binary 1 is 0.

Computer interface: A device which allows communication between a computer and the CPU of a PLC.

Contact: 1. In relay systems, one of the conducting parts that are energized or de-energized to make or break a circuit. 2. In PLCs, the juncture point that provides a complete path when closed.

Contact symbology: A set of symbols used to express user-programmed logic using conventional relay symbols.

Control relay: See relay.

Core memory: A nonvolatile memory used by early PLCs. Core memory uses magnetic rings, or ferrite cores, to store each binary digit as permanent magnetic fields.

Counter: A device capable of changing from one distinguishable state to the next upon receipt of an input signal. The output changes state when the preset number of counts is achieved.

CPU: See Central Processing Unit.

Crosstalk: Undesired energy appearing in one signal path as a result of coupling from other signal paths.

CRT: See Cathode-Ray Tube.

CRT terminal: A programming terminal consisting of a CRT and keyboard for entering programming instructions.

Current-limiting resistor: A resistor inserted in a hardwired PLC system to limit the flow of current to some predetermined value.

Current loop: A two-wire communication network which uses a 20-mA signal to represent binary 1. Four mA is considered binary 0.

Cursor: An illuminated position indicator on a CRT screen which indicates the point where data entry or editing will occur.

Cycle: An interval of space or time in which one set of events is completed.

Data: A term used to denote all numbers, letters, and symbols that can be processed by a PLC.

Data highway: A method of transmitting information between two or more communications points.

Data transfer: A PLC instruction that moves data from one memory location to another.

Debouncing: The act of eliminating unwanted pulse variations caused by mechanically generated pulses when contacts repeatedly open and close.

Debug: A method of detecting, locating, and removing mistakes from a routine or malfunctions from a PLC system.

Decimal number system: The base 10 system of counting. Uses the ten numeral digits 0 through 9.

Decrement: To decrease the contents of a register or counter by one.

Diagnostic program: A nonvolatile program used to test the various operating conditions of a PLC. For example, the CPU is tested automatically in most PLCs to detect and possibly prevent system failure.

Digital: A system of discrete states, high or low, ON or OFF, 1 or 0.

Digital device: A device that operates on the basis of discrete numerical techniques in which the variables are represented by coded pulses or states.

Digital-to-analog converter: An electrical circuit that converts binary digits to a continuous analog signal.

DIP switch: Acronym for Dual Inline Package. A group of tiny in-line, ON-OFF switches.

Discrete device: A device that can be in only one of two possible states, ON or OFF.

Discrete input module: A PLC modular input device that provides the interface between hardwired discrete components and the CPU.

Discrete output module: A PLC modular output device that provides the interface between the CPU and discrete output components such as motor starter coils, solenoid valves, etc.

Disk drive: An I/O peripheral device that reads data from a magnetic diskette and writes data onto a magnetic diskette.

Diskette: A flat, flexible disk on which a disk drive reads and writes.

Distributed control: A method of dividing process control into several subsystems. A PLC oversees the entire operation.

Dividend: In a division operation, the quantity that is being divided.

Documentation: An orderly collection of information regarding the hardware and software of a PLC system.

Double precision: The system of using two addresses or registers to expand the storage capacity of a memory location.

Down load: The process of loading data from a master listing to the user memory of an end device.

Down-time: The period during which a system or device is not operating due to internal failures, scheduled shut-down, or servicing.

Drum controller: 1. Synonymous with sequencer. When applied to a PLC, it refers to the electronic operation of a digital device as it steps through a multiple sequence of simultaneous ON-OFF states. 2. Electrical contacts made on the surface of a rotating cylinder, or by the operation of a rotating cam.

Dummy program: A program used when commissioning a PLC to verify I/O addressing.

Dump: To copy the contents of all or part of the RAM memory stored in a CPU into a peripheral device.

Duplex: Pertains to a simultaneous, two-way, independent transmission in both directions.

Dynamic memory: A memory having cells that tend to lose stored information over a period of time and must be *refreshed*.

EAPROM: Abbreviation for Electrically Alterable Programmable Read Only Memory.

EBCDIC: The Extended Binary Code Decimal Interchange Code. A code which is similar to ASCII, the main difference being it uses eight bits instead of seven.

EEPROM: Electrically Erasable Programmable Read Only Memory. A programmable integrated circuit chip which can be erased after use by applying electrical current to its terminals.

EIA: Abbreviation for Electronic Industries Association.

Electrical codes: A compilation of rules and regulations covering electrical installations, including PLC systems.

Element: A program instruction. Examples of program elements are coils, contacts, timers, etc.

Enable: To activate a function by energizing a PLC ladder network.

Encode: To convert data into coded form.

Encoder: A digital circuit that converts information into coded form.

EPROM: Erasable Programmable Read Only Memory. Same as EEPROM, except that memory erasure is accomplished by ultraviolet light instead of electric current.

Equivalent network: A circuit that, under certain conditions of use, may replace another network and provide similar operating characteristics.

Error correction: The process of correcting bit errors occurring in a digital code.

Even parity: A characteristic of a group of bits that has an even number of binary 1s.

Examine OFF: An instruction that is true only if the examined bit is 0, or OFF. If the examined bit is 1, the instruction is false.

Examine ON: An instruction that is true only if the examined bit is 1, or ON. If the examined bit is 0, the instruction is false.

Fail-safe: A method of controlling a process so that system operation is interrupted when the control power source fails.

False: A disabling logic state which occurs when prescribed conditions are not met.

Fault: A system malfunction which affects the operation of a PLC.

Feedback: A method of taking a portion of an output signal and routing it back to the input.

Feedback loop: The part of a closed-loop system that provides controlled response data allowing comparison with a reference command.

FIFO: First-In-First-Out memory.

File: A set of logically arranged data that is treated as a unit.

Flag: A character that signals the occurrence of a specific condition.

Floppy disk: A magnetic storage device; typically, a 5 1/4-in. flexible Mylar disk.

Flowchart: A graphical representation for the definition, analysis, or solution of a problem, where symbols are used to represent data, operations, and flow.

FORCE function: A mode of operation or instruction that allows an operator to override the processor to control the state of a device.

Frequency: The number of periods per unit time.

Full-duplex: Simultaneous bidirectional transmission of data on a transmission line.

Fuse: An overcurrent protective device.

Gate: A logic circuit that performs a specific logic function, i.e., AND, OR, NAND, etc.

Glitch: A voltage or current spike of short duration which adversely affects the operation of a PLC.

Gray code: A type of digital code characterized by a single bit change from one code word to the next.

Ground: A conducting connection between an electrical device and earth ground.

Ground potential: A potential of 0 volts with respect to earth ground.

Ground rod: A rod that is driven into the ground to serve as a ground terminal.

Half-duplex: A communication link where data are transmitted in one direction at a time.

Handshaking: The method by which two digital machines establish communication.

Hard copy: Any form of printed document, such as an I/O cross-reference, ladder logic, etc.

Hard disk: A storage medium used by computers and newer series programming terminals.

Hardware: The mechanical, electrical, and electronic components of a PLC.

Hardwired logic: Electrical devices interconnected through physical wiring, i.e., conventional relay logic systems.

Header: The control prefix in an asynchronous message sequence.

Hex: An abbreviation for hexadecimal.

Hexadecimal: A number system consisting of 16 characters. A number system with a radix of 16.

High: A status representation of binary 1.

High-level language: A powerful programming language in which each instruction corresponds to several machine-code instructions.

Holding register: A memory location in a PLC which is used for data storage and retrieval.

Host computer: A main computer that controls other computers or computer peripherals.

Hybrid control: Utilizing both analog and digital control to control a process.

Hydraulic operation: Power operation by movement of a liquid under pressure.

IC: An integrated circuit in which all components are integrated on a single silicon chip of a very small physical size.

IEEE: Institute of Electrical and Electronics Engineers.

Image table: A portion of the PLC's memory which is allocated for the storage of I/O data.

Increment: To increase the contents of a register or counter by one.

Input: A signal that provides information to the CPU.

I/O: Abbreviation for Input/Output.

I/O address: A unique number assigned to each input and output location in a PLC's memory.

I/O channel: A single input or output circuit.

I/O module: A plug-in type printed circuit assembly that interfaces between user devices and the PLC.

I/O rack: A chassis which houses I/O modules. Also referred to as a base by some manufacturers.

I/O update: The process of revising each binary digit in the image tables on a continual basis.

I/O update time: The time required, in milliseconds, to update all local and remote I/O. Also referred to as I/O scan.

Input register: A PLC register associated with input devices.

Instantaneous: A qualifying term indicating that no delay is purposely introduced in the action of a device.

Instruction: In a PLC system, the information that tells the CPU what to do.

Integrated circuit: See IC.

Interfacing: An electrical circuit that enables communication between the CPU and I/O devices capable of transmitting and receiving information.

Interlock: A device actuated by the operation of some other device with which it is directly associated. A device connected in such a way that the motion of one part is held back by another part.

Interrupt: The process of stopping the normal execution of a program in a PLC to handle a higher-priority task.

Inverse time: A qualifying term indicating that a delayed action is purposely introduced in the circuit operation.

Inversion: Conversion of a HIGH level to a LOW level, or vice versa.

Inverter: The digital circuit that performs inversion.

ISO: Abbreviation for International Standards Organization.

Jog: A control function that provides for the momentary operation of a rotating device. The momentary ON state is caused by depressing a spring-return switch or pushbutton. Also referred to as inching.

Jogging: The quickly repeated closure of a circuit to start a motor from rest for the purpose of accomplishing incremental movements of the driven machine.

Jump: A command in a ladder logic program that causes a change in the normal sequence of program execution. Causes program execution to jump forward to a labelled rung.

Jumper: A short length of conductor used to make a connection between terminals.

Label: An identification tag attached to the item of data that it identifies, i.e., registers, contacts, coils, etc.

Ladder diagram: An industry standard which uses successive horizontal lines with symbols to represent the logic operation of a control system.

Ladder element: Components used in ladder logic programming, i.e., contacts, coils, etc.

LAN: Local Area Network. A system of interconnected processing devices operating within a radius of a few miles.

Language: A set of representations, conventions, and rules which are used to convey data.

Latch: An electronic or mechanical device that causes a coil to remain energized after power is removed. The input state is stored until the latch is reset.

Latching relay: A relay that maintains its contacts in the last position assumed until released mechanically or electrically.

LCD: Liquid Crystal Display. A small light-emitting device used in visual displays.

Leakage current: Undesired current flow in certain components such as semiconductors and capacitors.

LED: Light-Emitting Diode. A semiconductor device which radiates light when energized.

Limit switch: A switch which is actuated by depressing its protruding arm.

Logic: A process of solving complex problems using the decision-making capability of logic gates in terms of true and false statements.

Loop: 1. A part of a PLC program in which a machine constantly repeats a portion of the program. 2. In magnetic bubble memories, the tracks on which the bubbles travel.

Loop control: A process control method that incorporates feedback.

Low: A state represented as binary 0.

Magnetic bubble: A small magnetic region created in a magnetic material by applying an external magnetic field.

Magnetic contactor: A contactor which is operated electromagnetically.

Magnetic core memory: See core memory.

Magnetic tape: A tape with a magnetic surface on which data can be stored by selective polarizations of portions of the surface.

Master control relay: A device used in logic circuits to control power to an entire circuit or to selected rungs in a program.

Matrix: A logic network which is an intersection of input and output connection points. In a PLC, it is a group of sequential registers which is generally 8-by-8 or 16-by-16.

Mechanical drum programmer: See drum controller.

Memory: A storage medium for binary data and programs.

Memory protect: A hardware circuit incorporated into PLC systems to protect user programs. Generally, a key switch mechanism.

Menu: A list of programming selections displayed on a programming terminal.

Microprocessor: A large-scale integrated circuit that can be programmed to perform arithmetic and logic functions and to manipulate data. A standard microprocessor consists of an arithmetic logic unit, instruction decode circuitry, temporary storage registers, bus interface, and a program counter.

Microsecond: One millionth of a second, or 0.000001 seconds.

Millisecond: One thousandth of a second, or 0.001 seconds.

Minuend: The number being subtracted from in a subtraction operation.

Mnemonic code: A short code, usually an abbreviation or combination of key letters used for easy recognition.

Mode: The operating state of a PLC, i.e., run mode or program mode.

Modem: Acronym for MOdulator DEModulator. A device that modulates digital signals and transmits data across conventional telephone networks. Also demodulates incoming signals and performs digital conversion.

Module: An interchangeable plug-in card containing electronic components.

Most-Significant Digit (MSD):   The digit representing the greatest value.

MOV: Metal Oxide Varistor. Used for suppressing electrical power surges.

Multiplex: To put information from several sources onto a single line or transmission path.

Multiprocessing: A method of applying more than one microprocessor to a specific function to speed up operation time and reduce the possibility of system failure.

NAND: A logic gate whose output is OFF only when all of its inputs are ON.

Negative logic: The system of logic in which a LOW represents a 1 and a HIGH represents a 0.

NEMA: Abbreviation for National Electrical Manufacturer's Association.

Nesting: A set of contacts located within another set of contacts.

Network: A group of interconnected logic devices.

Node: 1. A common connection point between two or more contacts or elements in a ladder diagram. 2. An interconnection point on a network bus where a secondary station is installed to transmit and receive data.

Noise: An undesired disturbance usually caused by radio waves, or electrical or magnetic fields passed between electrical conductors.

Noise immunity: The ability of a circuit to reject unwanted signals.

Non-retentive output: An output that immediately de-energizes when power is removed.

Nonvolatile memory: A type of memory that retains data even if operating power is lost.

NOR: A logic gate whose output is OFF when either one or more of its inputs are ON.

Normally Closed contact (NC):   A contact that is conductive when its operating coil is de-energized.

Normally Open contact (NO):   A contact that is conductive when its operating coil is energized.

NOT: A logic inverter function.

Null modem: A conductor that interconnects two RS232-C devices by acting as a dummy communications device.

Octal: The base 8 numbering system, which uses digits 0 through 7.

286

Odd parity: Refers to a group of binary digits having an odd number of 1s.

Off-delay timer: 1. In conventional relay circuits, a device in which the timing period is initiated when the timing coil de-energizes. 2. In PLCs, a timing function that is initiated when the logic rung goes FALSE.

Off-line: A programming technique where any changes made to the program have no effect on the actual operation of hardwired components. Isolates the processor from the I/O rack.

One shot: An action that occurs once per initiation. Once the action has been initiated, it continues regardless of any changes which occur at its input.

On-line: A programming condition where any changes made to the program will immediately affect the hardwired components. Links the processor to the I/O rack.

Operand: A number used in an arithmetic operation as an input.

Operational amplifier (Op-amp): A high-gain DC amplifier used to increase signal strength for devices such as analog input modules.

Optical Isolation: Electronic isolation between two electrical circuits by use of a beam of light. One circuit generates the light and the other responds to the change in light intensity.

OR: A logic gate that is ON if any one or more inputs are ON.

Output: An electrical signal sent from the processor to a connected device through an interface.

Output device: A device connected to an output module to receive programming information. Output devices include solenoid valves, motor starters, indicator lights, etc.

Output module: A modular electronic interface card used to provide a connection point between hardwired components and the PLC.

Overflow: The act of exceeding the numerical capacity of a device such as a timer or counter. The overflow can be either a positive or negative value.

Overload: A condition existing within or at the output module that causes a programming error due to a malfunctioning component. A load which exceeds the rated capacity of a device.

Overload protection: A form of protection that operates when current exceeds a predetermined value.

Parallel circuit: A circuit in which two or more connected components are connected to the same nodes. A parallel circuit may form an entire network or be a portion of a network.

Parallel transmission: A method of communication in which binary digits are transmitted simultaneously.

Parity: A method of verifying the accuracy of recorded data by counting the number of binary 1s.

Parity bit: A binary digit appended to a group of bits to cause the sum of all the bits to always be either odd or even.

Parity check: A method of testing to determine whether the number of bits being transmitted is odd or even.

PC: Abbreviation for Personal Computer. Also used as a reference to Programmable Controller.

Peripherals: Devices which are connected to, and controlled by, a central processing unit.

PID: Proportional-Integral-Derivative. A mathematical equation that provides closed-loop control of a process system. A sophisticated analog control network for inputs and outputs that is constantly changing.

Pilot device: Controls the operation of another device.

Pneumatic: A system operated by air pressure.

Pointer: A register or memory location that contains an address instead of actual data.

Polling: A method of communicating on a data highway. When an initial message is sent, a network controller will *poll* to obtain an answer to the original message.

Port: A connection point for a peripheral device.

Positive logic: The system of logic in which a HIGH represents a binary 1 and a LOW represents a binary 0.

Power supply: A device which supplies the necessary voltage and current levels to the system circuitry.

Preset: The upper limit specified for a timer or counter.

Priority: Order of importance.

Processor: See CPU.

Program: A sequence of instructions stored in memory, and executed by the CPU.

Programmable (Logic) Controller (PLC): A solid-state control device that controls machine or process operation. Consists of memory, input/output interfaces, a central processing unit, and a programming terminal.

Programming terminal: Also known as a *programmer*. A combination of keyboard and CRT which is used to insert, modify, and observe programs stored in a PLC.

PROM: Programmable Read-Only Memory. A retentive memory used to store data. This type of memory device can only be programmed once and cannot be altered afterward.

Protected memory: Instructions or data stored in memory that cannot be altered or erased.

Protocol: A formal definition of establishing criteria for receiving and transmitting data through communications channels.

Pulse: A signal of relatively short duration.

Rack: A chassis designed to hold I/O modules.

Radix: The base of a number system.

RAM: Random Access Memory. An integrated circuit chip that has read and write capabilities.

Read: The process of retrieving information from memory.

Refresh: The process of renewing the contents of dynamic memory.

Register: A location in a PLC's memory for storing information. There are three types of registers: input registers, output registers, and holding registers.

Register length: The number of characters that a register can store.

Relay: Operated by a change in one electrical circuit to control a device in the same circuit or another network.

Reliability: The ability of a device to perform a required function under stated conditions for a specified period of time. Can be expressed as either a decimal or percentage.

Report: An application data display or printout.

Resolution: The smallest distinguishable increment into which a quantity is divided.

Response time: The time required between an input transition at one node on a data highway and the corresponding output transition at another node.

Retentive output: An output that remains in its previous state when its rung is de-energized.

Retentive timer (or counter): A function block instruction having two separate inputs. One input allows the timing or counting cycle to be interrupted, while maintaining the accumulative value of the timer or counter.

RFI: Abbreviation for Radio Frequency Interference.

ROM: Read Only Memory. An integrated circuit chip which allows data to be permanently stored and read but not altered during operation.

RS-232: Electronic Institute of America (EIA) standard for data communications. Originally introduced by the Bell system, it defines signal levels, pin assignments, etc., for transmission of data in conductors less than 50 feet in length.

RS-422: An EIA standard for transmitting data using a digital interface in conductors less than 400 feet in length.

Rung: A grouping of PLC instructions that controls a single output. A single rung may have more than one horizontal control line.

Scan: The sequential examination of a ladder logic diagram, including the updating of all inputs, outputs, and storage registers.

Scan time: The time required to execute one complete scan of user memory and update the status of all inputs and outputs.

Schematic: A diagram that shows, by means of symbols, the connections and functions of a specific circuit arrangement.

SCR: Silicon Controlled Rectifier. A semiconductor device used to control power in DC circuits.

Scratch pad memory: A small, temporary storage area used for interim calculations by the CPU.

Sequence table: A table, or chart, indicating the sequence of operation of output devices.

Sequencer: A controller which sequences multiple tasks through a fixed series of ON-OFF conditions.

Sequential operation: A mode of operation in which instructions are executed consecutively unless specified otherwise by a jump.

Serial operation: The flow of information where only one binary digit is transferred at a time.

Servomechanism: A control system that incorporates a feedback circuit for process operation.

Shield: A housing or barrier that substantially reduces the effect of electric or magnetic fields.

Shift: To move binary data within a shift register or other storage device.

Shift register: A PLC function capable of storing and shifting binary data.

Signal: An electrical quantity that conveys information from one point to another.

Signal, error: A signal whose magnitude and polarity are used to correct the alignment between controlling devices and devices being controlled.

Significant digit: A digit that contributes to the accuracy or precision of a numeral.

Simulator: An I/O module used by a PLC to simulate the operation of an input or output device.

Snubber: A circuit used to suppress inductive loads.

Software: The user program that controls the operation of a PLC.

Solenoid: A current-carrying coil that provides magnetic action to perform a variety of work functions.

Solid-state device: An electronic component that controls current flow by use of solid materials such as semiconductors.

Start-bit: Used to initiate the transmission of data in a communications network.

Startup: The time between the installation of a PLC and full operation of the system.

State: The binary equivalent of an I/O device, e.g., an output which is ON is in the 1 state.

Status: The operating condition of a device, usually ON or OFF.

Stop-bit: Used to terminate the transmission of data in a communications network.

Storage: The process of retaining binary information for later use.

Subroutine: A programming technique in which specialized or repetitive operations are performed during the course of the main program.

Surge: A transient variation in current, voltage, or power in an electric circuit.

Synchronous: Having a fixed time relationship.

Table: A group of consecutive registers used to store data.

Thumbwheel switch: A rotating numeric switch with a series of small adjacent rotary wheels.

Time base: A unit of time generated by a microprocessor's clock circuit and used by PLC timer instructions. Typical time bases are 0.01, 0.1, and 1.0 seconds.

Timer: A programming function used for monitoring or determining specific timing values. After a predetermined time period has elapsed, an event will occur.

Timing relay: An auxiliary relay, or relay unit, whose function is to introduce a definite time delay in circuit operation.

Toggle switch: A small electrical switch with an extended lever.

Token: A binary pattern used in communication circuits.

Token passing: A technique where tokens are circulated between nodes in a communication network such as a data highway.

Topology: The structure of a communications network, i.e., ring, bus, etc.

Traffic cop: A term used by AEG Modicon which refers to how a CPU controls input and output data.

Transducer: A device which converts physical parameters such as pressure, temperature, weight, and humidity into electrical signals which can be processed by a PLC.

Transistor: An active semiconductor device exhibiting current or voltage gain. Also used in switching circuits.

Transition: A change from one level to another.

Transitional contact: A contact that allows power flow for exactly one scan of the CPU.

Transmission line: A conductor over which data are transferred from one point to another.

Triac: A semiconductor device capable of switching alternating current.

Truth table: A table listing indicating the status of one function and how it relates to the status of one or more other functions.

TTL: Transistor-Transistor Logic: A semiconductor logic family which is based on transistor switching circuitry.

Two's complement: A numbering system used to express positive and negative binary numbers.

Unlatch instruction: A programming instruction that causes an output to de-energize, regardless of how briefly the instruction is enabled.

Up-count: A counter sequence in which each number has a successively higher value.

User memory: The area designated in memory for application programs.

VA: Abbreviation for Volt-Amperes.

Value: A character located in a specified position.

Varistor: A two-terminal resistive element, composed of a semiconductor material having a voltage-dependent, nonlinear resistance.

Volatile memory: A memory whose contents are destroyed when operating power is removed.

Weight: The value of a digit in a number, based on its position in the number.

Word: A group of binary digits used to represent a number or symbol.

Write: The process of inserting information into a memory location.

Index